The Complete Idiot's Refere

Tips for Designing

- ➤ Start with a list of things you like in gardens, f... to individual plants.
- ➤ Stick with all cool colors or all warm colors until you gain confidence in putting colors together.
- ➤ Use different textures: linear or sword-shaped, fine or ferny, bold or large-leafed, medium or average.
- ➤ Create focal points, combinations of flowers that bloom at the same time. Scatter them around the yard, one more for each season.

Tips on Planting

- ➤ Always treat the roots with care. The health of the plant depends on their health.
- ➤ Loosen the soil around the hole you dig. Well-aerated soil allows ˋ the root area to expand.
- ➤ Place the plant at the same level. Don't leave roots out of the ground or put more soil on top of them.
- ➤ Firm the ground well around the roots, leaving no air pockets. Don't push down heavily, though, unless you have highly organic soil.
- ➤ Water well, using enough water to thoroughly soak the root ball.

Tips for Choosing Plants

- ➤ Suit the plant to the place. Make sure it fits into the ecological niche you're offering it.
- ➤ Use annuals for long-season color, perennials for yearly dependability and interesting foliage, trees, and shrubs for adding substance to the garden.
- ➤ Check out a plant's heat as well as cold tolerance. Some like cool summers and fail in hot, humid climates. Others require high temperatures to bloom.

Fun Things to do with Flowers

- ➤ Put them in salads and soups.
- ➤ Cut handfuls as you wander around the garden and stick them in small pitchers you find at thrift stores.
- ➤ Buy a hanging fuchsia and watch the hummingbirds dart around it.
- ➤ Put handfuls of dried lavender blossoms in your bath.

alpha
books

Gardening in Sun

➤ Place plants a short distance away from light-reflective walls to avoid burning leaves.

➤ Use drought-tolerant varieties in difficult to water areas. Water well until roots have a chance to get well established, though.

➤ Most plants need good drainage. Put only damp-soil loving varieties in constantly moist areas.

➤ If your soil is sandy and poor, choose types that like that condition unless you're willing to spend a lot of time digging organic matter into the whole bed.

Gardening in Shade

➤ Use lots of interesting textures in shady gardens to compensate for a lack of colorful flowers.

➤ You can add shade with trellises or trees.

➤ You can add sun by pruning certain branches off overhanging trees.

➤ Roots often compete for moisture. Plant drought-tolerant types of plants under thirsty trees and shrubs.

Tips for Buying Plants

➤ Look for vigorous, green leaves. Avoid those with yellowed or wilted leaves.

➤ Avoid plants that seem too large for their pots. Their roots are likely to be cramped and unwilling to expand into new soil.

➤ Check the needs of the plant carefully and make sure they match your own climate and yard conditions.

➤ Ask if there's anything you should know about your plants. Nursery professionals often have tips to share.

Tips for Maintaining Your Garden

➤ After planting, spread a mulch around your flowers. This prevents weed seeds from sprouting and helps keep moisture levels even.

➤ Water deeply and only as needed.

➤ Be sure to keep new beds well weeded. Your plants will spread and shade the soil soon, but right now they need help to keep weeds out.

➤ A few minutes a week will do more to keep beds neat than an hour a month.

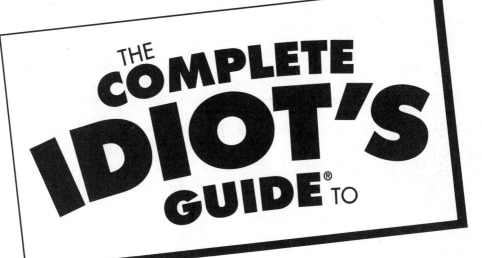

THE COMPLETE IDIOT'S GUIDE® TO

Flower Gardening

by Mara Grey

**alpha
books**

A Division of Macmillan General Reference
A Pearson Education Macmillan Company
1633 Broadway, New York, NY 10019

Alpha Development Team

Publisher
Kathy Nebenhaus

Editorial Director
Gary M. Krebs

Managing Editor
Bob Shuman

Marketing Brand Manager
Felice Primeau

Editor
Jessica Faust

Development Editors
Phil Kitchel
Amy Zavatto

Production Team

Development Editor
Nancy Warner

Production Editor
Francesca Drago

Copy Editor
Mary Flower

Cover Designer
Mike Freeland

Photo Editor
Richard H. Fox

Illustrators
Terry Marks
Brian Moyer

Book Designers
Scott Cook and Amy Adams of DesignLab
Insert designed by Holly Wittenberg

Indexer
Riofrancos & Co. Indexes

Layout/Proofreading
Sean Decker
Doreen Russo

Contents at a Glance

Contents

Foreword

Some people are born with the gardening gene. Seemingly without the slightest effort or uncertainty, they whip up colorful one-of-a-kind concoctions that dazzle year-round. This book is for the rest of us: the horticultural mortals who crave a bright floral backdrop to our lives and the satisfaction that comes with getting a little mulch under our fingernails, but need some help getting there.

The beauty of Mara Grey's guide is that she makes it so easy. Beginning with one of the biggest hurdles facing the novice gardener—that paralyzing intimidation of not knowing where and how to start—she not only helps you past that fear, but quickly has you standing by the front door, seeds and hoe in hand, impatiently waiting for daylight so you can get started. From mapping out your overall design, to picking a color palette and the flowers to make it come alive, to knowing everything necessary to keeping your garden alive and healthy, this book leaves no plot uncovered. Unsure what will work in your region? Comprehensive lists include the complete rundown on each flower, including color, expected height, recommended zones and typical blooming time and duration. Shrubs, trees, and vines are also covered in depth, along with suggestions on how to mix them all together. Nature lovers will especially appreciate the section on planting to attract hummingbirds and butterflies. Real-life considerations such as budget and soil condition help to make gardening an accessible pasttime for anyone, anywhere. The book even helps you evaluate what you're doing right and what could be tweaked so that you can make your garden even more spectacular next year.

To the novice gardener, an untouched plot of land, no matter what size, can be as daunting as it is inviting. Close your eyes and you can practically smell and touch the possibilities: the rich drama of textures and colors blending together into an ever-changing masterpiece. Before you open your eyes, panic, and consider leasing the yard to the local high school soccer team, give yourself a pep talk. Getting started is often the most difficult step. Pick up some gardening magazines, drive around the neighborhood. Realizing that imitation is the sincerest form of flattery, keep an eye out for what pleases you, think of how you could use those ideas in your own garden and jot them down. Instead of trying to mimic someone else's work, mix all those inspirations together to create your own. This is not your Great Aunt Marla's garden, it's yours, so it's crucial you create something that reflects your personality. Think of your garden as a big blank canvas and start planning it, one corner at a time. Perhaps there's a wire fence at one end of the yard. It's the perfect place to begin. A rapidly-growing vine will not only mask it, but will turn an eyesore into an attraction.

Experiment. Try different types of flowers. One good way to start is with seeds, since they're less cumbersome on the budget. Another is by returning to those yards you initially admired and asking for a few clippings. Chances are, the owner will be so flattered you asked, you'll be chatting for hours and leave with armloads of clippings of all varieties.

When you're mapping your space, also keep in mind that many flowers have limited show times. They might bloom for a few weeks, and then go on sabbatical for the rest of the season. Think about how that spot will look without them; perhaps you want to fill in the area with some longer-lasting annuals, or abut them with varieties which have later show-times.

Start small—a single bed perhaps—to give yourself a confidence boost. Mix colors and textures: Plant some blue spikey flowers in front of a purple bloom-producing vine. Surround it with white ground cover. Once you've gotten started, take note of what works and which sections could use more color or height. Part of the joy of gardening is in the experimentation. Keep in mind that your garden will probably not look exactly like the one behind your closed eyelids, and don't be disappointed. Instead, revel in what looks good. The most important part of gardening is getting a little dirty and having a great time, and *The Complete Idiot's Guide to Flower Gardening* will get you started.

—Kate Staples, author of *Plant Parenthood for Urban Gardeners*

Introduction

Here you are, faced with a small yard or a large estate. Why not plant the whole thing with grass and be done with it?

Because it would be unbelievably dull, of course. Lawn has its place as a cool green pool, as the space between elements of a garden design, but most people want something else, something more interesting: flowers.

You want to grow them. You'd love to have a garden filled with blossoms. But, you say, they die. Or they bloom for a while, then look pathetic. Your garden, the patch you had two years ago, ended up as yellow leaves and insignificant blossoms. You just don't have a green thumb, whatever that is.

In fact, when faced with a garden, you feel like a complete idiot. You aren't, of course. You just need a few pointers, some of the basic information, a push in the right direction.

Well, that's what this book is about. We all feel overwhelmed when faced with a new field, one in which the experts use language containing words like *cambium* and *transpiration*. All you need are the basics in plain, simple English. Welcome to the *Complete Idiot's Guide to Flowers*.

What You'll Learn in This Book

This book is organized into four parts, each focused on a different aspect of gardening. Let's look at them in turn.

Part 1, "Splashing Color on Your Garden," covers the whole process of creating one bed or a whole landscape, from getting ideas, through jotting ideas on paper, to buying and installing plants, to maintaining your yard.

Part 2, "The Stars of the Show," introduces you to the broad categories of plants available, from those that last only a single season to dependable yearly visitors. You'll also get a glimpse of the flowering trees and shrubs that give height and substance to a garden.

Part 3, "Matching Place and Plant," looks at plants from a different perspective. You'll travel through six environments, each one an ecological niche that requires a unique set of talents to grow there. Your own garden may include three or four of them no matter how small.

Part 4, "Expanding Your Enjoyment," looks at the pleasures of living with flowers after the work's done. For a few more minutes a week, you can increase your joy by bringing blooms indoors, planning beds for butterflies and hummingbirds, increasing your stock for free, and learning more about the flowers that fascinate you.

By the time you finish this book, you'll know which flowers you like and which ones will like your yard. You'll be able to walk into a nursery and choose a few to complement your landscaping and your taste. You'll have the confidence to call yourself a gardener.

You'll be well on your way to sharing your life with a host of fascinating, colorful, delightful flowers. You'll be on your way!

Extras

Besides all the explanation and advice, this book has lots of tidbits of useful or interesting information strewn here and there in sidebars throughout the chapters. The following icons set these tidbits apart.

Garden Talk

Gardening, like most activities, has acquired a number of terms unique to itself. Here are some quick definitions to help you understand your local nursery professional or your gardening-fanatic neighbor.

Take Care!

These are potential pitfalls, places where you could easily make mistakes.

Green Tips

These suggestions should help make your gardening life easier.

Floral Lore

People have been growing plants for many centuries. Here are samples of traditions and odd knowledge gardeners have accumulated over the years.

Acknowledgments

My thanks to my parents, grandparents and great-grandparents, gardeners all, who helped make plants a green frame for my life.

Part 1
Splashing Color on Your Garden

You start with a dream, a longing for color and fragrance, a desire to be surrounded by blooms. You want to end up with a visible, tangible garden bed. The process, however, seems like a mystery.

Don't worry. Here's the process of turning dreams into reality, laid out one step at a time. Each one builds on the foundation laid by the previous stages. It's as simple as making dinner for your friends.

Chapter 1

Creative Dreaming

In This Chapter

➤ Why plant flowers, anyway?

➤ Collecting dreams

➤ Get it down on paper

Give yourself a gift. Allow yourself to create the garden of your dreams. First, of course, you have to dream, to open up to the possibilities of your new venture. All gardens begin here, in the cultivation of hope and wishes. This is your first, and most important, chore.

Winter is a good time to work on this one. You can sit down with a cup of tea or coffee and page through magazines and books to your heart's content. No matter what the weather outside, your dreams can blossom.

Why Flowers?

Flowers. Who can resist them? They're a lover's gift on Valentine's day. A Neanderthal scattered them on a grave more than thirty-five thousand years ago and Dr. Andrew Weil, health guru, prescribes them for healing. Selling them is a $7 billion dollar a year business.

But could you, yourself, grow them at home, have a supply to pick for dining room bouquets or give away as gifts? Of course. No one has a monopoly on flowering plants. They're available at your corner grocery, from slick, colorful catalogs and as unwanted extras from a neighbor's garden. Once you start collecting them, you'll be constantly stumbling over opportunities to add to your store.

You can grow them in pots on a small balcony, or in great swaths around a country home. They can brighten narrow entries between buildings or curve around a doorstep to create an entry themselves. You might scatter seeds along a drive to make a casual drift of bloom or place them carefully in geometric shapes to create a formal garden.

You might end up with flowers above your head, on trees that provide a bonus of shade or on vines hiding an unattractive wall. You might have tiny daffodils on stems only a few inches high, or flat mats of flowering thyme like a lavender-pink carpet. Over, under, all around, you can fill your life with flowers.

But, you say, I'm not a gardener. I don't know the first thing about plants. Aren't they a lot of trouble? Perhaps I should just install a lawn and hire someone to mow it.

Well, yes, flowers are a little more trouble to put in than grass, but usually no more work to care for, often less. And the principles of planting are easy to learn. Chapter Four, for instance, will show you that roots need some of the same things you do: water, air, and room to spread out.

But before we get down to practicalities, let's dream a little, starting with some of the reasons to give yourself the gift of their presence in your garden.

Flowers Bring a Garden to Life with Color and Texture

Flowers are masters of color. In fact, you'll rarely find the exact tint of one flower duplicated in another. Some have a rich velvety sheen to them, others are translucent. Some are spotted with a contrasting hue, and still others shade from one color to another within the same petal. No wonder they've inspired artists to create endless studies and paintings!

And flowers have countless variations in form and texture, too. From massive sunflowers to clouds of baby's breath, or from flat single roses to spurred columbine, their various shapes and arrangements fascinate those willing to take the time to examine them.

You may choose to make intricate harmonies of tone and texture in a single bed, much as a floral designer does in a vase. Or you may take a single color and repeat it again and again with different flowers, making a white or blue garden. Even a mass of a single flower in front of a few shrubs can be beautiful.

Flowers Are Relaxing, Even Healing

If there is one malady common to almost all at the end of the twentieth century, it's too much stress. A little can be exciting, but a lot can contribute to high blood pressure and decrease resistance to disease. Finding ways to reduce stress is not only important for our peace of mind, it's essential for our health.

Floral Lore

Did you know that star-of-Bethlehem (*Ornithogalum umbellatum*) is used as a flower essence to aid healing from all types of trauma? This plant is so easily grown it's a weed in some places, but beautiful and useful just the same.

Who hasn't found a garden relaxing? And who hasn't stopped by a flower stand, simply to breathe in the fragrance and admire the brilliance of so many blossoms? Just saunter through a park on your lunch hour and notice how much more relaxed you feel in the afternoon. Or buy yourself a bouquet and feel the tension, the worry over tomorrow and its problems, dwindle and fade away.

In these days of heightened interest in using natural remedies as an adjunct to traditional medicine or as a means of building health, many people are trying flower essences, remedies similar to homeopathic medicines.

Practitioners match flowers to specific problems, especially emotional issues. They feel that, just as our friends have different qualities, each flower has a character. When we have a problem, we often want to spend time with one of our friends whose presence gently makes us feel solid again. Flowers can do the same, surrounding us with qualities that support and heal our emotional wounds.

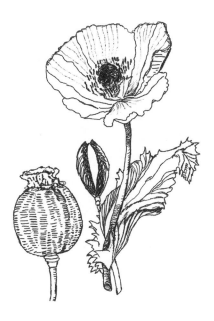

The white or opium poppy (Papaver somniferum) was originally used only as a medicine, being useful as an astringent as well as a sedative.

5

Flowers have also been used medicinally, as herbal teas and remedies. Mullein flowers are reputed to be good for asthma. Calendula, or pot marigold, is used to stop bleeding and help wounds heal. Chamomile is well known for relaxing and calming.

Flowers with Fragrance Expand Our Sensual Enjoyment

One of the most prized properties of flowers is their fragrance. Our sense of smell rarely gets as many treats as our sense of taste, but a spray of lilac, a pot of lilies, or a few roses will remedy that neglect. Put scented flowers on your desk at work and notice how many people smile and thank you for the gift.

As many writers have pointed out, a fragrance will recall scenes that we may have forgotten. Somehow, scents of which we're hardly conscious will become connected with the sights and sounds of a particular place. For instance, just try planting a scented plant that was in a childhood garden and watch the memories appear.

Perfumes take advantage of these qualities. With your own garden of fragrant plants, however, you can scent a room or a drawer with dried blossoms such as lavender and roses. Or you can make potpourri, a mixture of scented flowers and leaves.

Floral Lore

The word *potpourri* comes from the French words meaning "rotten pot." In medieval times, it was a mixture of herbs and flowers, both fresh and dried, that were layered with salt and left to ferment. Less sweet smelling than modern mixtures, it was probably used to repel fleas and other pests.

Flowers Attract Wildlife

A burst of bright flowers is beautiful. Now, add butterflies hovering over them and you have a dazzling picture. Color, movement, fascinating life cycle, butterflies have much of what we appreciate in nature. They look like flowers themselves as they dance from one end of the garden to the other.

Equally appealing are hummingbirds, whose iridescent colors and hovering flight make them a showy, welcome presence in anyone's garden. Often attracted to red, but willing to visit flowers of many shades, hummingbirds eat insects found at the flower base as well as sip nectar.

Even as flowers fade, their usefulness to wildlife often expands. Seeds and berries bring different birds to our gardens, some as colorful as the yellow and black goldfinch.

Planting flowers for wildlife is like taking a garden into a fourth dimension of friendship with nature. If you add the right ones, these creatures will come on their own, without any extra work on your part. And few pleasures match watching something wild favor you with their company.

Shopping for Ideas

One of the keys to making a great garden is to choose your models carefully. What, imitate someone else? Yes, of course. From how to dress to how to succeed in business, we choose styles, ideals, and patterns to follow that keep us from constantly reinventing the basics. Even the most original artists and thinkers start out by copying someone else. Later, when they feel more secure and knowledgeable, each one adds a unique slant to their creations.

Keeping in mind that no two gardens can ever be exactly alike, of course, simply because of differences in soil, weather, and site. Still, finding gardens you wish you could transfer to your own will simplify your decision-making process. Instead of asking, "What can I do here?" you can ask, "What would they do here? How can I make this look at least something like that?"

Magazines, books, botanical gardens, public parks, even your neighbors can all provide patterns for you to follow. Use them for inspiration, especially for ideas on color combinations. The specific plants used may work in your own garden, or may not.

Now, of course, you'll say, "But I don't have the time (money, space, knowledge, etc.), to create a garden like the ones in the magazines." Perhaps not. But right now, forget your limitations and let your imagination run wild. Free yourself of practicalities, of dos and don'ts, of shoulds, ought tos and can'ts. Why? Because limitations are never solid walls. Some may even be illusions. You'll never know what could be until you let yourself dream.

Picture Books

One of the cheapest ways to get ideas is to borrow picture books from the library. Obviously, you won't be cutting pages out, but this is a quick way to explore a variety of garden styles and notice which ones tempt you.

Get lots of books and spend a minimum of time looking through them. You're not looking for information or for details. You're looking for a sensation, a feeling of excitement, a picture that makes you say, "Wow!" Jot down the book and page number so you can find it again, then go on. Or make a quick photocopy of the page at the library to serve as a reminder.

Green Tip

While there are many books with pictures to inspire you, here are a few excellent possibilities to start with. *Color in Garden Design* by Sandra Austin; *The Natural Garden* and *The Natural Shade Garden* by Ken Druse; *The Garden Design Book* by Cheryl Merser, *Garden Design* magazine editor; and *Bold Romantic Gardens* by James Van Sweden.

What you're looking at here, really, is yourself and your own biases. Each picture that excites you tells you something about what you need. Each picture that makes you quickly turn the page tells you something too. Soon you'll notice a pattern. You'll have a clear sense of the sort of garden you want to create.

Magazines

Once you know what you like, look for magazines whose gardens tend toward that style and cut out as many examples of great gardens as you can. Make a collage and hang it on your wall. Even if you have no more garden area than a balcony, lots of pictures can be found of beautiful pots overflowing with flowers.

Don't hurry this process. It's not likely you'll find enough pictures in a week. A whole winter might be a better time frame. Trade magazines with a friend whose tastes are different. Go to a large bookstore with a well-stocked magazine rack and buy a new selection.

Take Care!

A subscription to one magazine right now might be a mistake. Yes, there are wonderful publications and you might well want to explore gardening in more depth with one of them, but right now, you want variety, you want flexibility and diversity.

If your local library has past issues of magazines, take some home and use them like the books. If you find a picture you can't live without, you can probably get that issue from the publisher by special order.

Your Own Neighborhood

Walk around your own town and find some gardens you admire. Chances are you'll find the gardener at work and can ask questions, perhaps take a few snapshots. Most gardeners are happy to share a few moments with a polite novice, and you can often get good advice on flowers that are easy to grow in your area.

Most towns and cities have public gardens and parks that are good sources for ideas. You may come across a plant you love or a combination that would be perfect in your own garden. The problem may be finding someone to answer your questions, but a phone call to the local parks department will usually get you the information you need.

Nursery Shopping

Local nurseries often have display beds to show off their specialties, offering you a chance to see a plant in person. Sometimes it is a mature individual (more likely in a petunia or a daylily than a dogwood tree) sometimes it is a baby, considerably less expensive than its older brother, the landscape-ready specimen.

Nursery professionals are available to answer questions, usually patient and eager to share their love of plants. Tags on plants often give cultural needs. They're excellent places for self-education.

One advantage a nursery offers over a book is that the information you get will be tailored to your local climate and soils. There's nothing like first hand experience with the quirks of local gardening.

Here you can experiment with mini-designs of your own. Take a flat or cart and fill it with annuals and perennials of different colors. (When you're done with your research, be kind to the nursery and put everything away.)

Which ones work together? Which ones clash? What happens when you add a plant with leaves blotched with yellow? When do you add a plant with purple leaves? If you can find a quiet corner, play around with trees, shrubs and flowers, make first one type of garden, then another. Colors, textures, height and breadth, they're all here to try out.

> **Garden Talk**
>
> Annual is a term applied to plants that sprout, bloom and die in one year. Perennial is used to describe plants that grow a permanent root system but without woody stems.

Don't buy anything just yet, no matter how tempting. Leave your credit card at home. This is window-shopping, an idea shopping excursion. Don't saddle yourself with starts to put in the ground yet.

Use Pen and Paper to Capture Your Dreams

Paper and ink are cheap and sketches are easy to change. Finished garden projects are much more solid, as well as more costly in both materials and time. You can't foreshadow a garden exactly with your sketches and notes, but you can solidify your own desires and ideas, changing vague feelings into specific intentions for your garden.

Start a Garden Notebook

The exact type of notebook will depend on your budget and your preferences, but consider these points:

➤ A loose-leaf, three-ring binder lets you add pages of pictures or a gardening article you really like. Beautifully bound and decorated blank books are available, but waterproof covers and adaptable format make the loose-leaf binder a better choice.

➤ You don't have to stick with white paper or black ink. You want color in your garden, so why not use colorful paper, stickers, and ink to keep your notebook from becoming dull and monotonous?

➤ Look for a notebook with a pen holder attached so your spur-of-moment inspirations won't be lost while hunting for something to write with.

➤ Clear plastic sheet protectors, available with three holes at the side, allow you to keep clipped photos with your notes.

Keep your notebook with you whenever you're in the garden, reading magazines or books, or walking through a public garden. You know you'll forget those ideas that flit through your mind before you sit down at your desk, so write them down on the spot.

Gather Your Dreams in Detail

Be specific. When you cut a photo out of a magazine, notice what gets you excited about it. Is it the color combination? Is it the style of fence behind the border? Is it the way a vine covers a wall and softens the gate? Make a small note on the back.

The whole composition may strike you as attractive, but the more aware you are of exactly what is pleasing, the more chance you have of duplicating its effect on you.

You'll probably find new dreams popping up occasionally. A chance article on herbs gives you the idea of growing lavender. You always loved the scent, so why not? A friend's comment on how easy her rugosa roses are to grow may plant the idea of a rose hedge in your mind. And so on.

Now Choose the Best

After a few months of idea gathering, sit down with your notebook and your collection of pictures and sift through for the ideas that seem the most important to you. Which ones are must haves, which ones are great, and which ones are nice but not necessary? Look for these points in particular:

➤ What styles attract you? You don't have to stick to just one; you can incorporate elements of several, but try to choose one to provide a unifying theme. Consider, too, the style of your house. A Japanese garden may look a bit out of place around a Victorian mansion. And a formal, geometric herb garden may look equally out of place surrounding a small cabin in the woods.

➤ What colors and combinations attract you? Do you tend to like cool pinks, light, primrose yellows, and sky blues? Or does gold, orange, and scarlet seem more your style? Do deep velvety tones seem most appropriate or light pastels? Which would go best with the color of your house? Are you in love with hot pink next to orange? Or does that make you shudder? Do you want a riot of color, or a more subdued composition with just a few colors, repeated in different places?

➤ What plants attract you? What are your favorites, the ones you go back to again and again? Many people particularly love roses, dahlias, iris, or delphiniums. Right now, don't worry about whether they're hard or easy to grow. This is brainstorming, remember? When you get down to practicalities, often you'll find tough disease-resistant varieties that do well in your part of the country, even when others are finicky.

Green Tip

You don't have to hold yourself to one color scheme. You might go for pastels in spring and vivid reds and oranges in early fall. Right now, just be aware of what you like most, especially what combinations excite you.

Once you identify your favorites, you can plan your garden around them, or plan a special corner, a display bed. If these are the type that need more attention than most, you can budget some extra time and energy to growing a few of these, then plan to surround them with easy ones who may not be so demanding.

What Would You Like to See?

What parts of your own yard seem to fit each idea? Is the tiny side yard perfect for the simple Japanese-style garden you want? Can you picture your yellow, gold, scarlet, and orange bed against the back fence? Is the wisteria perfect for draping over your patio?

Each place has its own problems and its own possibilities. You might not pay much attention to bog plants if you didn't have that wet ditch running through your property. And you don't really like orange, but the brown paint of the garage seems to call for warm tones. Perhaps a bit of orange in with yellows and golds might look just right.

You don't have to have a place for each idea, at least not right now. But places may spark new ideas, and seem to gather their own community of dreams. Write them down.

What Else Is Important?

Do you want to dry flowers? Cut them for indoor arrangements? Is fragrance a significant consideration? Is there a flower your grandmother grew that would remind you of her? Do you want to attract hummingbirds or butterflies?

Or conversely, are there things you really don't want? Are there scents that remind you of something you'd rather forget? Are there small children around who might eat poisonous leaves or berries?

How Do You See Yourself in the Garden?

What are you going to be doing in the garden? If you want to sunbathe on the grass you may want some privacy. Would you want spiny shrubs such as roses to act as a barrier? Or would you need something taller, hawthorn trees, perhaps, because of the two-story house next door?

Be sure to plan for your most beautiful show where you'll see it often. The front door is always on display, for both you and your visitors. In spring, when the weather is still cold, a bed next to the garage may be what you see most often. In warm weather, when you're ready to sunbathe, you'll be able to appreciate some sunflowers in the backyard.

If you simply want to admire the flowers from a window, make sure you plan for blossoms where you can see them. What draws your eyes when you glance outside? Perhaps you could plant a flowering tree there and add bulbs, perennials, and annuals for a lavish display later in the year.

The Least You Need to Know

➤ Flowers can expand the potential of a garden to give pleasure and relaxation, fascinating the senses with color, texture, and scent.

➤ Look at as many gardens as possible, either in person or through pictures, to find the styles and elements that please you most.

➤ Be patient. Idea gathering can take months.

➤ Don't rely on your memory. Use a garden notebook to collect your inspirations.

➤ Include yourself in your garden picture. In what ways will you enjoy the flowers? Plan for your own delight.

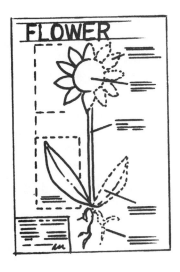

Chapter 2

Designing with Flowers

In This Chapter

➤ Every creation needs a frame

➤ Choosing your palette

➤ Texture's important, too

➤ Leaves can add more than green

➤ Final touches

Design. That's a word that scares a lot of beginning gardeners. It implies artistic expertise and years of study. Yes, some people with both these qualifications create stunning gardens. Does that mean you can't? Not at all.

Give yourself permission to play, to experiment, to have as much fun in your garden as a kid in a sandbox. Cut out the serious set-in-stone garden styles. Develop your own.

Move plants around, change the shape of the beds. Test out your ideas using garden hoses, poles, and colored paper. Build a whole display at the nursery before you buy it. Perhaps you like scarlet and pale pink combined. Even if your mother wouldn't approve, do it anyway.

Here are some ideas to get you started and spark your creativity. Build on them.

Frames Are Important

Paintings need frames, neat limits that separate the picture from the wall. Would a Van Gogh have the same effect if it just fuzzed off into space? The lines of your garden beds are just as important.

Even a meadow garden blending into forest looks better if the front edge is a definite line, perhaps a curve between mowed and unmowed grass. Even a woodland surrounding a cabin has a definite end at the doorstep.

How you shape these edges has a strong effect on the garden you will create. Your garden beds form the stage on which your play, the scenes of spring, summer, and fall blooms, will be performed. Theaters have stages of limited shapes. You, however, can create many variations on curves and straight lines.

What Do You Have to Work with?

What's there right now? The walls of your house, certainly. Perhaps there is a driveway and a walkway to the front door. Perhaps there are fences or other paths. All of these taken together are your starting point.

Perhaps you'll change them someday, building a new addition here or tearing out a walkway over there. But for right now, accept them as limitations within which to work. Maybe won't help you design a garden for next year.

What Can You Do Now?

Garden bed lines are the easiest to change. You can snake a hose out across your lawn, try one shape or another, change your mind and try again. When you're sure you like what you see, cut along the line with a shovel, first on one side of the hose, then the other, removing a two- or three-inch strip of turf to mark your place.

Green Tip

The small ditch you make to mark the bed can be your best defense against grass invading your bed. Just deepen it a little, to four or five inches, and occasionally remove any dirt that slides in.

Cover the new bed with a thick layer of mulch (6 inches to 1 foot depending on the density of the material) and in a month or two (depending on the weather) the grass will have decayed leaving good, diggable soil.

A new tree is a major vertical accent you can easily plant. Perhaps a cluster of three, a mini-forest, would work well in a corner, giving you shade for begonias, impatiens, hostas, and ferns.

Other major lines include paths and walkways. Stepping-stones, gravel, and bark are all easily placed materials that can separate one bed from another, or divide a single large bed into easily managed sections.

Make Strong Lines

Curves are nice, but too many ins and outs making wavy borders can seem timid or indecisive. A good rule of thumb is that the lawn should have a clear shape to it. A lawn that is oval, oblong, circular, square, or rectangular would leave attractive borders around it in most lots.

If a single shape seems too dull, try overlapping two of them, perhaps setting a circular section at the end of a rectangle. Try tipping the square so it angles toward the side of the lot instead of running parallel to it. You could even try a teardrop or S shape.

Simplicity makes life easier. If you find you have too many lines, try making them fewer and bolder. Remember, you're creating the background against which your flowers will glow. They'll give you as much interesting complexity as you could wish.

Backgrounds

Now consider the backdrop against which your play will be seen. What is the color of your house? Is there a hedge or a fence behind your border? What are the flower colors of any nearby shrubs? A background of purple-pink rugosa roses flowering sporadically through the fall may be the deciding factor in your color scheme.

Quick-growing vines are one way to change a background you dislike. If a chain-link fence isn't your first choice for beauty, but your budget demands it, silver lace vine (*Polygonum aubertii*) can cover at least twenty feet of it in one season. Just be sure it has room to keep spreading or be sure you're ready with the pruners every spring.

Don't forget texture. If your background shrubs have large leaves, you'll want to complement them with something fine and lacy. Perhaps some grasses or a clump of narrow-leaved Siberian iris would stand out. Any plant with leaves the same size as your background plantings would be almost lost in its expanse.

Garden Talk

Scientific names may look strange and be hard to pronounce but they're more accurate than the easy, vivid common ones. The first word is the genus name, usually a description of a broad category. Roses, for instance, are all *Rosa* whether they're wild or cultivated. The second name is the species, or subdivision of the genus. Both Shasta daisies and florist's chrysanthemums are *Chrysanthemum*, just different species.

Open Space

While some gardeners use flowers to create carpets of color, solid areas of flowers the length of their yard, many award-winning gardens have large areas of green that rest the eye. These may be shrubs out of bloom, nonflowering ground covers or evergreens.

These spaces serve the same purpose as the blank areas around print in a book. A page that is solid text is not only boring, it's hard to read. Smaller areas of print, or flowers, are easier to pay attention to and easier to design. They can be a bit like a pot of flowers or a large arrangement transferred to the ground.

What can act as white space in your garden? Lawn is an obvious choice. If you don't want the work of watering and mowing, consider planting a ground cover, a similarly restful area of green. Or using pavement to make a patio. There are endless possibilities.

Floral Lore

An ideal Elizabethan lawn was filled with daisies, daffodils, and other flowers. They would have thought our plush green acreage rather dull.

Now, let's move on to the main show.

Easy Paths to Color Harmony

Color. That's one of the main attractions of flowers. From satiny pastel tulips to orange-red oriental poppies, we marvel at the variety of shades we encounter in even the simplest garden. It's easy to feel overwhelmed when considering the complexities of which colors look good together, which ones to separate.

The key to using color in a garden is simplicity. Yes, Monet created amazing combinations, but few of us are artists of his ability. If we stick with some uncomplicated associations, who will blame us?

You Don't Even Have to Be Original

In fact, to make things really easy, we can copy someone else. Find a picture in a magazine that has a color scheme you like and use it. Snoop around at a florist's and take notes. Nobody will ever blame you for using the same combination of light and dark pinks with cream and touches of yellow that they did.

When you look at display gardens, consider only the colors for a few moments. Ignore everything else and ask yourself "Does this please me?" Write down the combinations that you particularly enjoy.

Most are made up of one or two main colors with touches of another and perhaps white or cream. You could easily duplicate any in your own garden, in a single bed or across the whole design.

Or Create Your Own

Perhaps you have a red rhododendron that dominates its section of the yard when it's in bloom and you want to add other plants to make a real show. How do you choose the colors? There are several possibilities:

➤ Choose similar colors. Your red rhody is probably a deep rose-red. Choose lighter shades of rose, all the way to pale pink. Contrast this with pale yellow, purple, or blue. If it's a deep blood red, you could try oranges and golds. The whole warm spectrum of yellow through red can give you bright stand-out bouquets, especially useful for small beds. Contrast with blue or purple. Blues and purples themselves can make a lovely garden, especially if mixed with lots of white and some yellows for interest. In fact, these cool colors mix well with almost anything. They tend to recede into the distance, however. Brighter colors will have more impact.

➤ Choose colors with a similar intensity. Velvety rich shades of dissimilar colors may look well together. Your red rhododendron may look well with deep sky blue and clear yellow. Try to keep the composition simple, though, and stick with only these three shades. If your rhododendron is pale pink, you might go for restful pastels. Apricot, pink, lavender, and light blue will give your garden an air of delicacy, especially when combined with gray-foliaged plants and lots of white.

➤ Find a multicolored flower such as a pansy that includes just the shade of rose you're looking for. Add a few bulbs or perennials that match other shades in the same blossom. This gives you automatic color coordination.

Many flowers have contrasting colors at the throat. Pink daylilies, for example, often shade to through peach to yellow. Or a yellow one may have a purple center. Matching each with another flower can give you a really spectacular grouping.

Bold or Dainty?

Think of a floral arrangement of roses framed by a mist of baby's breath. The contrast between the tiny white flowers of baby's breath and the substantial roses is one aspect of its appeal. You can do the same thing in your garden, using plants with masses of tiny flowers to fill in the cracks between larger, more weighty blooms.

Why bother with texture? Because creating enjoyable texture patterns takes the design-with-color pressure off you. They make simple color combinations more interesting. No matter how well-planned the color scheme, if all the blooms are about two inches wide it will lack excitement.

Large flowers, such as cannas and lilies, can be used sparingly, perhaps one grouping per bed. Tiny blossoms like baby's breath or sweet alyssum can be used in quantity, allowed to pool around and between larger plants. They become a living background.

Don't Forget Leaves

Why talk about leaves in a book on flowers? Well, what would flowers be without a backdrop of green? Its restful, calm tone provides an underpinning for contrasting colors. Leaves also come in many shades of green, with glossy or dull surfaces, and with many textures, from lacy to large and conspicuous. Just as a florist may add ferns to bouquets of roses, a good garden designer may add them to a bed of impatiens.

Green Tip

If you have trouble finding flowers for a shady area, look for interesting leaf textures and colors. You can combine colorful foliage with flowers for unusual effects. Hostas with yellow-spotted leaves, for instance, combined with yellow-flowered corydalis make an eye-catching arrangement.

Color?

Some leaves are striped or spotted with white or yellow. Others, such as coleus, have red, orange, or yellow markings. Many plants have the undersides of the leaves brushed with purple.

The flowering cabbage and kale often sold in fall have tightly packed heads of leaves shaded with pink, purple, and cream, making a large, long-lasting, flower-like display. All are edible.

Some plants have burgundy-colored foliage. Some have bright yellow or lime green leaves. You could create an entire grouping of colorful leaves and hardly miss the flowers.

But you needn't go to that extreme. Just look around for plants with interesting leaves to add as accents. Or look for varieties of favorite plants that have extra foliage interest.

Chamomile (Chamaemelum nobile) *has finely cut leaves that give it a dainty, mossy texture.*

Ferns, Grasses, and Other Textures

Once you start looking, you'll find that leaves come in myriad textures and shapes. Grasses are often long and fine, sometimes upright and stiff. Ferns may be finely divided or rather swordlike. And you won't have to contend with clashing colors, either.

Perennials are important sources of green texture, since most bloom for only a month or six weeks. When not adding their own flowers to the show, they can be restful patches of leafy background.

Iris are excellent vertical, swordlike accents. Daylilies and spiderworts (*Tradescantia*) are also narrow-leaved, but more arching in outline. Lily of the Nile (*Agapanthus*) has arching, strap-shaped leaves.

Hollyhocks have bold, round leaves. Foxgloves and hostas are also bold, but more oblong. Japanese anemones have large, maple-shaped leaves. You'll find more bold leaves as you look around, and it takes only a clump or two to add drama to a garden composition.

Delicate, ferny textures can be found in plants with small, narrow leaves, such as rosemary, or tiny, round ones, such as meadow rue. Others include corydalis, rue, and yarrow.

Take Care!

Foxgloves, while beautiful vertical accents, are poisonous if eaten. Keep them out of gardens where small children may be playing.

Even the surface of the leaves can be appealing. Lamb's ears (*Stachys byzantina*) has soft, feltlike gray leaves that seem to ask to be touched. Some plants have very shiny leaves. And some, such as *Rudbeckia* 'Goldsturm,' have prominent veins that give a patterned look to the foliage.

Putting Everything Together

If your bed is small enough, you can pretend you're creating a huge bouquet. Take your largest, boldest flowers and place them across the bed, as if they could fill it up by themselves. Now, working from medium- to fine-textured plants, fill in the spaces between them. You'll end up with a unified mixture that can stand on its own.

In a larger bed, however, this approach rarely feels satisfying. Individual plants may seem to get lost in the extra space or look spotty. Try grouping them in bunches of three or five. If you have a really large area to fill, try planting drifts five feet long, or more.

If you're placing more than a few of each type, you'll have to draw shapes in your bed to fill with your chosen plants. Ovals are often used, or even curving rectangles. If you have a formal garden, use geometric patterns such as squares or interlaced circles to guide you.

Now, in the cracks between your groups, sow sweet alyssum, forget-me-nots, or other easy-to-grow annuals. These will fill up the space, giving you quick color and satisfaction until slower-growing plants can catch up.

The Least You Need to Know

➤ Strong lines are the easiest piece of the design to create. Use the trees, fences, and walkways you have now and add shapes of beds to complement them.

➤ The easiest way to choose a color scheme is to imitate one in a picture, bouquet, or a prize-winning container at a garden show.

➤ Surround large flowers with masses of small ones for contrast.

➤ Use leaves to add more texture contrast, choosing one each from fine, medium, bold, and swordlike texture groups.

➤ Use each flower in a grouping proportional to the size of the bed. Use single plants, for instance, in a four-foot-long bed, but use five or seven of them in one twenty feet long.

Designing in the Fourth Dimension: Time

You have a satisfying three-dimensional design. The curves of your beds look good from the kitchen window. There's height in the form of trees or fences. You have the stage. Now think about the production.

Consider the fourth dimension, time, before choosing your flowers, your company of actors and actresses. As in any play, the performers move in a constant procession, in and out throughout the year. As director, you place them so that one follows another without conflict, without the colors of rival prima donnas clashing.

They also grow wider, taller, older. This year's play won't look exactly like the one next year or the one ten years from now. You aren't placing sculpture. You're orchestrating a living composition.

Feel overwhelmed? Don't worry. There are ways to simplify any director's job.

Seasonal Moods

You don't have to produce an extravaganza every week of the year. No one expects a solid carpet of flowers lasting from March through October. Be easy on yourself and settle for smaller shows.

If all your plants have colors that mix or match, you're assured of harmony no matter what time of year things bloom. This approach takes quite a bit of self-control. Though few people can stick with a limited palette all year, it's an effective technique. Look in chapter 2 for color schemes.

Small Spaces, Short Times

The beginning gardener often tries to create perfection, a constant succession of blossoms spread across the yard. Don't. Do your designing in small areas and small periods of time.

There may be no curtains dropping between scenes, separating spring show from summer show from fall show, but a change of planting bed does same thing. Even spring pastels and summer orange-reds can be kept from overlapping and shouting at each other if you put them on opposite sides of your yard.

Of course, some plants bloom longer than others and each area will probably have a few flowers long after its main show is over. Once you separate your stars, you can simply enjoy the extra bonus.

Give Each Season a Home

How much time you spend outdoors usually depends on the weather. On a wet spring day, you may only see the areas next to the front door and the garage or the view from your picture window. Choose one of these for your daffodils (*Narcissus*) and pink tulips rising out of a cloud of forget-me-nots.

Floral Lore

Socrates called narcissus the "chaplet of the infernal gods" because of its narcotic properties, which can cause a staggering gait and numbness of the nervous system.

Summer is the time to have an array of impatiens and fuchsias in a shady corner by the patio, where you can enjoy them on hot days.

In the fall, on the other hand, gold and rust may be just what brightens your mood as summer slides away toward winter. Put a tree with good red autumn color where you can see it from a window and surround it with chrysanthemums.

Each Season Has a Mood

Notice that the tone of the display changes with the season. You can choose your plants not only by color, but by paying attention to your feelings about each time of year.

What says spring to you? Perhaps it's snowdrops, apple blossoms, or the flowering quince your grandmother grew. Perhaps it's light pastels or bright Easter-egg colors.

Summer may be hollyhocks or lilies and roses. Do you need cool colors to compensate for high temperatures? Or do you want a passionate affair with red, orange, and velvety purple?

Autumn can be bronzy or it can be restful, with blue, purple, lavender, and pink asters. Colchicum, which look like giant pink crocus, can push up through a ground cover to cheer up a gray day. Even chrysanthemums can cooperate in pastel shades.

Winter itself can take on a new character when you plant clumps of hellebore, or a winter-blooming cherry. Even cool areas can have Chinese witch hazel (*Hamamelis*) that blooms with its bright yellow ribbonlike flowers in February in some areas.

Choose a few favorites for each season, flowers you'll look forward to every year. Plant lots of them. Even build a whole bed around them.

Focal Points Are Accents in Time as Well as Space

Focal points are compositions planned to draw the eye to a certain place. By separating your flowers into seasonal groups, you have the beginnings of a number of focal points.

Take your favorite plants for each season and picture them as a group. Pick one for the center of your composition, a tall perennial, a shrub, or a tree. Then mentally arrange the others around it. Now add some other plants with harmonious colors or contrasting foliage textures.

For instance, you might have a crab apple in bloom in April. If you're particularly fond of tulips, choose some in a harmonious color to plant beneath the tree, perhaps in a darker pink or pale yellow. Then add a ground cover such as white-flowered periwinkle (*Vinca*) then some clumps of hosta for their large, round leaves. Touches of blue from a few forget-me-nots (*Myosotis*) or a cluster of brunnera could complete the picture.

All you do is build, one by one, from the star specimen to those with supporting roles to minor characters.

Monkshood (Aconitum), with its spires of deep violet-blue flowers, can be the center of a summer focal point.

Green Tip

Most perennials flower for less than a month. Here are some that may bloom for two months or more, given their favorite conditions: golden marguerite (*Anthemis tinctoria*), feverfew (*Tanacetum parthenium*), avens (*Geum*), beardtongue (*Penstemon*), pansy (*Viola tricolor*), blue marguerite (*Felicia amelloides*), golden corydalis (*Corydalis lutea*).

What if you don't have room for five or six different compositions? Stack them. If your early spring bed is bare of bloom by early May, that's where the roses and lilies for June can go. Late spring flowers will make way for autumn asters and mums. If you don't want clashing colors, let bloom subside in one bed while another bed takes over.

Or you can search out the longest-blooming perennials and mix them with annuals that flower until frost if old blossoms are removed. Add seasonal interest with just a few perennials, bulbs, and flowering shrubs in colors that work with your main show.

Go for simplicity rather than ornate and complicated arrangements. One wisteria in bloom can cover the roof of a patio or the side of a house. What else do you need?

Focal points can include other things besides flowers. Any tree standing by itself is a major focus of interest. Statues, birdbaths, reflecting balls, and driftwood are all centers of attention. To support rather than supplant these objects, use simple color schemes, perhaps only a single color plus a variety of foliage textures.

And don't forget pots and planters. These can be wonderful focal points for entries and patios. Commonly planted with annuals and bare in winter, they can house shrubs and small trees with trailing vines to soften the edges. Look at chapter 21, Barrels, Tubs, and Pots for more ideas.

Fussing Over Details Can Be Fun

Many gardeners spend hours planning just the right combination of plants. It's part of the fun of creating. But remember, it should be fun, not a headache. If you have lots of flowers in your garden, no matter how many changes you'd like to make, your visitors will be full of complements. They'll be much less critical than you are.

Bloom Times Can Be Tricky

How do you know which plants will bloom to-gether? Unfortunately, observation and rough guesses from gardening books are your only guidelines. Bloom times vary from place to place, even from year to year.

Even well-established plantings may veer from schedule depending on the weather. Some may be more delayed by a cold spell, or hurried by heat, than others. Don't bet your savings on bloom by an exact date.

Garden tours, trips to public display gardens, even walks around your neighborhood are all good for gathering ideas. If you want to create an April focal point, drive around in April and see what's avail-able.

You can also pick blossoms from one place in a yard and carry them around, looking for partners. This is a good way to catch subtle combinations, a pink that picks up the center of a daylily with peach, pink, and yellow shading. Put together they can be synergetic favorites.

Take Care!

Small pots dry out more quickly than larger ones and plants may wilt when you're away for the weekend. Clay dries more quickly than plastic or wood. For easier care, make up a few large planters rather than lots of small pots.

Green Tip

You can ask advice from your local nursery professional but don't assume that what's blooming in the store will bloom again at the same time next year. Many have been grown in warm greenhouses that persuade them to flower earlier than normal. Some have been shipped from warmer regions.

Fill Those Gaps

Some plants take time out while others are just starting. Autumn crocus (*Colchicum*), for instance, flowers in fall, and sends up leaves in early spring that only last until June. You need to leave space for them, but you don't want bare ground through the summer.

One solution is to plant in a ground cover. It's green whether or not the leaves and flowers are there, and it can even keep the flowers from falling over. Narcissus is particularly good in both grass and ground cover.

Another is to plant long-blooming annuals among the leaves. They'll hide the browning foliage (don't cut the yellowed leaves off until they have finished feeding the bulbs) and add color long before the colchicum. Just be sure to choose a shade that will harmonize with the lavender-pink of the colchicum blooms later on.

Some late-sprouting perennials work well with early-fading blooms such as tulips and daffodils. These include baby's breath, threadleaf coreopsis (*Coreopsis verticillata*), and leadwort (*Plumbago*).

Infants to Patriarchs

Plants grow, and keep on growing. Even a shrub listed as five feet tall may be much taller at twenty years of age. (See chapter 8 for tips on pruning to contain growth, a short-term, high-maintenance solution.) Perennials expand. How is any gardener supposed to plan around all this change?

One option is to look at the ultimate size, then give your plants room to grow to their full extent. Your garden may look a bit sparse at first, but you can add lots of annuals and fast growing perennials to compensate. There's no need for bare expanses of soil or mulch.

Take Care!

The heights listed in gardening encyclopedias for shrubs and trees are for an average specimen at ten years of age. Don't expect them to quit at that age! Growth may slow down, but it never stops.

This is a good plan to follow if you're planting lots of shrubs. While you can transplant them, it isn't a good idea. You'll lose some roots and set them back at least a year's growth. Add height with annuals like cleome and sunflowers.

You can also plant close and plan on dividing and transplanting. If you know that you'll be starting a new bed in the backyard in a few years, there's no reason you can't plant a bit closely this year, and then transplant starts to your new area. You'll have the advantage of a few years growth at no extra money as well as a well-filled garden.

Be sure, however, that you don't plant so closely that your flowers interfere with each other. Three daylilies planted within six inches of each other will grow as one plant, making a large clump. Those planted farther apart, though, will eventually cover a larger area because their roots are able to forage farther.

You can try planting fast-growing specimens and removing some later. This is a bit risky, since you may not want to cut down the galloping silver lace vine (*Polygonum aubertii*) that was so cute as a youngster. Or you may find yourself battling it with pruning sheers twice a year. Or you may not be able to get rid of its suckers. Still, if you're impatient some plants will give you all the growth you want, now.

Thinking Ahead a Year

Part of the fun of gardening is planning new combinations, new possibilities. Once in a while walk around the garden with a cup of coffee or a glass of wine in your hand to keep yourself from feeling guilty for looking instead of weeding. Think about what you'd do differently next year.

Then, while your ideas a fresh, take a few moments to write them down! You may have great ideas in May on what you would do for next year. You'll never remember them in September without prompting from your notebook, never.

You can't move plants during hot weather or put more crocus in during April. Plants aren't furniture to be rearranged at every whim, much as it would be convenient and rewarding to do so. They're growing organisms whose needs must be considered if you want them to live with you.

Transplanting and adding new plants sometimes ends up being done long after you planned it. A notebook is your only guide; depend on your written ideas to direct you toward your ideal garden.

Green Tip

Some snapshots taken every few weeks are easy, precise memos on the state of your yard that can supplement your written notes. You may also notice more readily that the tall cleome and sunflowers overwhelmed the little bed by the back door when a photograph frames the picture.

Take an Assessment

Occasionally letting your imagination run free can produce lots of new ideas. First, sit down and write down everything you wish you'd done better. The seeds that didn't get planted until too late. The petunias that should have been watered more. The daisies that should have been fertilized. Get it all out.

Now, look at what went right. Perhaps the verbena really took off, surprising you with its energy and its outpouring of blossoms. Perhaps you got some compliments from relatives on the little bed next to the door you really put some work into. Perhaps you think the lilies you tried just for fun are so beautiful you'd plant dozens if you could afford them. Put all these memories down on paper.

Now compare the two lists. Maybe the mistakes make a longer column than the successes but that's all right. If nothing else, you know exactly what you do not want to do.

Then do some planning.

Build on Your Successes

First, take your successes and expand them. If one verbena did well, where you could you use more of them? If the bed by the door was such a success, would you want to make it larger? Or do another one just like it somewhere else? Would you want to add some daffodils for extra spring color or some winter pansies to bloom into December? Where could you put some more lilies? And could you squeeze some money out of the food budget by eating cheap for a week?

You probably have lots of ideas, if you let them come out. Was there a particular color combination you liked, such as pink hollyhocks with vivid magenta rose campion? Or a combination of leaves that looked especially good, like round hosta with ferns?

Use your notebook to jog your memory.

The Least You Need To Know

➤ Simplify your garden by concentrating seasonal blooms in small beds.

➤ Build focal points by choosing a favorite plant with star quality and adding a supporting cast.

➤ Give your plants room to grow. Crowding only slows them down and creates more pruning and transplanting work.

➤ Write down your inspirations for next year. Don't rely on your memory.

➤ Do more of whatever went right last year, lots more. Even a thirty-foot border of poppies is better than weeds.

Chapter 4

Here and Now: What You Have to Offer

In This Chapter

➤ Light: the essential

➤ Soil: the foundation

➤ Water: the unpredictable

➤ Air: the invisible

Sunlight, water, soil, and air. These make up a plant's total world, everything that's available for them to use during growth. You, the gardener, have a unique blend of these to offer. Sometimes the characteristics are subject to your control—and sometimes not.

Though there are hundreds of annuals, perennials, bulbs, shrubs, and trees available for you to choose from, each comes with strings attached, namely preferences for specific combinations of light, water, soil, and air. Some prefer the environment of a dense, warm jungle, some prefer an arctic plain.

If their tastes don't match the circumstances you have to offer, the plants won't grow. It's a little like putting the wrong puzzle piece in place. Though one part may fit, if it doesn't match all around, you better look for another.

Remember, you don't grow a plant. It will grow itself. Your job is to put it in the right place.

Light Is Important for Food Production

You wouldn't try to grow a daisy in a dark closet, would you? Of course not. It needs light to make food, to convert oxygen, carbon dioxide, and water into carbohydrates. This process, called photosynthesis, is the basis for all plant growth. However, getting the proper amount of light is essential.

Garden Talk

Photosynthesis refers to the process that takes place in leaves by which plants manufacture food. Using the energy of light, they turn simple materials such as oxygen, carbon dioxide, and water into carbohydrates.

Different Plants, Different Needs

All over the planet, sunlight varies from one place to another, from dim rain forest floors to exposed desert sands. Some plants have leaves that are broad, catching every available ray. Some have narrow, tough blades that can take intense light without burning. Each one has a preference for a lot or a little light.

What happens if there's not enough light? Put your daisy plant in a dark corner and it will try its best to find the sun, extending long, skinny shoots. These will be pale, light green, or even white, because green chlorophyll can form only with adequate light. In addition, all available energy will be channeled into leaf growth, leaving none for flowers. Even a slight lack of sun can cut flower production dramatically.

What happens if there's too much light for a shade plant? New leaves are smaller, sometimes crinkling or rolling up to reduce the leaf area. Sometimes they burn, showing irregular brown patches or spots. Sometimes the leaves simply become pale or yellowish or bleached-looking. Leaves droop even when watered, retreating from the harsh light.

Sometimes plants that enjoy full sun can burn if they're suddenly moved from a shady spot. The leaves just haven't adjusted to the abundance of light. Take off any browned foliage and be patient until new, more sun-resistant leaves appear.

Be wary of south- and west-facing walls that may reflect more light than any but the toughest sun-lovers can take. Try moving your flowers farther away from the wall or plant a heat- and sun-tolerant vine to cover it.

Your Job

Changing the amount of sunlight is usually impractical so make sure you put plants that like shade in dim corners and plants that like intense sun against south walls.

Be aware of how the strength of light changes through the seasons. Ground beneath a tree may be sunnier in early spring before the leaves expand than later in the year. A

Hellebores (Helleborus) enjoy shade, where their bold leaves can contrast with finer-textured plants.

bed on the north side of the house may be shaded in April but partly sunny in July. Only occasional observation will mark the changes.

Soil Provides a Firm Foundation

What's soil? You might say, dirt, meaning dark particles that get your hands dirty. Soil, however, is more than dirt. It's a mixture of grains of rock, air, partially or fully decayed leaves and other once-living material, water, and microorganisms.

The mineral part of the soil is most obvious. Grains of broken up rock, from sand grains $1/12$ inch in diameter to flat flakes of clay less than $1/12,500$ inch in diameter. These provide bulk and sometimes nutrients needed for plant growth.

Take Care!

Shade has many qualities, from the dappled broken shade under high-branched trees to the deepest shade between a wall and a dense over-hanging tree. What grows in light shade may fail in the other.

31

In the breakdown process, these mineral particles become mixed with organic matter, with decaying leaves, roots, and the bodies of earthworms and other small organisms. The fungi and other life that helps this process of decay are also important parts of the soil.

Garden Talk

Nutrients are the elements plants need to carry out their growth processes. The six needed in the largest quantities are nitrogen, phosphorous, potassium, calcium, magnesium, and sulfur.

What is good about organic matter? It holds lots of water, it breaks down into compounds easily assimilated by plants, and it holds nutrients. If you water with a fertilizer solution, for instance, a soil high in organic matter will hold the fertilizer longer than one that is mainly minerals. It acts as a sponge, slowly absorbing and releasing both water and nutrients.

One of the most important components is the space between particles of soil. Why? These can be filled with water or allow excess water to drain away. Then they can fill with air, giving needed oxygen to the roots.

Sometimes soil is compacted by pressure from feet or heavy equipment. The grains become pressed together and few spaces are left for water and air. Roots have more difficulty developing and the plant grows poorly.

pH Demystified

In technical terms, pH numbers measure the concentration of hydrogen ions, which are electrically charged molecules. In practical terms, a pH of 7 is a neutral state, with a balance of hydrogen atoms. Numbers less than that are acid, with a soil of pH 5 being strongly acid, and numbers more than that are alkaline, with a soil of pH 9 being strongly alkaline.

Why bother? Why do you need to know this? Plants have acidity preferences that you need to consider when planting. Few are restricted to a narrow range of pH, but many, such as azaleas and camellias, prefer definitely acidic conditions.

What is your soil's pH? Test kits sold by nurseries are good for getting a general idea, but are not accurate to the nth degree. In general, soils in areas with light rainfall tend to the alkaline side; soils in more rainy areas tend to be acid.

Should you try to change your pH? Perhaps. If the flowers you want need slightly acid conditions and your ground is alkaline, adding lots of slightly acidic organic matter may allow you to have the garden of your dreams. Or perhaps building raised beds would be a permanent solution, allowing you to fill with soil of a proper pH.

You can raise the pH of acid soil by mixing in ground limestone, though many flowers will do quite well in anything above pH 6. Unless you know a particular plant needs a higher pH, don't bother.

Your Job

Know the qualities of the soil that you have and then decide whether to find plants that enjoy those qualities. Or change the soil, making it less acid, more fertile, higher in organic matter, softer, or less claylike. These changes can make your garden suitable for a wider variety of plants, but they'll take some work.

Effort put toward improving the soil, however, will probably improve your garden more than anything else. Whatever helps plants develop deeper, stronger root systems will be more than paid back with healthy leaves and flowers.

First priority should be loosening compact soil, then adding organic matter, which will, by itself, improve the fertility, water-holding capacity, and texture of your bed. Not bad for simply digging in some steer manure, is it?

Green Tip

Roots can dig farther than you think. Sweet alyssum roots may go down a foot or more, tulips two feet, and camellias five feet.

Water—a Delicate Balance

Water is just as essential to plants as it is to us. Since water enters through the roots and exits through pores in the leaves, a constant flow is needed to maintain that balance.

Like sun, water is unequally distributed over the globe, not to mention within a particular garden. And different years bring different amounts of rainfall.

What happens if there's too much? Water fills the spaces in the soil, and roots die of suffocation. The leaves turn yellow and wilt, sometimes giving the impression that the plant needs to be watered even more. Lacking roots, it is indeed dying from lack of water, but adding more won't help.

What happens if there's not enough? Water evaporates through pores in the leaves and as it continues to flow out without any replenishment, leaves become limp, eventually yellowing and dying. Stems last longer, but they too will eventually succumb.

Your Job

If you stocked your garden with plants that enjoy life with no more than the rainfall nature gives you, you'd have the least amount of work to do. (See chapters 17 and 19 for drought-resistant flower gardens.) However, garden hoses do allow you to compensate for deficiencies. Just be aware of the extra work involved when you plant thirsty beauties. And be aware that even the most drought-tolerant plants need extra watering until their root systems are securely established.

Air Is More Important than You Think

Plants need oxygen to manufacture carbon dioxide in the chemical processes that in humans we would call breathing. Air, however, has other properties, a certain weight that we feel as wind when it moves, and a wide variation in temperature and dryness, or humidity. Unlike us, plants can't retreat or put on and take off clothing to adjust. That doesn't mean however that they don't have likes and dislikes.

Temperature

Temperature and humidity, summer and winter, play a major role in determining whether or not a plant will succeed in your area. And you have almost no control over these.

Take Care

Air envelops the leaves. You don't have to worry about giving them more. However, do concern yourself with the amount of air the roots receive. Remember, soil is composed of spaces between mineral grains, tiny air pockets that give oxygen to the roots. Jumping on moist ground or driving equipment over it compresses the soil, reducing the amount of oxygen available so don't.

Yes, you can pile straw over perennials to insulate them from drying winter winds and you can create small microclimates of higher humidity if you're in the desert, but these are minor adjustments. You'd be better of working with what nature hands you.

Some plants die at 32°F, some at -40°F. Some languish when the thermometer dips below 50, others when it goes above 90. You can't change your climate. All you can do is choose the plants that are most likely to feel at home with your summers and winters.

How? A good garden encyclopedia will tell you a plant's likes and dislikes (see chapter 25), listing the hardiness zones that indicate the minimum temperatures at which a plant can be expected to survive in that area. These were created by the U.S. Department of Agriculture in cooperation with the National Weather Service. See page 341 for a display map of the zones across the United States. Here's a summary:

- ➤ Zone 1: below -46°C (below -50°F)
- ➤ Zone 2: -46 to -40°C (-50 to -40°F)
- ➤ Zone 3: -40 to -34°C (-40 to -30°F)
- ➤ Zone 4: -34 to -29°C (-30 to -20°F)
- ➤ Zone 5: -29 to -23°C (-20 to -10°F)
- ➤ Zone 6: -23 to -18°C (-10 to 0°F)
- ➤ Zone 7: -18 to -12°C (0 to 10°F)
- ➤ Zone 8: -12 to -7°C (10 to 20°F)
- ➤ Zone 9: -7 to -1°C (20 to 30°F)
- ➤ Zone 10: -1 to 4°C (30 to 40°F)
- ➤ Zone 11: above 4°C (above 40°F)

You want to know if a plant will freeze out in your toughest winters, the ones that come every ten years or so. Hardiness, however, is not an exact science. Shrubs that have been allowed to go dormant in late summer are hardier than those forced with extra water and fertilizer to bloom up to the last minute. And low temperatures in January, after a slow cooling process, are less damaging than those in October or November.

Snow on the ground all winter, is a natural insulation that will keep perennials beneath considerably warmer than those bared to winter winds. If your summers are hot, ask for flowers that will stand up to high temperatures. If they're cool, look for those that prefer a cooler summer.

Garden Talk

Hardiness is a measure of a plant's ability to survive your area's winters. This depends not only on the type of plant, but on whether or not it has time to ripen and become completely dormant before a hard freeze. Extra early frosts can kill branches and roots that aren't prepared for them.

Humidity

The inside of a leaf is moister than the air surrounding it, and though water needs to evaporate through the leaf surface, plants have created ingenious ways to minimize this loss. Some have waxy surfaces, some have reduced the leaves to thin, tough needles, some have fuzzy hairs protecting the exterior.

Dry winds can pull water out faster than it can be replaced; leaves wilt, then brown and die. If these are common in your area, look for plants whose leaves are adapted to dry conditions. On the other hand, if humidity is high and summers warm and moist, make sure the plants you choose do well under those conditions. Some get diseases that flourish in these favorable conditions, some simply won't grow. Find out ahead of time what grows well in your area.

Take Care!

Air pollution may be a problem in your area. Some plants grow beautifully with smog, some refuse to develop at all. As always, ask for local advice on the best plants to choose and be aware that those you order from other places may not do well for you.

Wind

Wind has its physical effects, too, pushing over or even snapping off tall stems. Spires of delphinium and hollyhock may not survive a day of strong gusts without staking, so put stakes in when you plant as a precaution in exposed areas. Roots are smaller and less liable to be damaged by a stake than they would be if you waited until the plant was full size. As the stems grow, tie them to the stake, substituting a taller one if you need to. When you're done, your flowers should be safe from all but extraordinary blasts.

Lilies, delicate as they seem, are resistant to wind damage, as are agapanthus, marguerites, daylilies, and common geraniums.

The Least You Need to Know

➤ For easy gardening, match plant needs to the conditions you have to offer them.

➤ With too much sun, leaves turn yellow or get spotted with brown. With too little, plants never bloom and send out long, pale shoots.

➤ Most plants grow best with slightly acid or neutral soil.

➤ Having loose, well aerated soil is more important than having rich soil.

➤ To let air reach the roots, soak deeply whenever you water, then allow the soil to dry slightly.

➤ Before you plant, find out whether a perennial or shrub can take your area's summer heat as well as your coldest winters.

Get Ready, Get Set . . .

The pictures in books and magazines are nothing to the beauties in your mind right now. You can see exuberant billows of blossoms outside your front door so clearly you can almost touch them.

Now it's time to get down to practicalities, to the techniques of turning dreams into here-and-now reality. Don't get discouraged. Creating a feast is a step-by-step process; so is creating a garden.

So be realistic about your resources. You're going to be laying out both labor and money before you receive a bonus of flowers. Though overextending yourself is easy, information and understanding can substitute for work and dollars if you're careful. First, however, look at what resources you have available.

A Time Budget

How many spare hours and whole weekends can you spend on this garden? If you divided your yard into weekend-long projects, how many weekends would you need to complete them?

The beginning stages, the installation, will be more time-consuming than the maintenance required later, provided you choose easy-care varieties of plants. But be sure not to plant an area larger than you can water and weed easily, or you'll lose plants to drought and quick-growing invaders.

How much time can you put into creating your garden? A few hours a week? A day a month? How much can you put into maintaining each bed after it's finished?

If you're short of time, can you hire help for digging and planting? A few hours from an experienced gardener can get you started and you can handle the rest. If you have a large area, can you gather enough patience to install a landscape over five years instead of one?

What you need to do is plan now to minimize maintenance. Watering and weeding will be your main chores, so take some time to choose strategies to reduce them.

Drought-tolerant plants can mean fewer hours spent watering, though they need regular soakings the first few years. Even half the yard planted with less thirsty shrubs and perennials can make a difference, significantly lowering your water bill, too.

A drip irrigation system on a timer is another option. The combination of a watering system with a substantial mulch to keep soil moist can be a great help to busy gardeners during a hot spell. If a timer turns the water on automatically, you won't lose new transplants to drought just because you forgot to turn the sprinkler on.

Mulches and ground covers can reduce weeding by preventing seeds from sprouting. They can't kill plants with strong roots like dandelions and quack grass, so you'll have to remove these weeds before you add them. Set aside some time for this chore, too.

Does creating a low-maintenance garden sound like a lot of work? Consider it a one-time investment, paid back by time saved next year, and the years after that. Do it right once, and you can relax.

A Money Budget

Gardens don't need to be expensive. Many flowers can be grown from packets of seeds spread outdoors in early spring (see chapter 10) or from free starts provided by a neighbor. Still, a few sprees at the local nursery can be fun.

Settle on a reasonable amount to spend on each bed. Shrubs and trees will be more expensive initially than smaller plants, so set aside the largest amount to cover their cost. If you can't afford all of them this year, get the most important now and wait until later to buy the rest.

Most perennials will get larger each year, often allowing you to divide them into three or four smaller plants so decide to spend a fairly large amount for these.

What do you have left? Extra money for splurges can get you instant color in the form of 4-inch pots of annuals or lots of packets of seeds to experiment with.

Flowering tobacco (Nicoti-ana) often reseeds, saving you the expense of new plants.

Small Is Better

Perhaps you have three hours on Saturday, to make your garden look more colorful. When you step out the front door you may not know where to begin. Everything looks like it needs work.

So you buy a flat of annuals at the nursery and put a few petunias in the backyard, some marigolds in the front yard, and spread the rest along the driveway. When you stand back and look at what you've done, you feel a little disappointed. Nothing looks as good as you thought it would.

What went wrong? You simply need to focus on your efforts. A little bit here and a little bit there sometimes adds up to nothing at all. Most people get more satisfaction out of creating beauty in a 3 × 4 -foot bed than they would if they spent the same amount of time and planted the same number of flowers over much larger area.

Yes, the rest of the garden still needs to be weeded, but at least you have a small piece that's just the way you want it. That gives you an incentive to do the next piece and the next. Soon you've finished the whole yard.

Prioritize before You Plant

What's your garden's most prominent feature? Which bed do you see the most? If you walk from the garage to the front door every day, it could be part of the entryway. Or perhaps it's the corner of your front yard you see when you pull into the driveway. Or the view from your kitchen window.

Make a list of the places you notice most often, then rank them. Work your way from most important to least. Put most of your money and your energy into the most conspicuous areas. Don't let the weeds in the back corner interfere with planting iris and lilies in the front bed.

Don't be too serious about this, though. Perhaps the area around the entry and the bed next to the patio are important. You can put them both at the top of the list and let your mood decide which one you start on first. The point is to have fun, not to slavishly follow a schedule.

Preparing the Bed

Now you're faced with the reality of a blank page on which to write. Or is it blank? Perhaps the first task is to get it to the stage of receptive possibility.

Get Rid of Perennial Weeds First

Perennial weeds such as quack grass and creeping buttercup have runners that can turn one plant into ten if not removed promptly. And when you dig them out, new plants start from every piece left in the ground. Nasties, for sure.

If you have trouble with these, wait a month before you plant any bed. Remove all the weeds, then see what sprouts and remove that. If you get them quick enough, before they start spreading again, this second weeding will clear the ground completely.

Dandelions, dock, and thistles have a single deep root. If this breaks as you pull it out, the surviving part will send up new shoots. Don't try to pull it. Get a garden fork or shovel and loosen the soil around it, perhaps four or five inches on each side. The plant will slide easily out of its place.

Annual weeds can be gotten rid of whenever you see them.

Take Care!

How can you tell whether a weed is a perennial that can come back to trouble you or an easy-to-get-rid-of annual? Look at the roots and side shoots. Annuals don't send out runners to expand their territory and usually have fine roots that decay easily. They put most of their energy into flowers and seeds.

To Dig or Not to Dig?

How much work do you have to put into preparing the ground? Well, that depends. If you have loose, fairly dark soil (which means with organic matter in it) you may be able to get away with just planting your plants and watching them grow.

Notice the word *loose* in that description. One of the most important components of soil is air. A hard, compacted soil is a poor environment for roots no matter what its fertility. First judge the spaces in the soil. Do you have chunks you have to break up with a shovel? Or do the crumbs of soil trickle through your fingers? Some roots can push through blocky soil, but the fine fibrous ones of many annuals and perennials do much better with room to expand.

Most new homes are surrounded by ground that's been compressed by heavy equipment. You may even think, "This must be clay, it's so hard!," when it actually has only partial clay content. Once you break it up, the soil will be fine.

What's the best way to break it up? A garden fork is easier to shove into dense soil than a shovel, though shovels are good for breaking up lumps. Try to dig as deeply as possible, two feet if you can. Roots spread farther than most people expect and the better the environment you can provide for the roots, the healthier your plants will be.

What about improving soil fertility? If you're planting nasturtiums, don't bother. They'll give you lots of leaves and few flowers in good soil. If you're planting delphiniums or dahlias, yes, definitely.

Try to keep plants needing the same fertility together. You might want your favorite roses and lilies close to the house. This is a bed to put as much work into enriching as you can. You may also plant some less fussy shrubs toward the back of the yard and spend less time on their needs.

If you're going for drought-resistance, however, added organic matter and extra-deep loosening of the soil is a definite plus. You want deep roots in a soil that can hold as much moisture as possible. The work you save in watering will pay back your efforts.

Add Organic Matter

Organic matter, the partly decayed remains of something that was once alive, is an excellent addition to any soil. It makes sand more able to hold water and nutrients. It loosens clay and actually helps the tiny, platelike minerals clump together into larger pieces.

Most organic matter, as it decays, will release nutrients into the soil. It also acts as a sponge to hold fertilizers and water. Great stuff. No wonder gardeners go into ecstasies over compost and manure.

Garden Talk

The term *organic matter* refers to the remains of once-living organisms, usually fibrous material such as rotted wood and dead leaves. In a partially decayed state it can loosen heavy soil and hold moisture. When completely decayed it can bind clay minerals together into granules.

41

The kinds depend on what you have available. Many people will simply buy bags of manure at the store. Steer manure has less fertilizer than chicken, about right for most purposes. You want its bulk more than its nitrogen.

If you have old straw, decayed leaves, well-decayed sawdust, or even compost, add them.

One caution: conifer needles often make the soil more acid, as does peat moss. Unless you have neutral or somewhat alkaline soil, you may want to use something else.

What about sawdust, which is cheap? What's wrong with it? The microorganisms that break down new sawdust need extra nitrogen and will take it out of your soil. You might mix sawdust with nitrogen-rich grass clippings for a quick compost. This will heat up and decay just as more complicated compost mixtures do. Just be sure the clippings are from a herbicide-free lawn.

Other Improvements

While you're turning over the soil, you might as well add anything else the plants might need. Bone meal is an excellent choice. High in phosphorous and potassium, the nutrients that strengthen roots and stems and promote flowering, it's especially good for bulbs.

Acid soil may need some ground limestone added if you're growing baby's breath (*Gypsophila*), scabiosa, or other plants that need soil close to a neutral pH.

On the other hand, somewhat alkaline soil may demand peat moss if you're to grow your favorites. Hard to wet, peat moss is best mixed in thoroughly and never allowed to dry out.

Just before Planting

Water thoroughly the day before you plan to plant. Dry soil shocks the roots and sets them back. Wet soil can become compacted and like concrete, losing the air spaces roots need for growth.

Green Tip

Check your tools. Make sure you have everything you need, including a sharp knife to open the matted root balls of rootbound plants.

Make sure you have some mulching material ready to put around your new purchases. If you can mulch before their first watering, you'll preserve the open, porous soil structure you've worked so hard to establish.

Why? Grains of soil exposed to drops of water tend to slop together into a uniform mass that soaks up water more slowly. When dry, it forms a water-resistant crust. A mulch lets the drops trickle down without disturbing the spaces.

Get some starting solution, preferably one containing hormones that help roots grow. You'll use a small amount to make up a watering can full of solution, the first soaking for your plants. Fertilizer isn't really helpful for newly planted flowers. This is.

Now you're ready to bring home the plants.

The Least You Need to Know

➤ Be realistic about your limitations of time and money.

➤ Use the resources you have to create one small plot at a time, as much as you can finish in a weekend.

➤ Perennial weeds must be removed before planting. This is your only chance.

➤ Make sure your soil is loose and easy for roots to move through.

➤ If your soil needs to be enriched, use organic matter such as steer manure or aged sawdust. Both sand and clay soils can benefit.

➤ Make sure the soil is moist but not wet on planting day. Wet soil can turn into mud when worked, losing its air spaces and becoming brick-hard on drying.

Chapter 6

Buying without Busting Your Budget

> **In This Chapter**
>
> ➤ A growing investment
>
> ➤ Design counts more than ever
>
> ➤ Try a few at first
>
> ➤ Plants for free
>
> ➤ Seeds are cheap
>
> ➤ Shopping the nurseries
>
> ➤ Choosing a healthy plant

Now we get to the fun part of gardening—ordering seeds from those tempting catalogs, filling flats with pots of budding annuals, and picking out bushes awash with bloom.

If money grew on trees we'd never have a problem. For most of us, however, money's a limited, finite resource that needs to be doled out sparingly. Does this relegate your garden to the mundane? Not at all. It simply means that patience, ingenuity, and creativity become as important as dollars.

A Small Investment Yields Big Rewards

Very few things you buy get more valuable as they get older, do they? But look at the relative price of a 4-inch potted perennial and one in a gallon can. The first may be a dollar fifty to three dollars, the second may be five to seven dollars. The difference between them? Anywhere from two months to a year's growth. Now that's a good return on your money! Patience, obviously, can save you money.

Buy perennials and annuals in small sizes. They take off quickly and will usually double their size in a few weeks. Why pay someone else to watch them grow?

Green Tip

Many trees and shrubs are available at discount prices first thing in the spring. During their dormant, leafless season, they're shipped bareroot with sawdust, not soil, covering the roots. They're cheap and often available in large sizes.

Some perennials may only be available in larger sizes. You can console yourself by thinking of the three or four new plants you can divide this one into in the fall. (Read about dividing plants in chapter 24.)

Shrubs in 5-gallon cans are usually a year older than those in gallon cans, and often three times the cost. Unless they're a prominent part of the plan, plant them small.

Highly visible display beds, the ones you pass every day, may deserve gallon-can perennials to start, just because you need *something* to admire and congratulate yourself on creating.

Trees, if they're major pieces of your landscape plan, should be bought large enough to stand out. A foot-high seedling may take three or four years to reach visibility in a landscape. Go for one at least 6 feet high if you can.

Spend the Time to Design Well

Go to a Japanese garden and imagine it without plants. Still beautiful, isn't it? Bold, good-looking patterns cost no more than mediocre ones and look stunning with just a few easy to grow plants. Even the rocks that lend strength and interest to a naturalistic garden can be less than exorbitant, if you transport and arrange them yourself.

Before you buy a single flower, your garden can look great, if the basic design is exciting. Don't count on blossoms, pleasing as they are, to pull the weight of the garden. Add a garden sculpture (ask for it as a gift) or a piece of driftwood you picked on your last trip to the beach.

Your yard, taken as a whole, is a sculpture. Lines of paths and beds, circles of lawn, and informal drifts of ground cover, form the framework of this creation. You may not have total control over the way your plants grow, but in this you are the king, president, and CEO. Why settle for second-rate?

Now, go back to the first chapter and read about idea gathering. Time spent here costs nothing and will save you the fee of a professional or the frustration of spending hours of work installing a disappointing landscape.

Start with Just Three

No matter how easy and tough a plant is reputed to be, your garden is unknown territory. Some thrive, some sulk and refuse to put out more than token growth, some concede defeat and die. As every experienced gardener knows, there'll always be a few failures.

Don't put in a ten or twenty of anything until you've tried three. Often, out of those three, one will often grow much better than the rest, or much worse. If you started with a single individual, how do you know its demise was not due to an individual quirk?

Occasionally, plants that grow well one summer will disappear over the winter, despite a catalog's assurance of hardiness. If you're counting on its presence in great swathes, a year's test is a worthwhile precaution.

How to Get Plants for Free

Many of the toughest plants spread rapidly by offsets or seed and neighbors may be happy to have you come and dig a few. These can be just as attractive as the prima donnas who need extra attention, with the benefit of making quick masses of impressive color.

Your success in transplanting starts may depend on the weather. Pick a cloudy, cool day, with the prospect of rain the next. Why? Your new plants will lose roots in the process and a sunny, warm day can draw water out of the leaves much faster than it can be replaced. Result: wilted, possibly dying plants.

Take Care!

Though you'll be assured that these free goodies like your climate, soil conditions may vary within short distances, going from sand to clay within the same yard. Before you dig, check that your soil is the same as where the freebies grew.

Being free, you may be inclined to try just about anything. Stop. Refuse any plant you don't really like, Once it's growing happily, are you going to feel any more like digging it up and throwing it in the trash? You'll feel even guiltier throwing it out later. And this is *your* yard. You have a perfect right to shut the door on even friendly, eager-to-grow plants that you don't like.

Some may be too aggressive. There are some plants that you simply don't want to let loose in your yard. As pushy and difficult to remove as a noxious weed, they can be killjoys of the worst kind. Which ones? That depends on your area of the country. Just spend a few moments talking with your neighbor. Is this likely to be trouble unless confined in concrete? Or is it simply gently expanding?

If you do find a neighbor beset by one of the attractive bullies, you can take starts for an easy to maintain container garden. Undeterred by neglectful watering or poor soil, these are ideal plants for pots on your deck.

Should you dig in the wild? No, no, and no. Plants will likely die owing to root loss and because you can't give them the conditions they need. The only allowable exceptions are plant salvages made when the land is going to be scraped and built on. Otherwise, let them alone.

Hundreds of Plants for a Few Dollars

A packet of sweet alyssum contains about a thousand seeds and each plant may be six inches in diameter. That's 250 square feet of bloom for no more than a few dollars! This is plainly an area that money-short gardeners should explore, especially since many of these plants will come up from seed the next year without help from you.

What Do They Need?

Seeds won't sprout or grow well if not kept evenly moist until their roots are able to gather moisture deeper in the soil. Either you or nature must provide water.

Seeds need soil that's clear of weeds. Not that most can't abide the company of chickweed or dandelions, but how are you going to pull up one and not the other?

Seeds need light to grow once they've sprouted. Seeds started in a kitchen window can languish if not given the sunlight they need, or at least a strong artificial lamp.

Drawbacks

Some annuals, termed hardy, can be planted in your garden before the ground warms up and nature stops watering as frequently. Others need warmth, and you may have to supply the water. Either use a sprinkler set on a timer or resign yourself to frequent soakings.

If started indoors to keep pace with greenhouse annuals, seeds need light and diligent watering. Are you up to this much extra responsibility? Then there's planting them outside, getting them used to the cooler air, a process called hardening off.

At this point, most people head for the nursery, especially if they need only a few plants of each kind.

Where to Use Them Best

Sweet alyssum is great as a filler, easy to scatter, and quick to sprout. Many annuals are similarly attractive in masses, especially the hardy ones you can sow outdoors during the rainy season.

Others are larger, making imposing specimens by the end of summer. Since these make a great show in the garden, they're sometimes worth starting yourself. A fence line of sunflowers, after all, adds a flamboyant touch that three or four can't match.

How to Shop Without Feeling Overwhelmed

Walk into any nursery in spring and you'll be assailed on all sides by color, fragrance, and temptations of every kind. Is it possible to maintain a sane grip on your checkbook? Is it possible to come home with plants that match your garden conditions *and* your fantasies? The key to shopping without grabbing every charmer you see is in having a strategy. Here are a couple of possibilities.

The Definite-List Trip

You have a plan, as any practical, efficient gardener should. You're going to buy the plants you've listed as the best for your yard. Great.

Nurseries, however, are more like train stations than grocery stores. In spring, shipments of bareroot trees come in, then leave. Perennials and annuals come in, then leave. Other flowers take their place. Some of the items on your list may have just left, some may be coming six months from now.

Before you gnash your teeth and tear your list up in frustration, talk to a nursery professional. He or she can help you plan your purchases, pointing out the ones that are better left until later.

If you're clear about the general type of plant (sword-shaped leaves, about 2 to 3 feet high) you can substitute one for another. What aspect is most important? Height? Color? Texture?

Think of your plan as a year-long project. You add one piece now, another in a few months. Your goal can still be a completed landscape. It simply happens more slowly than you expected.

The Exploratory Trip

The description in the book sounds great, but you'd like to see it first. Or you just want to find out what's available. A trip to a good nursery is in order.

Your strategy here is openness to possibility. Your wallet stays at home, but your notebook comes with you. You appreciate the velvety pansies, delicate columbine, and fragrant roses, take notes, and plan for splurges later.

Green Tips

Use your research trips to experiment with design. When you see a plant you like, look around for others that like similar conditions, then group them. Mix shrubs and annuals, or set pots of bulbs around a tree. Check out the effect of a ground cover by massing small plants. But most important, have fun.

*The European elder
(Sambucus nigra)* comes
*in a purple-leafed form
that is instant temptation.*

There's nothing wrong with surrendering to temptation occasionally, but impulsively buying a blooming zinnia when all you have is shade will only lead to disaster. No matter how much you want a plant, remember that you must provide the right mixture of sun, soil, and water or it will weaken and die.

The One-Bed Trip

One of the best schemes is to combine focus with openness to opportunity. Take on a small project, the bed nearest your front door, for instance. Know the environmental conditions, have a few ideas of plants that you think you'd like, then spend an hour or two nursery shopping.

You may buy some on your list. You may find some you'd never heard of that would do quite well. You may have an absorbing conversation with a nursery manager who has some suggestions, some of his or her own favorites to recommend.

The bed and its environment is your frame. Within those constraints you can mix and match plants with only your pleasure to consider. You can have bold colors and large plants, or large grouping of plants like lavender that seem to blend into the background. You choose.

If You Can't Find the Plant You Want

Perhaps you've set your heart on golden corydalis, an excellent choice for dry, shady areas, but you can't find them anywhere. What do you do?

Ask if the nursery has had them and, if so, when they expect more. If it appears to be unavailable in your area, you have several options:

➤ You can try to find a mail-order source. Check out tips in chapter 25.

➤ You can grow it from seed. This is a wise choice if you want ten or more since the money saved makes up for the work involved.

➤ You can ask around to find someone you can get a start from. Gardeners are often generous with plants that expand quickly, either with seedlings or by widening clumps. This is a good way to get some of the tougher plants that seem to be weeds to fastidious gardeners.

Green Tip

Corydalis often self-sows, a hint that you could sow the seeds in fall and have new plants the next spring.

Now that you have found your plants, which ones do you want?

Get the Healthiest Plants You Can Find

Skip the bargain table, at least until your garden's well on its way to satisfying you. Yes, they're cheaper, but they're risks that may never do much. Usually they're far larger than the pot allows and they may have dried out a few times. They won't get going as fast and may even be permanently set back.

Is the root system strong? Remember, all growth depends on good roots. If you have a chance to look at those of a bareroot shrub, for instance, are they shriveled or plump? Is it a spreading root system or has it been chopped off to fit into a bag?

Does it look vigorous? Some plants look vigorous and ready to get going. Others seem to languish, having a few yellow leaves and an air of making the best of a poor situation. While some plants are inherently more vigorous than others, try to pick the greenest, most flourishing you can find.

Yes, many will perk up when you get them home and in good soil. Until you have a sense of your own limitations as a gardener, though, pass them by. You need a successful introduction to growing flowers, not a job playing nursemaid.

Does It Have Yellow Leaves?

One sign of a plant that has been allowed to dry out in its pot is yellow leaves at the base. Though plants can usually survive one or two wiltings, they may not be as quick to start out as those that have not been stressed.

Even the best nursery can have watering problems and your local grocery store probably has no one who's really experienced with plants. They may put out a rack of annuals in spring, but that's about it.

If you want the best starts, find out when new shipments come in to your local nursery and get them as soon afterward as possible. They'll be exactly the right size and in great condition.

Are the Roots and Top in Proportion?

A fountain of greenery or sparkling color sells plants. Roots don't. That's why you'll see beautiful plants rising over pots a third their size, when in nature roots spread deeper and wider than the top growth.

Go for the smaller specimens, even if they're just starting to bloom. Why? If the plant has outgrown its pot, when you come to slipping the plant out of its pot, you'll see a mass of interwoven roots, sometimes so thick you can't see any soil. As you're planting you'll have to untangle this mess, at least partially. Sometimes the best solution is to take a sharp knife and slice off the outer edges of the root ball, or at least make a number of cuts in it. Drastic, but effective in getting roots to find freedom.

The Least You Need to Know

➤ Buy large specimens only for high-visibility areas. Smaller plants are much cheaper. Practice patience.

➤ Before you plant masses of any type of flower, try three or five for a year. Even those that do well for your neighbor may decide your garden isn't for them.

➤ Seeds are cheap and an excellent way to start flowers in quantity. Perennials and hardy annuals can be sown outdoors in fall, eliminating transplanting.

➤ Make sure you get a good healthy root system when you buy a new plant. This is the basis of all its growth. Take time to get the best you can.

Chapter 7

Getting off to a Good Start

In This Chapter

➤ After you bring them home

➤ Where do they go?

➤ Roots are priceless

➤ Final touches

Here you are, full of excitement and the proud possessor of armloads of flowers. What's next? Planting, of course. Think of it as the connecting link between your dreams and the reality of blossoms and compliments a few months from now. Worth doing right, isn't it?

Planting can be simple, if you take it step by step, without haste. Give yourself a whole afternoon to create your bed of flowers, arranging your purchases to your satisfaction, then giving each a gentle tucking in. Welcome them properly and they'll settle down and grow without hesitation.

Care at Home

Buying plants is fun, exciting, addictive even. But when you get home, the temptation is to put them aside and make dinner or watch TV. But if you forget them you may neglect to take a few simple steps that can keep your plants ready to grow.

You should water right away. Even plants fresh from the nursery can be dry, so drench them before planting. If one or two seem exceptionally parched, put them in a bucket of water for a few hours. Bareroot trees and shrubs, in particular, benefit from a good soaking.

Take Care!

Never plant into soggy soil. Its naturally crumbly texture will disintegrate, leaving you with a mess more suitable for making mudpies than putting around roots. It dries hard, too, without the air spaces so necessary for good root growth.

While you're at it, make sure the soil of your waiting bed is moist, but not wet, in perfect condition to receive plant roots.

Make sure you give them some shade. Even sun-loving starts should go in part shade until they're planted. This reduces chances of drying out and helps greenhouse-grown plants get used to outdoor conditions. If you're worried about sun scalding delicate leaves unused to strong light, put them in full sun for part of each day until they're toughened up.

Try to plant them as soon as possible. You may decide to plant tomorrow. Just don't let tomorrow stretch into three or four days. Forgotten plants may get dry and even wilt without being noticed.

If you have to wait, create a holding bed, a square of prepared ground where plants can be stuck quickly, higgledy-piggledy, without order or reason. The roots will stay cool and moist until you're ready to put them in their permanent positions.

Deciding on the Best Place

If you're the perfectly organized gardener, you'll have the ground prepared, weeded, loosened, and watered before you go to the nursery. If not, go back to chapter 5. Now you're ready to transfer your plan onto the garden.

Try arranging them before you remove the pots. Though it's hard to visualize the exact size and shape of a mature plant when all you have is a youngster, your imagination can fill in the gaps. Now, make adjustments. Every design needs a bit of fine tuning as it's positioned, so play around a little with the arrangement.

How Far Apart?

It may be hard to believe that some of your purchases will be 3 feet high and wide in a few years, or even next year, but if that's the stated size, you'd better pay attention to it. Leaving room for full-grown specimens may make your planting look thin, but plants rarely grow to their full size in crowded beds and may even be smothered by more energetic neighbors.

You can fill spaces with creeping annuals, if you wish. Or, if you promise to transplant to locations with more room at the end of the season, you can group three perennials into the semblance of a single larger one. Just be sure to give that composite individual space to expand.

Sudden Inspirations

Your nursery browsing will probably have focused on one or two beds, but spur of the moment inspiration frequently adds a few more plants you can't live without, but don't know what to do with.

If you can, fit them into existing plantings, at least temporarily. They'll be better cared for as part of an existing group and you can transfer them to their new home later.

What if you planned carefully, but the perfect plant for the back of the border wasn't available. What do you do now? You can substitute or you can fill with a tall annual in the same color. Or you can just wait. Remember, patience is as necessary as a shovel if you're going to have the garden of your dreams.

Roots Are the Key to Plant Fitness

Roots are the base upon which plants create health and exuberant growth. Care for them as you would for a new baby. After all, they aren't supposed to be hanging out in the open air. This is an unnatural situation and one demanding extra care.

When you get a plant, they'll be covered, either with a plastic or fiber pot, burlap, or moist sawdust. Keep them covered until you're ready to plant! This is important.

Naked Roots Are Vulnerable

The most important part of a root is practically invisible. These are the tiny root hairs, only a cell thick and more fragile than the daintiest china. These microporous walls are where water and nutrients enter, nourishing the plant. Important places!

In nature, roots are surrounded by darkness and moisture, never experiencing the drying sunlight and wind that strikes them as soon as they are unwrapped or taken out of a pot.

After a minute of nakedness, the roots you see may look healthy and plump, but the root hairs are gone, shriveled into oblivion. Yes, they can be replaced, but why force your plant to go to the extra trouble? As soon as you remove the protective covering, cover the root ball.

Remember, drought and desiccation are enemies of roots.

Uncover Carefully

Water a few hours before planting, if the soil feels dry. Here are a few techniques for getting a plant out of its container:

Plastic or metal can. Squeeze the pot gently all the way around. Turn upside down and tap gently on the base, or tap the rim of the pot on the side of a table.

Fiber pot. Even if it's supposed to decay naturally when put in the soil, the roots may be chasing each other around the inside of the pot. If left tangled, they may continue circling without reaching out into new soil. Either follow the techniques for unpotting from a plastic pot or, if it's a large shrub or tree, place at the proper height in the hole and tear off the fiber wall.

Bareroot. Shake the packing material off gently and keep moist, perhaps sticking them into a pail of water for a few minutes to counteract any dryness.

Burlapped. Place at the proper height in the hole and gently remove the cloth, immediately firming soil around the root ball. If you try to take the cloth off before setting it in its permanent place, the ball of soil may crack, breaking off roots, as you move it.

Most evergreen shrubs, such as rosemary (Rosmarinus) *are sold in pots. Only deciduous shrubs and trees are transported as bareroot specimens.*

Spread out the Roots

You want a wide and deep root system, capable of reaching out to the largest area of ground for nutrients and water.

If your newest perennial comes to you in a pot, a common method of growing and selling flowers, when you remove the container you'll often find the roots visible on the outside of the soil, their path already set in a circle. Sometimes you'll find a whole mat of intertwined roots.

Now if you were one of these roots, put into the ground without having your direction changed, where would you go? Around, not out, probably. You'd never see the good soil prepared for you. The leaves you nourish would never develop the size they would have if you'd been ready to push outward.

Take your fingers and gently untangle some of these roots, pulling them outward where new soil can be dribbled around them.

Garden Talk

The term *rootbound* refers to a plant whose roots are tangled and entwined. The roots are prevented by the walls of the pot from reaching out so they grew inward. To help them move into new soil, you'll have to unwind or cut them.

If you have a solid mat, take a sharp knife and make some cuts on each side, exposing new surfaces to a new life. Even, perhaps, shave some of the roots off, sacrificing them to this new start. Radical measures, certainly, but the wall of old roots has to be broken down before healthy new growth can replace it.

Put the roots in the hole (check orientation so you get the best branches or leaves pointed toward the admirer) and spread them out.

Don't Plant Too High or Too Low

Place the plant so its original ground level is the same as the level of your soil. In other words, don't leave the roots high and dry above ground. A root ball dries out easily if it's exposed.

And don't add earth on top of the roots, possibly suffocating them. Some plants, particularly rhododendrons and azaleas, have fine roots that need to be near the surface. If you put three inches of soil on top of them, your rhododendron will turn yellow and die.

Add dirt around the roots. Now, push down, lightly, to firm it, giving a stable surrounding to the root system. Bear in mind that you want spaces between the grains of soil, but you don't want caves. Poke the soil in with your fingers, but don't mash it down.

A Few Last Chores

Once your plant is securely in the ground, you need to spend just a few more minutes helping it settle into its new home.

Spread a thin layer of mulch. Water sinks in more easily when applied over the mulch than over bare ground.

Soak the planting area. This step settles the soil around the roots and eliminates any dryness. Plain water is often adequate, but one with an added starting solution containing rooting hormones is helpful.

If your new purchase has lost roots in the transplanting, accidentally dried out, or is finicky, continue to water with starting solution for several weeks.

Garden Talk

Diatomaceous earth is a dustlike powder made up of the microscopic skeletons of tiny organisms. These are so sharp that they pierce the soft tissues of insects and slugs, causing dehydration. Be sure to use the type sold as an insecticide rather than that sold for filtering swimming pools, which may be harmful to pets because of its high silica content.

Some starts may be coming out of greenhouse conditions for the first time. If you're transplanting into the hot sun, rig a shade for a few days to keep them from wilting before they adapt to the full sunlight. If your humidity is low, try sprinkling them with water a few times a day to help them make the transition.

If you have problems with slugs, they'll flock to a newly planted tidbit. Either put a physical barrier, like a fence of chicken wire, around it, use slug bait, or one of the natural controls such as diatomaceous earth or traps made of empty cans half filled with beer. Barriers of sawdust, wood ash, or copper strips may also be effective. If you use commercial slug bait, be sure it doesn't come in contact with any plant you'll be eating.

Last, look at your handiwork from a short distance, five feet to ten feet. Does it look balanced? Does it please you? Yes, it's bare, but a year or so will take care of that. Remove any leaves that have gotten crushed or broken, and any old buds. You want to be able to feel a sense of satisfaction when you walk by.

The Least You Need to Know

➤ Try to get plants into the ground as soon as possible. If you can't, put them where you'll remember to water them.

➤ Make last-minute adjustments to your plan when you place plants on the ground, using your imagination to fill them in to their adult sizes.

➤ Care for roots as if they were priceless resources. They are.

➤ Don't forget to water thoroughly after you're done.

Minimizing Aftercare

Here you are with a whole bed of new flower starts, properly planted. Doesn't the bed look orderly and well groomed? And don't you feel proud of yourself?

Now, to make sure you feel just as contented with your creation next month and six months from now, let's look at the care small plants need to get them started right. Your efforts now will be well repaid by a shorter list of chores later on.

If You Want Fewer Weeds, Mulch

First, take some precautions to prevent weed growth. Put a layer of mulch around your newly planted treasures. Why? Because mulch will reduce or eliminate the sprouting of weed seeds that are already in the soil. In addition, it keeps the ground cool and evenly moist, a favorite condition for most plants.

You need something that shades the soil and keeps them dark. Some seeds, of course, need darkness, but weeds usually colonize bare soil and spring up quickly when any cover is removed. So both thickness and density are important.

A light, airy mulch such as straw needs to be used in quantity, 4 to 6 inches thick at least. A more dense material such as aged sawdust can be put on in layers of only an inch or two. Pine needles are best used about 2 inches thick. Packaged steer manure could be applied 1 to 2 inches thick.

You'll want to make it attractive-looking, too. An old piece of cardboard or plastic will do all this, certainly. But beauty is important in your garden. Attractiveness and tidiness are other qualities to look for.

In fact, the proper mulch can add to a garden's appeal. Dark brown mulches such as bark and packaged steer manure make excellent backgrounds for bright colors. Pine and fir needles add a delicate texture. Small gravel can complement drought-tolerant plants, especially in rock gardens.

Take Care!

If your area gets strong winds, you may prefer a heavy mulch such as gravel rather than straw or pine needles.

Water and Air Need to Get to the Roots

To keep the soil evenly moist, a mulch must let water pass through. And some plants, such as rhododendrons, have small roots that smother easily. So the spaces in a mulch are just as important as the substance itself.

In fact, one of the reasons why plants do so well under a mulch is that water goes through it into the soil more easily than if the surface was bare. Drops of rain often push the top grains of soil together into a crust that will shed water once it dries. Mulches protect the soil's porous structure.

Look for Long Life

Since most organic mulches decay slowly, finally forming a fine bed for a weed seed to sprout in themselves, durability is important. Look for a size of shredded bark, for instance, that will hold up for a few years.

On the other hand, if the size is too large, 2-inch nuggets of bark for instance, any weeds that do sprout will be much more difficult to pull out. And, eventually, weeds will come up in any mulch whether it is thick, thin, large, small, organic, or crushed rock.

Is It Easy to Weed?

Always consider what you'll do when the weeds appear. You may be able to use a herbicide in a path but around plants you must get them out by hand. Sharp-edged rock, for instance, is a particularly hard substance to weed around. Avoid it.

While gravel has the advantage of durability, you'll have a difficult time pulling weeds out from among large pebbles. Choose a small pea-size gravel that is round and easy to dig into.

Dandelions are difficult to remove if you try to pull them up by the leaves. They'll slide out easily, however, if you take a shovel or garden fork and loosen the soil around them.

Buy Cheap and Use More

You'll probably be able to get a better price on a truckload of mulch than on a bagged product. Call nurseries and landscape suppliers to get quotes. Use it generously in all areas of your yard.

If you're on a small budget, try mixing sawdust with bagged steer manure or grass clippings from a lawn untreated with herbicides. Sawdust by itself can compete with the plants for nitrogen as it decays, but nitrogen-rich clippings balance it out. A slow-release high-nitrogen fertilizer can also help.

Strategic Watering

Now, water enough in the next few months, but not too much. What does that mean? It means you need to balance the water and air.

Green Tips

Recommended mulches: Packaged steer manure (contains some fertilizer, but not enough to burn small plants, mainly sawdust with manure added); fine or medium bark; fir or pine needles (tend to make the soil more acid); sawdust mixed with grass clippings.

Moisten thoroughly, then resist the urge to water again until the top inch or so feels dry. This first fills the soil spaces with water, and then lets air flow back into them. Roots need both. If you water again before the soil has time to dry out a little, the roots may die from lack of oxygen.

Garden Talk

The terms *drought-tolerant* and *drought-resistant* mean that a plant can survive with little or no more water than nature usually provides. Obviously, a plant that is drought-tolerant in Oregon may need extra water in Arizona. And a plant that has had only a year to become rooted will need more water than one that has had ten.

How do you know when the soil has dried out enough? For small starts, water again when the surface of the ground is dry. When your plants are a few months older, let the top half inch dry out. When they're mature you can wait until one or two inches of soil are dry.

Of course, different plants need different amounts of water. For some, the surface of the ground should never dry out. Others will quickly rot if not allowed to dry deeply between soakings. Most fall between these two extremes. Be sure to get watering instructions when you buy a new plant.

If in doubt, err on the side of underwatering slightly. This will often cause roots to go farther down in the soil, making a more drought-tolerant plant. And a few wilted leaves will revive. Rotted roots cause the plant to suddenly collapse, a disaster from which they rarely recover.

Deep Watering for Deep Roots

Many people don't realize that even a small annual may grow roots that go down two feet or more. When you buy one, it has a neat package of roots, a four inch mass of intertwined threads that would spread out in all directions if they hadn't been restricted.

You can untangle roots a little during planting, but you also need to help them find their natural place deep in the soil by giving them an incentive to go down. If the surface is somewhat dry, the ones that are deepest will grow most quickly. The ones toward the top will languish.

Take some time to find out how long it takes to water your soil to a depth of a foot. It may take longer than you think. Sandy soil allows water to pass through quickly. A soil high in clay fills up slowly. It dries out slowly, too, which is an advantage. To do this, wait until the soil is fairly dry, water for 15 minutes, and then dig a hole to see how far it has penetrated. Repeat and see how much further you've moistened. This should give you an approximate idea of time needed to wet the soil one foot.

Once you know the time to allow per foot, you can make sure your sprinkler is on long enough to soak the bottom roots. Trees and shrubs may need watering to several feet.

Never let the soil dry out completely or you'll lose your new addition, but remember that roots need air. If the soil is always wet the plant will probably drown, the roots dying from lack of oxygen. Strike a balance, watering fully, drenching the root system, then letting the soil return to a moist-but-not-dry condition.

Use Fertilizers with Care

If you believed every ad on TV and in magazines, you'd think plants are dependent on us for their food. They, of course, make their own food using the energy from sunlight. They do need some nutrients from the soil and growth can slow if these are absent.

Plants have widely varying needs for nutrients. A rain forest vine has evolved to use what it finds there. A desert cactus will find different nutrient patterns as well as different amounts of rainfall. A perfect fertilizer for one may not suit the other.

What Is a Fertilizer?

Fertilizers are materials containing nutrients that plants need for growth, especially those that may be in short supply in the ground. Some are organic, made by living beings, such as manure and compost. These are usually used in a state of partial decay, decay being a process that makes the nutrients available to plants.

Some fertilizers are chemically produced, composed of compounds similar to those found in organic fertilizers, but in a forms that are more quickly available to the plant.

Green Tip

Rhododendrons, camellias, and mountain laurel (*Kalmia*) benefit from an acid fertilizer. You'll often find this type marked as rhododendron and azalea food.

What Do the Numbers on the Label Mean?

Though some fertilizers may have micronutrients, elements needed in very small quantities, three elements make up the main menu. The percentages of these are listed as three numbers, 5-10-10, for instance. The first number is nitrogen, the second phosphorous, the third potassium. The higher the number, the greater the percentage of that element.

As you look around the nursery shelves, you'll notice that fertilizers have many different combinations of these elements, each one formulated for a different purpose. Before you choose, you need to know how each element affects plant development. Then you can pick the right combination for the result you want.

Nitrogen promotes green, leafy growth. A high nitrogen fertilizer may give you large plants, but not flowers.

Phosphorous and potassium are necessary for strong stems, good flower and fruit production, and healthy roots.

Most fertilizers have all three elements combined, some with more nitrogen than others, some with less. You'll often see one marked for bloom with a 5-10-10 composition, for instance. Though you want small plants to put out leaves quickly, it's best to avoid putting high nitrogen fertilizers on flowers. Save them for your lawn or for a group of hostas and ferns.

Garden Talk

The term *harden off* means to condition plants to low temperatures or low humidity. Seedlings raised in a greenhouse, for instance, need gradual exposure to drier air and cooler nights. Woody plants go through a natural preparation for winter temperatures. Early frosts, for instance, may injure them more severely than later ones because they haven't had enough time to harden off.

Liquid or Granular Fertilizer?

Determining whether liquid or granule fertilizer is best depends on your situation. Liquid fertilizers act quickly, but need to be applied often. Granular fertilizers may break down or dissolve more slowly, but they're available for a longer time. You can even buy pellet fertilizers for single-application, all-season feeding.

If you want a hanging basket or container garden to fill in quickly use a liquid fertilizer, perhaps a 10-10-10. If you're feeding a fully grown flowering shrub, use one that has less nitrogen and that will be available while the new leaves are maturing, about a month.

When fertilizing shrubs, remember that they need little or no feeding in late summer. In fact, any new growth at that time may be winter killed. Let them harden off by watering a little less, too.

Is It Possible to Use Too Much Fertilizer?

You can use too much fertilizer. If you do, the plant may spurt new growth without flowers, or dark spots may appear on the leaves.

A few weeks after your planting session, give the bed a dose of complete liquid fertilizer, a quick boost. After that? Well, it depends on which plants and which time of year. Know why you're applying a fertilizer, what result you want to see. Then choose the right kind.

Always apply fertilizer to moist soil. Dry soil may soak up more than the recommended amount. Use the following as a guide:

➤ Annuals: You want lots of bloom, over along period of time. Use a 10-10-10 if you still need quick growth, otherwise a 5-10-10 will do.

➤ Perennials: You want balanced leaf growth and flowering. In most soils a fertilizer with equal elements is called for. If you're growing plants in an average garden that need rich soil, such as aconites or delphiniums, add some extra nitrogen.

➤ Shrubs and trees: These need nutrients when new growth is coming out, usually in spring and early summer. Roses are often fertilized throughout the summer to promote the bloom that comes on new growth. Do allow them to slow down in fall, though.

Floral Lore

Did you know that plants can absorb fertilizer through their leaves? It's a quick way to boost growth, but not a substitute for long-term feeding. Use a water-soluble fertilizer at the rate recommended on the label and apply when temperatures are below 85 degrees.

Pinching and Staking

Occasionally nature needs a bit of help in making a plant with a neat appearance. Some plants are naturally bushy, some need encouragement to branch out. Some plants are able to hold their stems upright no matter how much wind and rain assaults them. Others need support. Here's how to keep plants from flopping.

Pinching

When a stem grows upward, the tip takes precedence and receives most of the growth energy. This is called the terminal bud. Side shoots may appear, but they're definitely subordinate to the tip.

What happens when you remove that growing point? All the buds along the stem start sprouting, giving a branchy, stable silhouette rather than a slender one. Why is this called pinching? Because the terminal bud is so soft that you can literally remove it by pinching between thumb and forefinger. No clippers or other equipment needed. You can do it on the spur of the moment.

Garden Talk

The terminal bud of a plant is the one at the tip of a stalk or branch that is responsible for continuing the growth of that stem. The buds at the side of the branch often remain dormant until the terminal bud is removed. When you take off the bud without any of its stem, the process is called pinching.

Sometimes plants that have a little too much shade put out long slender branches that benefit from pinching. Sometimes too much fertilizer produces the same effect. Whenever you notice this happening, pinch.

Of course, you may not have time to be constantly pinching out leggy, sprawling plants. In that case, try to chose kinds that have a naturally branching habit.

Staking

If a stalk, especially one heavy with flowers, doesn't have enough strength to hold itself upright, tying to a securely planted stake may be necessary. You don't want the tying to detract from the flowers, so it needs to be done discreetly. Here are some possibilities:

➤ For light support, place twiggy branches on top of the ground just before the plant begins to grow. The new shoots will push through the twigs, anchoring themselves. This is especially good with many stemmed perennials such as Shasta daisies.

➤ You can buy wire hoops or cages ready made to place over the small plants. Peonies, for instance, do well supported in this manner.

➤ You can place one stout stick slightly behind the clump and run a length of drab string in and out of the stems, catching a few then taking a turn around the stick, then catching a few more. This gives a more graceful shape to the clump than simply surrounding it with string and pulling up tight.

➤ Tall stems may need to be individually staked. Make sure your piece of wood or bamboo is deep enough in the ground to be secure itself. The best time to do this is before your plant has a large root system. You want to get this as close to the center of the plant as possible but you don't want to hurt the roots. Do it early.

➤ Bulbs such as lilies need particular care since damage to the bulb may kill the plant. Though most varieties of lilies rarely need staking, you may want to prepare a hole just in case. When you plant the bulbs, put a short piece of wood next to them. If the lily stem needs support, just take the short stick out and substitute a longer one.

Garden Talk

Deadheading is the removal of faded flowers before they ripen seeds, a process that often sends a signal to the plant to stop blooming. Seed formation may also use energy gardeners would rather channel into growth.

Deadheading and Cutting Back

A plant's whole cycle is oriented toward producing seeds. Often, when a few flowers have achieved this goal, it will slow down on forming new buds. Many gardeners cut off the spent flowers to avoid this result, in a process called deadheading. Though some plants bloom for months without it, most will give you more flowers if you take the trouble to deadhead.

Depending on the plant, you might choose to cut off one dead flower at a time, or take a whole branch, or even shear large groups off. Just remember that the purpose is to remove old blooms before they set seed and you'll do fine.

If a plant is flowering at the end of leggy stems, you can cut it back to the new buds just sprouting at the base. You'll have a few weeks of green, then lots of new flowers. Though perennials usually flower for a month or six weeks, if you cut them back before they are completely finished you'll often have another burst of bloom.

Green Tip

Some plants with attractive seed heads include poppies (*Papaver*), love-in-a-mist (*Nigella*), stonecrop (*Sedum*), and yarrow (*Achillea*).

These aren't a required chore for gardeners, just nice touches. If you want to enjoy the seed heads and save your time for other things, go ahead.

Pruning Tips

Since shrubs, vines and trees have branches that persist from year to year, you'll probably find yourself doing some pruning to keep them growing in pleasing proportions or to keep the specimens from becoming too large.

Before you pick up your shears, picture your desired result in your mind. Plan your cuts to give you the kind of specimen you need.

If you want a smaller, bushier plant, cut the tips of branches off. If you want a smaller but open shrub, cut shoots back to a main branch that will take over the growth. If you have tangled mass of stems, a problem with some vines, choose the ones you want to keep, then cut out everything else.

If you prune flowering shrubs at the wrong time, you may find yourself without flowers the next year. Why? A forsythia, for instance, that blooms in early spring, will have next year's buds formed by midsummer. Cut branches in fall or winter and you've done away with spring flowers.

Green Tip

It's safe to prune a rose severely in early spring because all its flowers are borne at the end of new twigs. It's safe to prune a flowering quince in June because the new growth that sprouts won't flower until next March.

It's usually safe to prune right after flowering. The exception is summer- and fall-blooming plants that might put out tender new growth just in time for frost. Early spring is a suitable pruning season for these.

Another way to think of it: spring-blooming shrubs flower on branches produced last year; summer-blooming shrubs flower on this year's wood.

The Least You Need to Know

➤ Mulches cut down on weeding by preventing weed seeds from sprouting. They also keep the soil cool and moist, improving plant growth.

➤ Water deeply and infrequently for best root growth, but make sure that small starts don't dry out.

➤ Use fertilizers to get plants off to a quick start. Hold off on further applications if they seem to be growing well. You may not need any more.

➤ Know why you're pruning. Taking the tip off forces out bushy growth beneath it. Thinning lower branches gives an open airy effect.

Chapter 9

Help! Something's Wrong!

In This Chapter

➤ What do you do first?

➤ Is it in the wrong place?

➤ If you want to doctor it

It happens to everyone. Suddenly your petunia wilts or your peony has brown patches on the leaves. There's something chewing holes in the rhododendron leaves. The hosta is almost gone. You found three slugs on its stalks, so that one's no mystery. But what do you do now?

Magazine pictures to the contrary, gardens are not always green perfection. Plants are not as predictable as engines. They get sick, they get eaten, they die.

Gardens, however, can live on.

Don't Panic

When a plant starts turning yellow or if it hasn't put out any blossoms or the leaves wilt, you'll probably feel confused and unsure. Perennials don't come with instruction manuals covering every possible problem. Annuals don't come with the phone number of a hotline to call if they don't grow. What do you do?

Take a Closer Look

First, take inventory. What, exactly, is the problem? Are the leaves yellow all along the stem, or is it just the bottom leaves? Can you see insects or just some holes that might be made by insects? Is the whole plant wilted or just a few leaves? Does it recover when you water it?

Some of these details may mean nothing to you. Still, write them down, perhaps in your garden notebook. If you decide to ask a more knowledgeable gardener for help, you'll be able to give a precise description that contains (hopefully) key points he or she needs for a diagnosis.

Unless it's in danger of being eaten completely, spend a week or so watching. Do the leaf spots get bigger? Do they change shape or texture? Do the aphids come back after you hose them off? Do more leaves turn yellow? Or is the plant putting out healthy new growth above them?

Most problems can be ignored. A butterfly bush may drop some lower leaves but replace them with strong new growth. The aphids may cause some leaf curl, but soon move on to another place. Nature never intended for every leaf to stay picture-perfect.

Take Care!

If you're using pruners to snip off leaves or shoots, be sure to dip them in denatured alcohol to kill any disease before you use them on another plant. And put your clippings in the garbage can. Composting them only risks spreading the problem.

Keep Diseases from Spreading

One thing you can do right away if you notice spots on the leaves, wilted shoots or yellowed foliage is to remove the affected part as quickly as possible.

You're not making a diagnosis yet. The leaf spots could be produced by a disease or by other causes such as too much fertilizer. The wilted shoots could be caused by the accidental loss of some roots on that side of the plant. Yellowed leaves may be caused by lack of water or insects or disease.

Don't despair. Yes, diagnosis is a complex process but you have your task. Just get rid of the unsightly foliage. Why? Because spores from those leaves may infect others. You're containing the problem by removing sources of infection.

What If It's Dying?

Chances are nothing you could do would save it. If the roots are rotted, they rarely grow back. If your maple gets a disease that causes new growth to wilt, you may not be able cure it.

Insects and other munchers such as snails and slugs, however, may simply take all the leaves from a plant, a drastic form of pruning. Though the bare stalks look pathetic, your specimen will usually put out new growth if protected from further assaults.

New transplants are often vulnerable, needing protection when small, but tough enough to survive an occasional bite when older. Give them the attention they need to get started, but if you find yourself putting slug bait around a plant the whole summer, consider putting another one in its place.

Environmental Problems Are Most Common

Believe it or not, three quarters of all plant problems are environmental rather than caused by disease or insects. That means that your problem is likely a misfit between plant and place.

Think about what conditions the plant has been experiencing. Has it been underwatered? Sometimes newly planted flowers have such small root system that they dry out much more quickly than you'd expect. Or has it been so wet that the roots might have rotted?

Could it have gotten too cold? Too hot? Too much sun? Not enough sun?

All these factors can put a plant under stress, if it isn't adapted to those conditions. And like us, plants get sick or fall prey to insects when they're pushed to the limit of their tolerance.

Even if you see insects, don't assume that they're main problem. A weak plant is more vulnerable to their attack. A strong healthy plant may be bothered no more by a passing encounter with aphids, for instance, than you would be by a cold.

Here are some things to think about:

➤ Is the watering right? This is your most controllable environmental factor and the one that's most likely to cause problems if you use too much or too little. Even drought tolerant plants need regular amounts of water when they're small. They don't have the deep, wide roots that will sustain them next year. They're dependent on you for a while.

➤ Is it still adjusting? Sometimes newly transplanted starts have trouble settling in. Their root systems haven't had time to spread and stabilize. But if this plant has had a few months to establish itself, you may want to look for another variety.

➤ Can you relocate it? Many experienced gardeners will try a plant in one place and, if it doesn't thrive, then move it. Often a little more sun, or less, a little more of one thing or another, will make a difference. A failure in one place becomes a success in another. Look up this plant in a garden encyclopedia. Read as much about it as you can. Are there any clues that will help you place it properly? If it's from the Mediterranean, that might indicate a liking for warm, dry summers. Perhaps you could move it to the base of a south-facing wall. If it does well in wet areas, you may not need to keep it soaked, but don't let it dry out completely.

If you ask any experienced gardener if every plant she's ever tried grows for her, you're likely to get a laugh or a look of astonishment. No one has a 100 percent success rate. And sometimes there seems to be no explanation for the failures. The plant just didn't want to be there.

It May Not Be Your Fault

Too often, beginning gardeners blame themselves. They think they just don't have a talent for growing plants. Yes, you may make a mistake and put a plant in the wrong place. Yes, there are proper techniques to learn. But many attractive gardens are built more by persistence than green thumbs.

In other words, if a plant fails, try another one. Try twice as many flowers as you think you'll want. Plant at least three of each kind. One of them will probably be smaller than the others. If you had just that one, you'd think, "I just can't grow this plant," and give up on it.

Garden Talk

Plants that self-seed are masters at growing without the help of gardeners. Without any help from you, they sprout and grow in all sorts of odd places. If you wish them to stay put, cut off the fading flowers before the seeds ripen.

Be Willing to Try Again, and Again

Plants don't read books. Many flowers that self-seed will turn up in places that they don't belong according to the best books available. Be open to the possibility that someone else's garden has had a different effect on a plant than yours.

Gardening is an adventure. You can't play it totally safe. Dare to grow twenty or fifty or a hundred kinds of flowers. If you do, you'll find a large and benevolent group of them who seem to think your garden is just right. You just need to find them.

Should You Try to Save It or Not?

There's no point in trying to keep a finicky, borderline specimen alive when there are so many attractive flowers that would grow easily in your yard. So consider throwing it out.

Green Tips

If a plant in full sun looks pale and its leaves are small, put it in part-shade. If a plant has long thin stems and few flowers, give it more sun.

What? Just get rid of it without a fight? Yes. If it makes you feel better, give it to friend. But don't waste your time on it. You might leave it alone if the damage isn't too obvious. It may recover. Or you may decide to replace it with something better.

Can You Put up with Imperfection?

Often pests and diseases don't actually kill a plant, they simply make it unattractive. Most of us don't like seeing chewed, yellow, or spotted leaves on our prized specimens. It's not beautiful any more and we want to get rid of it.

Floral Lore

If you see neat circles cut out of your rose leaves, don't panic. Leaf-cutter bees did the damage, rarely taking more than a few bites out of each bush.

Can you increase your tolerance for what is, after all, a part of life? Nature seems to enjoy an intricate medley of life, including organisms we call pests and diseases. They have their place. Can it include your yard?

When Should You Put up a Fight?

Acting to save a plant may be best if you're particularly fond of that specimen. Your aunt gave it to as a wedding present. Or it's the main feature of your entry. Or it reminds you of a trip to France the summer after you graduated from college. Whatever the reason, you don't want to let it go.

Maybe it has five or ten years' growth and would be hard to replace. Trees, in particular, leave a noticeable gap when they die. The time and trouble to replace it make it worth saving. Of course, if it grew well for such a long time, it's probably well-adapted to your spot anyway.

It's just getting started and you want to give it a fair chance. Once it settles in, any plant is more resistant to insects and disease. Some flowers do need more time than others to get over transplanting and start growing vigorously. It's wise to give any plant a fair trial.

Can You Find a Substitute?

Roses, for example, come in all shades of disease resistance. If you love roses but two of the three you planted are sickly, consider looking for hardier varieties. You don't have to forgo your favorite plant, but you don't have to nurse weaklings either.

If you identify just what you like about a flower, you may be able to find similar ones that grow better for you. Is it fragrance? Or a particular shade of blue? Do you like its ferny leaves? Or is it the satiny texture of the petals?

Spend time exploring the nurseries. Plants in bloom sell quickly so many stores have them up front, giving you an opportunity to see a lot of flowers you may never have heard of. You may fall in love with two or three that will do just as well as the one that's failing.

*Foxglove (*Digitalis*) is a tough plant, somewhat drought-tolerant, that is rarely attacked by anything. Consider it an alternative to more delicate spirelike plants such as delphiniums.*

Guidelines for Doctoring

You want to save this plant. You won't stand back and let nature take its course. You won't give up without a fight. Now what do you do?

You can't do anything until you find out exactly what's wrong. A cure for one ailment is unlikely to help another. So where do you find a plant doctor?

You can try your own hand at the skill with some of the books listed in chapter 25. If you want to expand your own knowledge and have some time to spare, this is an excellent route to self-education as well as problem-solving.

Or you can ask a neighbor or friend. You can even take a piece of the problem plant into your local nursery and ask for help. Make sure you bring a section large enough to be helpful. If you see insects, put a number of them in a small bag or box.

Cooperative extension services in many states have a master gardener program with clinics you can go to for advice. Master gardeners are skilled home gardeners who have been given extra training by experts and who volunteer their time to help others sort out problems.

One caution: even experienced horticulturists sometimes disagree. Some plant problems are obvious and easy to name, others may have three people giving three different answers. All you can do is choose the best advisers you have available and trust them.

Green Tip

Try looking under county listings in your phone book to find a number for your extension service. It may be listed as a division of your state university, as "Washington State University Cooperative Extension Service" for instance.

Chemical or Organic?

Now that you know what the problem is, what do you do about it? Again, even experienced horticulturists may differ. Here are the options:

1. Do nothing. Let natural processes take over. Insect attacks, for instance, often diminish because of weather change or an increase in their usual predators. This, obviously, is the least work for you.

2. Try nontoxic organic controls. These may range from simple techniques such as spraying aphids with soapy water to complex, creative changes such as attracting birds to your yard. In general, these are earth-friendly and people-friendly. You won't accidentally cause problems for your neighbor's children if you stick with these.

3. Apply man-made chemicals. These may be effective, or may not. Follow every caution on the label to the letter, use in as limited a manner as possible, and take the manufacturer's claims that of quick decay with a grain of salt.

Take Care

If you have caterpillars chewing leaves, you may be told to spray with *Bacillus thuringinensis*, an organism that kills caterpillars but is completely nontoxic to humans. Be aware, however, that this kills all caterpillars it comes in contact with, including those of the brilliant butterflies everyone welcomes.

Research has shown that chemicals may break down more slowly under average conditions than the optimum conditions used during trials. These substances are harmful to people, to animals and to other organisms. Treat them with respect.

Applying Chemicals Properly

A pesticide label is the only instruction manual you can follow for that material, but here are some general guidelines:

Green Tip

If your roses, for example, get black spot (it's worse in some years than others) you can remove the affected leaves and sprinkle sulfur on the new growth. This is an essentially non-toxic fungicide that often works well if applied regularly. Or you may buy a stronger fungicide. Just don't expect to remove the spots that are already there.

➤ Some fungicides act to prevent spores from sprouting. You need to apply them before you see the disease, as preventative. Don't bother, unless your plant has gotten it before, or your neighbors have a fungus on the same plant.

➤ Sprays for other diseases may need to be applied at different times. Consult the label.

An insecticide is useless unless the insect is actually there to come in contact with it. Preventative spraying may leave a residue for a few weeks—either on the surface or in the tissues—that kills pests that come in contact with it, but unless you know one will arrive, wait. When you know you have a problem, when you're sure it's destructive enough to warrant pesticides, spray if you must.

The Least You Need to Know

➤ Many problems can be ignored. Either they go away or they stay at a tolerable level or they're an indication that this plant is in the wrong place.

➤ There are so many sturdy, good-looking plants available that if one fails you can easily fill the empty spot with another.

➤ Every gardener has had flowers die for mysterious reasons. The ones with the luscious yards simply keep trying new ones.

➤ Before trying to doctor a plant, get a diagnosis of its problem from a knowledgeable source. Make sure your cure will be appropriate.

➤ Only use chemical sprays as a last resort on specimens that must be saved.

Part 2
The Stars of the Show

Plants fall into broad categories depending on how they grow. Some arrive, grow and are gone in the space of one year. Others, such as tall trees, may last a century. Here's an introduction to flowers divided by form and habit.

Remember, though, that this is the tip of the iceberg. There are thousands of plants in cultivation, and some of the easiest plants to grow in your area may be known only by collectors. Every year more species make it into the neighborhood nursery. Cultivate an acquaintance with them.

One-act Wonders: Annuals and Biennials

When you see pictures of containers with colorful blossoms cascading down their sides, and garden beds that look like oversize florist's bouquets, chances are you're looking at annuals. They're the blazing reds and yellows lining nursery tables and the pinks and blues outside your grocery story. Instant, or at least quick, color is their specialty.

Annuals and Biennials are Short-lived

An annual is a plant that lives its whole life in a year. From seed to flowering and then to shriveled old age, they're here today, gone tomorrow. Well, not that quickly. In fact, many are willing to bloom their hearts out until frost. Why? Because their presence next year depends on a massive output of seeds. There's no bulb, no dormant root system to put out new growth next April. Seeds are the thing, the only thing, they put their hope in.

Since annuals survive the winter as seeds, winter-hardiness is not a problem. They do vary, however, in their temperature requirements for germination. Here are some of the types you'll find:

Hardy annuals: These are tough little beauties, such as forget-me-nots, who are able to sprout early in spring, surviving frost and storm, then burst out with blooms before store-bought annuals have much of a chance to get started. Tending toward the short-lived, though much depends on the species, these are best used to fill in the spring and early summer border. You can seed them later, but your easiest flowers come when you leave them alone.

Half-hardy and tender annuals: The distinction between these depends on how much frost they will take. Half-hardy annuals may stand a touch of frost, but not as much as the hardy varieties. Tender annuals are black and wilted the next morning.

Biennials are little more leisurely about life. They sprout and grow substantial plants one year, then shoot up flowering stems the next, finally dying after pouring their energy into seed production. Foxgloves are one of the best known of these. Angelica, Queen Anne's lace, and mullein are also biennials.

Hardy or tender biennials? Certainly. The difference depends on your climate. Some can overwinter with temperatures down to 0 degrees Fahrenheit, or lower, some may freeze out. Seeds are better able to withstand lower temperatures.

What Are the Advantages?

If your garden is bare, annuals and nursery-grown biennials will make it look well filled in a single season. Choose sunflowers (*Helianthus*), cleome, foxglove (*Digitalis*), and Canterbury bells (*Campanula medium*) if you want something substantial.

Many flower for months, even up until frost, especially if old blooms are picked off, or if they're trimmed back to new growth halfway through the season. Remember, they want to set seed and they'll put out flowers until they've reached their goal.

What Are the Disadvantages?

When cold weather kills tender annuals, they're gone. Leaves, roots, stems, nothing's left. If they've set seed, a few may emerge next spring, but often too late to put out much of a show.

Hardy and half-hardy annuals are better off since their seeds have a good chance at starting a new life. They may not come up in the place you chose for them originally, however. In fact, many make an attempt to colonize every spare corner you have but they're easy weeds to pull and charming guests if you don't bother.

Pointers for Planting

Annuals need a running leap into life to get their work done. Lack of water or nutrients can slow them to a crawl, resulting in stunted plants later on. For most, decent soil is a prerequisite, though fertilizer can compensate for many shortcomings. If yours is poor, try sowing some of the hardy annuals in their permanent positions in early spring. The strong root systems they form, unchecked by transplanting, seem better able to cope with less-than-perfect soil.

Outdoor sown annuals need a bed free of weeds, with a bit of mulch to make sure unwelcome seeds on the surface of the ground don't sprout. Scatter hardy annual seeds any time from fall through early spring and cover with more mulch, the amount depending on the size of the seed. Half-hardy annuals can go in a few weeks before last frost.

You can allow the plants to seed themselves at random, or save the seed and replant yourself. Just don't cut the flowers off until the heads of seed are dry and ripe.

Time of bloom depends on planting; fall-sown seed usually flowers much earlier than that scattered in May.

Though requirements vary for biennials, from almost any soil for foxgloves, to rich, moist conditions for angelica, do whatever you can to foster good leaf growth the first year. Fertilizer high in nitrogen, plenty of water, and mulch are all helpful for the first few months. Slow down on the water and fertilizer in late summer and fall, though, to allow them to harden for the winter. By next spring the plant will have enough growth to bloom well.

Introducing the Flowers Themselves

Here are your stars, the flowers that can turn a bare patch of ground into a bouquet of blossoms. If you don't find some of your favorites such as snapdragons (*Antirrhinum*), heliotrope (*Heliotropium*), and pansies (*Viola*), take a look at the tender perennial section.

Also, be aware that these are the plants that do well with sun and regular water, though some may be adaptable to other conditions. If you're landscaping a shady area, look at chapters 18 and 19.

A Bouquet of Hardy Annuals

You'll find a lot of Great-Grandmother's favorites here, a hint at their easy generosity. How much time did Great-Grandmother have to fiddle with flowers? She needed tough, independent pioneers willing to fill extra space with their seedlings. So, possibly, do you.

Green Tip

A note on names: common names are colorful, descriptive, easy to pronounce, and easy to remember. Why use cumbersome scientific names? Accuracy. For instance, at least six totally unrelated types of plants are called lilies. Ask for *Lilium regale* anywhere in the world, however, and you will be given plants bearing the same fragrant funnel-shaped flowers.

If you're in a hurry, you can usually find them in six-packs, but with forethought you can have more flowers by scattering the tiny seeds over the ground, topping with a skiff of soil, and keeping them moist.

Calendula pot marigold

> Needs: good drainage, any soil, modest amounts of water
>
> Character: large yellow to orange daisylike flowers on plants up to $2\frac{1}{2}$ feet with medium-size light green oval leaves
>
> Possible drawbacks: seeds prolifically, may sprawl, older varieties not resistant to heat

This plant may be found in named varieties from a soft primrose yellow through bright orange. Its big seeds and quick growth make it a good choice for children's gardens. Colonies will bloom through light frosts and begin again early in spring.

Floral Lore

This plant is named calendula because in mild climates it may bloom on the *calends*, the first day of every month.

Centaurea cyanus cornflower, bachelor's buttons

> Needs: average soil, sun, average or light amounts of water
>
> Character: somewhat stiff stems to 3 feet with bluish green leaves topped by blue, white, pink, or rose flowers, about 1 inch across

Grow these and you'll understand why cornflower blue is a synonym for clear, vivid sky-blue, especially striking with California poppies. 'Jubilee Gem' is an excellent dwarf strain. Cornflowers may self-sow, but not so prolifically as to overwhelm other plants.

Cleome hassleriana cleome

> Needs: sun, good soil, average water

> Character: globelike clusters of pink or white flowers top 3–4-foot stems

Attractive in both formal and informal gardens, cleome gives height without overwhelming smaller plants. Easy to grow from seed planted in spring, it also self-seeds prolifically.

Consolida ambigua larkspur

> Needs: sun, deep, rich soil, plenty of moisture, cool temperatures

> Character: spikes of blue, white, or pink flowers, up to 4 feet tall, above ferny, much divided leaves. Dwarf varieties a foot high are available.

A close relative of the majestic perennial delphinium, larkspur is just as useful for adding height to a design. Once sprouted, an extra application of mulch will help keep the soil cool and moist, prolonging bloom. Seed directly into garden for best results.

Convolvulus tricolor dwarf morning glory

> Needs: sun, average soil, good drainage, average water

> Character: spreading, foot-high mounds of oval leaves bear trumpet-shaped flowers of purple-blue and white

A close relative of moonflower and morning glory, this hugs the ground, mounding rather than vining, but can also be used to drape over the sides of containers.

Cynoglossum amabile Chinese forget-me-not

> Needs: sun, semishade in hot areas, average to less water, not for humid summer areas

> Character: clear, blue fragrant flowers, about $1/4$ inch across, in loose clusters on foot-high plants with bluish leaves, effective in masses

Reminiscent of true forget-me-nots but with deeper blue flowers and more sun and drought tolerance. An excellent filler to sow among more stout plants.

Gaillardia blanketflower

> Needs: sun, average soil, average to little water, tolerant of heat

> Character: large daisylike blooms in bright, warm colors on 1–2-foot plants with grayish leaves

Here's another cheerful daisy, almost as good as sunflowers for raising your spirits. Best if sown in place.

Gypsophila elegans annual baby's breath

> Needs: sun, average soil, good drainage, regular to little water

> Character: frothy sprays of white or pink flowers mound to 2 feet accompanied by narrow, grayish leaves

Few plants are as dainty as this one. Use as a florist would in a bouquet, to fill in space between larger plants and add a sense of unity to a composition.

Helianthus annuus sunflower

> Needs: sun, average soil, good drainage, average water

> Character: quick-growing plants up to 10 feet high bear huge, showstopping yellow, bronze to orange flowers with large, deep brown centers. Some varieties are lower, 3 or 4 feet, with smaller cream to yellow flowers.

> Possible drawbacks: tallest types may need staking, bottom leaves drop off leaving them looking leggy

Favorites for their size and their air of jaunty cheerfulness, sunflowers are easy and rewarding. Medium- or small-flowered varieties are best for mixing with other flowers. Groups of large-flowered varieties can be striking alone.

Floral Lore

Native to Mexico and Peru, sunflowers were revered by the Aztecs. Priestesses were often crowned with their blossoms and carried them in their hands.

Iberis umbellata annual candytuft

> Needs: sun to part shade, average soil, good drainage, regular water

> Character: low mounds, to 1 foot, are covered with pink to purplish or white clusters of flowers

This is a cheery plant with undemanding tastes, just right for the front of a border.

Lavatera trimestris annual mallow

> Needs: sun, average soil, average to little water, best with cool summers

> Character: hollyhocklike with flat, satiny blossoms, pink or rose, on stalks 2–5 feet (depending on variety) with soft, lobed leaves

An easy plant for substantial summer color, this can be helpful in filling bare new gardens. It's worth a place of honor in mature gardens, too.

Linum grandiflorum 'Rubrum' scarlet flax

> Needs: sun, average soil, occasional watering

> Character: rose-red flowers, 1 inch wide, on slender stems, to $1^1/_2$ feet

This is a beautiful plant for mixing with gray leaves or white flowers. It sprouts quickly, and because the plants are so slender, sow it thickly.

*Scarlet Flax (*Linum*) often reseeds but is rarely so enthusiastic that it becomes a pest.*

Lobularia maritima sweet alyssum

> Needs: sun to part shade, average soil, average water

> Character: tiny flowers in white to lavender-pink and purple hide the small narrow leaves

This is one of those plants that should be in all gardens, washing into every available space, eddying around larger clumps, a delicate tide of blossom. Choose one color and let it seed across the garden so you have a dependable shade to work with.

Nigella damascena love-in-a-mist

> Needs: sun to part shade, average soil, good drainage, average water

> Character: feathery leaves, flat, 1 to 1$^1/_2$-inch flowers in blue, white, or rose give a dainty, fragile effect

> Possible drawbacks: short-lived, must be sown repeatedly for bloom throughout summer, taproot makes transplanting difficult

'Miss Jekyll' is a lovely sky-blue variety, especially good in masses. Seed capsules are like small papery globes, decorative even when the blooms are gone.

Papaver rhoeas Shirley poppy

> Needs: sun, average soil, average water

> Character: thin, crinkled petals in many shades of pink through red open from fat hairy buds, up to 2$^1/_2$ inches above the clumps of leaves

Best in large groups, Shirley poppies were selected from the wild red poppy, producing double, semidouble, and single flowers in a whole range of colors. Easy to grow from seed, they look best in groups and will self-sow into wide areas.

A Bouquet of Half-hardy Annuals

You can plant these while the soil is still cold, but don't expect heroic frost tolerance.

Ageratum flossflower

> Needs: sun to part shade, average soil, average water

> Character: fluffy blue, pink, or white flowers top neat plants up to a foot high

An easy-care garden standard, ageratums are handy for creating colorful edgings to beds and containers.

Brachycome iberidifolia Swan River daisy

> Needs: sun, average soil, average water

> Character: spreading, foot-high plants are covered with 1-inch daisies in purple, blue, pink, and white, with finely divided leaves

These are good for any area where you want fine detail such as rock gardens and small display beds. Good for edging and trailing over the sides of containers.

Cleome spider flower

> Needs: sun, good soil, average water

> Character: globelike clusters of pink or white flowers top 3–4-foot stems

Attractive in both formal and informal gardens, cleome gives height without overwhelming smaller plants. Easy to grow from seed planted in spring, it also self-seeds prolifically.

Cosmos bipinnatus cosmos

> Needs: sun, average to poor soil, modest amounts of water

> Character: open, airy plants, up to 6 feet high, with daisylike flowers in many shades of pink, rose, lavender, and white

Though tall, this species is so delicate that it gives the impression of being, if not shy, at least demure. Many varieties are available, including bicolors, doubles, and flowers with quilled petals. Resistant to heat.

Cosmos sulphureus 'Klondike' yellow cosmos

> Needs: similar to *C. bipinnatus*

> Character: bold, smaller in stature, but with gold, orange, or red flowers that step out and claim their share of attention. Dwarf 'Klondike' strain grows to $1^{1}/_{2}$ feet.

Use this Cosmos for bright accent beds and for mixing with sunflowers, purple salvia, and crocosmia 'Lucifer,' listed under bulbs.

Tropaeoleum nasturtium

> Needs: sun to part shade, average to poor soil, average water

> Character: open tubular flowers come in many shades, mainly warm oranges and golds, but pink varieties are available, vining or compact plants have round leaves

An edible plant, with flowers appropriate for salads or soups and seeds that can be pickled like capers, nasturtiums are easy if sown directly into the ground when the weather is cool and damp. Rich soil or extra fertilizer will produce lavish growth but only scattered flowers.

A Bouquet of Tender Annuals

Most of these are heat lovers, plants to put against a south wall or grow in warm-summer climates. Don't plant them too soon in spring. They'll only sulk and succumb to mildew or rot if the ground is too cold.

Celosia cristata cockscomb

Needs: sun, average soil, modest amounts of water

Character: 1–2-foot plants with strangely shaped flower clusters in brilliant shades

With a somewhat tropical appearance, these can be hard to mix with other blossoms. If you want rich, stand-out color, however, these are hard to beat.

Coreopsis tinctoria calliopsis, annual coreopsis

Needs: sun, most soils, modest amounts of water, dislikes hot, humid weather

Character: yellow to bronze flowers banded with mahogany, dark centers, $1^1/_2$ to 3 feet

Bright, cheerful daisies good for informal gardens. Best if sown in place in a slightly dry soil.

Petunia hybrida petunia

Needs: sun to part shade, average to poor soil, average watering

Character: open, slightly funnel-shaped, round 2–4-inch flowers, sometimes ruffled, in most colors, some striped and double varieties, on 1-foot plants with broad, slightly sticky leaves

These deserve their popularity, being easy to grow and colorful. They make a low mass of bloom in that can spill over the sides of window boxes or hanging baskets or simply make a bold ground cover. In mild, humid summer areas they are grown for winter and spring bloom.

Portulaca moss rose

> Needs: sun, most soils, regular to light watering

> Character: bright jewellike flowers on flat plants with narrow succulent leaves

Given sun and enough warmth, this will thrive, perhaps seeding itself for next year. Few others do so well with heat and drought or give such clear rich color.

Salvia horminum Joseph sage

> Needs: sun, average soil, regular watering

> Character: cool blue, pink, or white spikes, to $1^1/_2$ feet

As willing to blend with other plants as scarlet sage is to stand out, this is a lovely middle of the border accent among sprawlers such as petunias and sweet alyssum.

Salvia splendens scarlet sage

> Needs: sun, good soil, regular watering

> Character: dense, upright clusters of warm-red flowers, 1 to 3 feet

No one can miss this accent plant. If you want to create an eye-catching display, surround this with yellow marigolds, white petunias, and gold daylilies. Strains with purple, pink, and white flowers are available.

Sanvitalia procumbens creeping zinnia

> Needs: sun, good drainage, regular to modest amounts of water, warmth

> Character: yellow or orange daisies with purple-brown centers on trailing branches, 6 inches high

Though not a true zinnia, this looks like it should be, with similar leaves and neat flowers that mimic its larger relatives. Doesn't like transplanting, so seed it in its permanent position as soon as the soil warms up.

Tagetes marigold

> Needs: sun, good soil, regular water

> Character: fluffy, pale yellow to gold and orange flowers, from 6 inches to 3 feet depending on variety; feathery leaves with a strong odor

Another of the garden standards, available almost everywhere. Rarely bothered by pests, marigolds are a rewarding plant for beginners to grow from seed as they sprout quickly and take transplanting well. You may plant taller varieties deeply to help support their stems.

Zinnia elegans zinnia

> Needs: sun, good to sandy soil, good drainage, regular to occasional water, warmth

> Character: upright, somewhat formal plants with flowers in almost any color but blue, from double daisies to exotic quilled and crested forms, 1–3 feet

These are hot weather standouts with lively clear colors and large flowers. Give the taller ones good soil. Once zinnias are established they can stand a bit of dryness, but water regularly when young. They may get mildew if leaves stay moist overnight. Resistant varieties are available.

A Bouquet of Biennials

Get these started by June so they'll have time to expand before winter. Remember, the bigger the plant this year, the more flowers you'll have next spring. You'll need to pay attention to hardiness zones here because they need to survive your winters. For a discussion of these, see chapter 4. For a map, see page 341.

Angelica archangelica garden angelica

> Needs: part shade, good soil, regular to frequent watering

> Character: huge, flat clusters of white flowers on 6-foot stalks above divided leaves that may reach 3 feet in length

> Season of bloom: summer

> Hardiness: zone 4

This is a standout, it's bold leaves commanding attention all season. It's deciduous, though, dying back to the ground each year. You may have it several years before it blooms, but be sure to sow the seeds as soon as they're ripe for new plants next year. They sprout poorly if stored.

Campanula medium Canterbury bells

> Needs: sun, good drainage, average soil, average water

> Character: 3–4-foot spikes of 2-inch long white, lavender-blue, or pink flowers, rising out of clumps of lance-shaped leaves

> Hardiness: zones 5–8

> Possible drawbacks: may need staking

This is an old favorite for cottage gardens. Use it to add height to a design or simply for the charm of its bell-like blossoms.

Digitalis purpurea foxglove

> Needs: sun to shade, average soil, average to modest amounts of water

> Character: drooping purple-pink flowers on 4-foot spikes rise out of clumps of large leaves

> Hardiness: zones 4–8

> Possible drawbacks: poisonous

A tough, adaptable plant, willing to reseed almost anywhere. The white form is especially beautiful in groups behind other flowers. Other varieties are available with larger flowers in pink, apricot, and yellow. Rarely needs staking in spite of its height.

Lunaria biennis honesty, money plant

> Needs: sun to part shade, average to poor soil, good drainage, average to modest amounts of water

> Character: attractive mauve flowers, like a purple mustard, with clumps of coarse, dark green leaves followed by flat seed pods that leave silver dollars lasting for weeks after the seeds are shed

> Season of bloom: spring

> Hardiness: zones 4–9

A weed, but a lovely one both in bloom and afterward. Allow it fill odd corners, perhaps with foxgloves as a partner, and you'll never have to sow it again.

Matthiola incana common stock

> Needs: sun to light shade, good soil, good drainage, average water

> Character: bushy, 1–3-foot plants bear fragrant spikes of flowers in shades of pink and lavender

> Hardiness: zones 6–9

Another cottage garden plant, stock is best in cool weather so plant early if your summers are hot. Its scent and good performance as a cut flower makes it worth growing no matter where you live. Stocks seem to be annual, biennial, or perennial depending on the climate.

The following tender perennials often treated as annuals:

> ➤ *Alcea*–Hollyhock

> ➤ *Antirrhinum*–Snapdragons

> ➤ *Bellis perennis*–English daisy

➤ *Dianthus barbatus*–Sweet William

➤ *Erysimum*–Wallflower

➤ *Gerbera*–Gerber daisies

➤ *Heliotropium*–Heliotrope

➤ *Tanacetum parthenium*–Feverfew

➤ *Verbena hybrida*–Garden verbena

➤ *Viola*–Pansies

The Least You Need to Know

➤ Get the annuals you buy in packs at the nursery off to a running start with good soil and regular watering.

➤ Seed hardy annuals during moist fall or spring weather. They'll develop good root systems before dry spells arrive.

➤ Plant tender annuals after the ground warms up or start in a greenhouse. Most weaken in cool weather, becoming more susceptible to disease.

➤ Biennials need three or four months of good growth one year to flower well the next. Plant them early.

Chapter 11

Flowery Carpets: Ground Covers

In This Chapter

➤ What do you mean by ground cover?

➤ Using ground covers creatively

➤ Planting tips

➤ A bouquet of annual ground covers

➤ A bouquet of perennial ground covers

➤ A bouquet of shrubby ground covers

Bare ground grows weeds. That's a fact of life. Want to delete weeding from your to-do list? Plant something that spreads to form a solid mat of leaves, shading the ground and keeping it cool and weed-free. Sounds idyllic, doesn't it?

Perhaps. But before weeding can become a thing of the past, you have to choose the right plants, get them off to a good start and care for them faithfully during their infancy.

What Do You Mean, Ground Cover?

Something that covers the ground. Well, a forest does that. So does a field of rye. In gardens, the word is usually applied to plants a foot and a half high or less that fill in space between larger plants or within the confines of a bed. The smaller the space, the lower the ground cover needs to be to give a carpet effect.

Lots of plants can sprawl across the ground but only those that score high in three areas can qualify as good ground covers. These three areas are as follows:

Take Care!

These plants are too rambunctious for most situations. Confine them in pots, in concrete-surrounded beds, or in the driest, poorest soil you can find: *Aegopodium podagraria* (bishop's weed), *Cerastium tomentosum* (snow-in-summer), *Convallaria majalis* (lily of the valley), *Lamium galeobdolon* (yellow archangel), and *Lamium album* (dead nettle).

➤ Density. Open, airy growth lets light get down to the soil, letting weeds sprout. And weeds twined among ground cover roots and stems are twice as hard to pull out as those in bare ground.

➤ Ability to spread fast, but not too fast. You need plants that grow with enthusiasm, expanding rapidly to form a thick mat within a year or two. However, some plants grow by leaps and bounds, overrunning everything else. The distinction between the two is sometimes blurred. After all, you want the plants to spread. It's just that they just don't know when to stop.

➤ Neatness. You don't want to trade weeding for hours spent cutting off dead blossoms or old stems. Choose plants that keep their attractive appearance without your help. Some types, especially woody low shrubs, need a yearly shearing to stay dense enough for weed control.

Using Ground Covers Creatively

A single expanse of green or of a single blossom in its season can be just what you need to provide a background for other plants, but consider these alternatives:

➤ Shapes and patterns. Divide a large area into smaller ones with straight lines or curves, then plant each with a different ground cover, or with different colors of the same one.

➤ More than one. For a natural look, choose two or three ground covers and allow them to mix and mingle. The evergreen carpet bugle (*Ajuga reptans*), for example, combines well with deciduous wood sorrel (*Oxalis oregana*) in shady areas.

➤ Matching colors. To complement a flowering shrub, surround it with a ground cover whose flowers are a similar color. For instance, the dainty pink-flowered soapwort (*Saponaria ocymoides*) is an excellent companion to weigela, whose tubular, rose-colored flowers attract hummingbirds.

➤ Varied textures. Fine, ferny ground covers such as creeping veronica (*Veronica prostrata*) can set off the bold leaves of bergenia and the linear ones of daylilies

(*Hemerocallis*). On the other hand, bold-leaved lady's mantle (*Alchemilla*) is a perfect partner to the delicate yellow corydalis (*Corydalis lutea*).

Planting Tips

Success with ground covers depends on getting them off to a vigorous, healthy start. Here's how:

Green Tip

You can see an annual ground cover such as sweet alyssum (*Lobularia maritima*) in between starts of a slower-growing perennial or low shrub. The annual will keep the weeds down and the permanent ground cover will eventually shade out most of the seedlings.

➤ Choose one that fits your site. If you have sun, pick a sun-lover. If you can't water regularly, find one that's drought-tolerant. If you have deep, solid shade, get one that loves shadows. Every plant grows thicker and more dense if given its favorite conditions.

➤ Try a few first. Don't plant a hundred before you're sure the plant will settle in well. Sometimes even the best match of garden and plant fails for no apparent reason. Try your ground cover in a small area and if it succeeds, then go for the whole yard.

➤ Thoroughly remove all weeds, roots and all. Some weeds sprout from the roots and any piece left in the ground is a potential menace to your new planting. Grass, for instance, can grow through a foot of stems and leaves to gain sunlight. Don't let it get started.

➤ Improve the soil. Loosen the soil deeply and add some organic matter. Avoid peat moss as an additive; it sheds water when dry. You'll be glad you did the extra work as the ground cover fills in and your weeding time starts to dwindle.

➤ Mulch to keep weeds down. As well as keeping the soil cool and moist, mulches fill in for your plants until they can carpet the ground themselves. Make sure you remove any weeds that sprout in the mulch. If they get a foothold in your planting now, you'll have twice the work removing them later.

➤ Water well until filled in. New plants should be treated well, never allowed to dry out completely. Even drought-tolerant plants can't do without regular watering until their roots spread wide and deep. Skimping now means waiting longer for your ground cover to reach maturity.

➤ Fertilize several times the first few years. You want cover as quick as possible. That's what fertilizers are for, isn't it?

A Bouquet of Annual Ground Covers

Annuals are good for filling space while you're waiting for slowing growing plants to spread. They may not keep weeds down as well as perennials unless planted thickly, however.

All are summer bloomers in any zone and may return next year by scattering seeds around your garden.

Gypsophila elegans baby's breath

> Needs: sun, good drainage, can take some drought

> Character: clouds of small white or pink flowers on foot-high plants

Short-lived, only a month and half, but will seed itself every year once established. Use as a delicate complement to larger plants.

Lobularia maritima sweet alyssum

> Needs: will grow almost anywhere except deep shade, drought-tolerant

> Character: tiny white, pink, or purple flowers on plants 3–6 inches high

A standard quick cover for most gardens. The white variety is especially nice under roses. Also seeds readily, so you'll have them coming up in unexpected places next year, a most welcome weed.

Portulaca grandiflora rose moss

> Needs: sun, good drainage, drought-tolerant, takes heat well

> Character: roselike flowers in vivid colors and succulent leaves on plants only a few inches high

Tuck these into dry, out of the way corners and you'll be surprised at the way they bloom without any care. Reseeds in some areas.

Sanvitalia procumbens creeping zinnia

> Needs: sun, good drainage, takes heat well

> Character: looks like a small, spreading zinnia about 6 inches high, with yellow petals surrounding dark brown centers

A native of Mexico, this is not a true zinnia, though it looks like one. Great in hanging baskets and as an edging for planters.

A Bouquet of Perennial Ground Covers

Perennials offer stability. Returning every year, spreading by runners and side shoots, they usually thicken quickly and without much work on your part. You can take some of the side shoots off and plant them other places, too.

Deciduous plants, those that die back in winter, may need the old growth cut off and may be vulnerable weeds when dormant. But they may be just the one you need otherwise. You be the judge.

Since these live over the winter, you'll have to pay attention to hardiness zones. For a discussion of these, see chapter 4. For a map, see page 341.

Aegopodium podagraria bishop's weed, goutweed

> Needs: some shade, not much water, average to poor soil with good drainage
>
> Character: flat clusters of white flowers above attractive, medium-size green leaves; deciduous
>
> Season of bloom: late spring
>
> Hardiness: zones 3–9

Attractive but extra vigorous. A variety with white-edged leaves is available that is slightly less likely to overrun your garden. Worth the trouble of finding a tough spot for it to spend its vigor and great in pots.

Ajuga reptans carpet bugle

> Needs: best in shade, even deep shade, can take wet soil or some drought if well-shaded
>
> Character: 6-inch spikes of small purple flowers above spoon-shaped leaves that may be green, purple, or variegated with pink in different varieties; evergreen or semievergreen in coldest areas
>
> Season of bloom: late spring
>
> Hardiness: zones 3–8

A garden standard, spreading from runners that sprout new plants at the tips, filling in quickly. May invade the lawn, but takes well to mowing.

Arabis caucasica wall rockcress

> Needs: some shade in hot climates, well-drained soil
>
> Character: white flowers thickly cover 6-inch plants that spread rapidly to a foot across
>
> Season of bloom: early spring
>
> Hardiness: zones 4–10
>
> Possible drawbacks: short-lived where summers are humid

Excellent cover for spring-flowering bulbs, good in rockeries.

Arenaria montana sandwort

> Needs: good drainage, regular water, sun (part shade in warm climates)
>
> Character: up to 4 inches high with small bright green leaves and inch-wide white flowers, dense and attractive
>
> Season of bloom: late spring, summer
>
> Hardiness: zones 4–9

Cerastium tomentosum snow-in-summer

> Needs: sun (some shade tolerated in hot areas), well-drained soil, even pure sand, average to infrequent watering
>
> Character: small white flowers cover silvery plants up to 6 inches high; deciduous
>
> Season of bloom: early summer
>
> Hardiness: zones 2–8

Make this one work for a living! In good soil it spreads quickly and strongly and is likely to pop up anywhere. Starve it, ignore it, contain it, and you'll be pleased with its appearance.

Ceratostigma plumbaginoides leadwort

> Needs: sun to part shade, not particular about soil or watering
>
> Character: excellent $1/2$-inch blue flowers on plants 6–10 inches high with bronzy fall color, deciduous
>
> Season of bloom: late summer to fall
>
> Hardiness: zones 5–9

Though slow to leaf out in spring, the fall display this plant puts on is worth waiting for. Could be planted with bulbs to hide their yellowing leaves and provide a later show.

Chaemaemelum nobile chamomile

> Needs: sun to part shade, occasional watering
>
> Character: small daisylike flowers above finely cut fragrant leaves, to 1 foot
>
> Season of bloom: summer
>
> Hardiness: zone 4

This is one of the few plants that can be mown to make a soft-textured lawn substitute, a sweet-smelling ground cover that takes foot traffic. It's easily divided, but if you need to cover a large area, consider starting it from seed.

Chrysogonum virginianum goldstar

> Needs: part shade to shade, sun with faithful watering
>
> Character: inch-wide golden yellow flowers above bright green, hairy leaves, about 6 inches high; deciduous to semievergreen
>
> Season of bloom: spring, fewer flowers in summer, again in fall
>
> Hardiness: zones 5–9

One of the best for moist soils, with one of the longest flushes of bloom you'll find. Combines well with other warm-toned flowers such as orange geum, yellow-flowered swamp iris (*Iris pseudacorus*), and bronzy bee balm (*Monarda*).

Convallaria majalis lily of the valley

> Needs: best in shade, most soils, can take some drought
>
> Character: small, fragrant white bells above bold 6-inch leaves; deciduous
>
> Season of bloom: spring
>
> Hardiness: zones 2–8

Another lovely invader, excellent when contained but a determined traveler when let loose. It can hold its own against other ground covers, however, and a mixed planting of this with ajuga or Labrador violet (*Viola labradorica*) has great possibilities for contained beds with poor soil and too much shade.

Floral Lore

There is an English legend that the lily of the valley sprang from the blood of Saint Leonard, who died fighting a great dragon in the woods of Sussex.

Cymbalaria muralis Kenilworth ivy

> Needs: shade to part shade, average soil, tolerates alkaline soil, regular to little water
>
> Character: round, scalloped leaves are accompanied by tiny lilac flowers that look like miniature snapdragons
>
> Season of bloom: summer
>
> Hardiness: zones 3–9

A quick-growing, delicate trailer often sold as an annual for hanging baskets. Often seeds itself into cracks in walls and pavement.

Fragaria 'Pink Panda' flowering strawberry

> Needs: sun to part shade, well-drained soils with average watering
>
> Character: 1-inch rosy pink or red flowers on 6-inch plants with shiny, attractive leaves; deciduous
>
> Season of bloom: spring
>
> Hardiness: zones 3–9

Not for fruit, this strawberry has showy flowers and a spreading but well-mannered habit. Useful for large swathes of color.

Gallium odoratum sweet woodruff

> Needs: partial to full shade, moist to somewhat dry soils, will take wet soil well
>
> Character: tiny white, fragrant flowers cover 6–8-inch high, fine-textured plants; deciduous
>
> Season of bloom: late spring
>
> Hardiness: zones 4–9

Used for making May wine, the flowers are delicate and airy, a perfect counterpoint to larger-leafed shrubs and perennials. Spreads quickly but will not overwhelm any but the smallest plants.

Lamium dead nettle

> Needs: some shade, average soil, average water

> Character: silver-spotted leaves, masses of small, white to pink flowers, making a mat about 6 inches high

> Season of bloom: spring

> Hardiness: zones 3–10

The varieties 'Beacon Silver' and 'White Nancy' are less invasive than the species, which can cover whole shrubs in rich moist soil. These are lovely, bright carpets for shade.

Lamium galeobdolon yellow archangel

> Needs: not particular about anything

> Character: small, yellow flowers on a vinelike plant with silver-spotted leaves; semievergreen to evergreen

> Season of bloom: spring

> Hardiness: zones 3–9

Will drape itself over walls and over other plants, but is great for tough areas. Requires cutting back in spring to look good.

Lysimachia nummularia creeping Jenny

> Needs: likes moisture, best in part shade but can take sun in the north, not particular as to soil

> Character: flat mats of round leaves dotted with golden yellow flowers; semievergreen to evergreen

> Season of bloom: spring

> Hardiness: zones 4–10

Sends out runners that root from beneath the leaves, making it a sprawling, somewhat open spreader, but thickens with age. There's a golden-leafed form that brightens dark spaces.

Mazus reptans mazus

> Needs: sun to part shade, average water, average soil
>
> Character: low, only 1 inch high, with purple flowers marked with white and yellow; evergreen in mild-winter areas
>
> Season of bloom: late spring
>
> Hardiness: zones 5–7

One of the few ground covers that takes some foot traffic, best in small areas. Can grow too quickly if given good soil and extra water.

Saponaria ocymoide rock soapwort

> Needs: sun, regular to less water, good drainage. Not for areas with hot, humid summers.
>
> Character: can grow 1 foot high and 3 inches across, sprawling, with small pink flowers
>
> Season of bloom: spring
>
> Hardiness: zones 2–7

Easy to grow and dense enough to make an excellent ground cover.

Sedum 'Cape Blanco' stonecrop

> Needs: sun, part shade, can take drought or average watering
>
> Character: thick, succulent bluish leaves, yellow flowers, about 4 inches high; evergreen
>
> Season of bloom: early summer
>
> Hardiness: zone 5

Many varieties of sedum aren't thick enough to keep down weeds. This one is. Though it takes its time spreading, you can rapidly expand your planting by breaking off stems and sticking them in the ground. Each one will grow into a new plant.

Viola labradorica Labrador violet

> Needs: some to lots of shade, average soil, average to little water
>
> Character: small purple flowers rising above 2–4-inch-high mats of purple leaves
>
> Season of bloom: spring
>
> Hardiness: zones 2–9

Few violets are as tough and generous with seedlings as this one. Not only an excellent carpet for dryish shade but an attractive filler almost anywhere.

A Bouquet of Shrubby Ground Covers

Arctostaphylos uva-ursi bearberry, kinnikinick

> Needs: sun or light shade, well-drained sandy to good soil, regular to occasional watering
>
> Character: drooping clusters of white to pink vase-shaped flowers followed by red berries, plants to 1 foot; evergreen
>
> Season of bloom: spring
>
> Hardiness: zone 2

This is one of the best ground covers you could find, attractive all year with both flowers and berries for interest, and glossy green leaves that turn purplish in winter.

Bearberry (Arctostaphylos) is a drought-tolerant ground cover that grows well at the seashore as well as in the mountains.

Ceanothus gloriosus Point Reyes ceanothus

> Needs: sun, well-drained soil, drought-tolerant, best in cool summer areas
>
> Character: clusters of tiny, brilliant blue flowers, shrub spreading to 4 feet wide with small, shiny leaves
>
> Season: spring
>
> Hardiness: zones 7–9

A beautiful, fast-growing ground cover with the density needed to permanently weed-proof your garden.

Erica and ***Calluna*** heaths and heathers

> Needs: sun to part shade, well-drained, acid soil, average watering
>
> Character: tiny white or pink flowers, needlelike leaves, give a delicate, fine-textured effect
>
> Season: early to late spring, depending on variety
>
> Hardiness: zones 5–9, depending on variety

An excellent ground cover in masses, though many varieties need a once a year shearing after flowering to keep them dense.

Helianthemum sun rose

> Needs: sun, well-drained, rather poor soil, drought-tolerant
>
> Character: small leaves, bright flowers like single roses on foot-high plants
>
> Season: late spring
>
> Hardiness: zones 4–10

Native to the Mediterranean region, this ground cover comes in many shades, from pale yellow to red and orange. Some varieties need to be sheared after flowering to keep them dense.

Iberis sempervirens candytuft

> Needs: sun, well-drained, average soil, average watering
>
> Character: clusters of small white flowers on deep green plants, 6–12 inches high; evergreen
>
> Season of bloom: spring
>
> Hardiness: zones 4–9

A cheerful spring accompaniment to tulips and daffodils, neat if sheared after bloom, often used in rock gardens.

Lavandula angustifolia lavender

> Needs: lots of sun, average soil, average to little water
>
> Character: spikes of tiny, fragrant purple flowers cover the gray-leaved plants
>
> Season of bloom: early summer
>
> Hardiness: zones 4–10

A native of the Mediterranean region, lavender takes heat and drought well. It may not grow as fast if given better soil and more water, but the plants grow more densely. Water and fertilize until established, then forget it. Needs shearing after flowering.

Floral Lore

The herbalist Sydney Parkinson said that lavender is of "especially good use for all grieves and pains of the head and brain."

Rubus calcynoides flowering blackberry

> Needs: average, well-drained soil, sun to shade
>
> Character: small, white single-rose flowers on a compact, spreading shrub about 6 inches high, whose neat, rounded leaves turn bronzy in fall
>
> Season of bloom: late spring
>
> Hardiness: zones 7–9, possibly farther north

This well-behaved blackberry is becoming a favorite for its neat but spreading habit and fall color.

The Least You Need to Know

➤ Ground covers can shade out weeds and keep the ground cool.

➤ Match a plant's needs to your own site.

➤ Ground covers need extra care the first few years to get them started off vigorously.

➤ Best ground covers for sun: sweet alyssum, leadwort, mazus, and candytuft.

➤ Best ground covers for shade: carpet bugle, goldstar, and sweet woodruff.

Chapter 12

Sudden Entrances: Bulbs

In This Chapter

➤ What do you mean by bulbs, corms, and tubers?

➤ Planting tips

➤ A bouquet of hardy bulbs

➤ A bouquet of half-hardy bulbs

Who would believe that the dry, papery globes you plant in October would turn into purple crocus? Or that the pointy, onionlike bulbs marked narcissus would turn into daffodils with long, yellow, trumpetlike blooms?

If there is proof of magic, it is surely in the transformation of these odd shaped bundles, merely dropped into the ground and forgotten, into beauty.

What Are These Terms?

Plants have a number of ingenious ways of storing food to get them through periods of dormancy or drought. Clever gardeners take advantage of these sizable, easy to handle storage systems and plant as many as they can afford.

While the average gardener calls anything a bulb that is vaguely round, brown and dry and that sprout when planted, a botanist uses an exactly defined term for each type. (Botanists, like other scientists, like to be precise in the names they use.) Not only will you impress your friends when you learn them, but you'll also know more about expanding your plantings for free.

True Bulbs

Onions and garlic are good examples of true bulbs. When you cut an onion or a clove of garlic in half you can see the embryonic plant at the base, surrounded by thick, protecting layers of leaves. You can often see the roots that grew from below it.

Daffodils are similar. A new bulb starts like a new clove of garlic and gradually separates as it gets bigger. You can take these off if they're about half the size of the mother bulb and plant them nearby. They'll grow faster in good soil of their own.

True lilies (*Lilium*) look more like loose heads of garlic, but what looks like a clove is actually one of the leaves that protects the shoot. New bulbs grow slightly apart from the mother bulb. Lilies don't like being disturbed so separate these only when the clump is quite large.

Corms

Corms are a like the base of the onion, but larger and able to store more food. The bud is at the top, exposed, not surrounded by puffy layers. It is often, however, covered by the papery remains of previous season's leaves. At the end of summer, a plant produces a new corm on top of the remains of the old one.

Look at a gladiolus corm. You'll see the pointed, papery top, and the plate at the base from which roots grow. This is where tiny seed corms bud off, five to twenty per plant. If you put these in good soil, they'll flower in two or three years.

Tubers

Like a corm, a tuber is an enlarged stem base. Rather than one point at which roots emerge and one at which another stem grows, the whole lower surface may sprout roots and a number of shoots may grow from the top.

Halves of a tuber may be planted separately to make two plants if you make sure each one has a growth bud on the top.

Rhizomes

Rhizomes are less organized than bulbs or corms, being thickened stems that grow underground. The long brown fingers of oriental ginger used in cooking are a good example.

Like all stems, it has a number of buds or growing points along its sides. Simply cut the rhizome in two or three pieces, each with several buds, and you have new plants. Most rhizomatous plants are classed with perennials rather than bulbs, but you may find such plants as bearded iris and calla lilies on your nursery shelf with the bulbs since the thick stem stores just as well.

Tuberous Roots

Potatoes are tuberous roots, enlargements of a section of root rather than stem. Each eye is a potential growing point and roots, too, can grow from almost anywhere. Each one can be cut into pieces, or the small ones planted whole.

Dahlias are similar, though the swollen roots are connected at the top, where the growth buds occur. This makes them look like a cluster of long potatoes connected by a narrow neck. When you dig them up, be careful the fragile neck doesn't break. Cut them so that at least one growth bud stays with each tuberous root.

Plant for Long Life

Planting bulbs properly means investing in the future. The bulbs you buy have plenty of food stored for first season bloom. Unless you plant them in soil so wet that they rot or so dry that they wither, your show is assured.

Your display next year, however, depends on whether or not the plants get their preferred conditions from you. Care in planting and making sure nutrients are available is important.

Most bulbs, however, are willing to make do with average soil and watering, asking only a decent start in life. Like gold pieces in the bank, they're willing to flower year after year with little more effort on your part.

> **Green Tip**
>
> Some of the best bulbs for ordinary soil and less-than-attentive watering are flowering onions (*Allium*), bluebells (*Hyacinthoides*), and grape hyacinths (*Muscari*).

Add Nutrients

Some bulbs are greedier than others, hybrid tulips being among the touchiest to keep going for more than a few years. All, however, appreciate loosened soil with some bonemeal mixed in. Why bonemeal? Ground-up bone decays slowly, so there's some left for next year, or even the year after. It's also high in phosphorous and potassium, nutrients that bulbs use to make new offsets. You can also use other slow-release fertilizers.

Because roots go down farther than most people care to dig, match your bulbs to your basic soil type. Alliums do well with sandy soil; callas do well with lots of moisture. Be realistic about what you're offering your purchases.

A few others, like camas and *Narcissus* 'Actaea', do well in wet soil, but most bulbs rot easily if kept too damp. Good drainage is important if you're going to grow crocus, hyacinths, and many others.

Putting Them in the Ground

Bulbs are formed underground, at the base of a main stem or on roots, and for best growth need to be placed in a similar position. Plant too deep and the shoots use up too much energy trying to find the sun. Plant too shallow and plants are floppy and subject to frost and drought damage.

What's right? For true bulbs and corms, digging a hole about three times the bulb's diameter is often recommended. A daffodil bulb about $1^1/_2$ inches thick would need a hole $4^1/_2$ inches deep. Other types need depths specific to the species. These instructions will be included with your bulbs.

In practice, individual holes are tedious to dig for more than a few bulbs. Since they look best in groups, dig a broad hollow, mix fertilizer with the soil in the bottom, set your bulbs in at the proper depth, and cover.

Moisture Is Important

Now water thoroughly. You may not see any growth for six months but the plant is growing a web of roots deep in the soil that will nourish its growth later. This rudimentary root system needs to be kept moist, no matter how drought-resistant the mature plant becomes.

Winter rains may take care of watering until flowering or you may have to soak occasionally yourself, depending on your climate. Just remember that the roots are down below the base of the bulb and add enough water to drench them.

While They're Growing

Again, remember that you're investing in the bulbs that come after flowering and growth. Fertilizing with high phosphorous-potassium solutions or pellets can insure good bloom next year and compensate for lean soil.

Most important, learn to tolerate the yellowing, drying leaves that mark the end of a life cycle. The nutrients and food from the leaves is being transferred to the bulb. If you cut them off too soon, you'll starve next year's embryonic plant.

A Bouquet of Hardy Bulbs

Here are some of the best of the bulbs, though if you become addicted you can find many more in specialty catalogs. If you're looking for ideas for a shady spot, there are more suggestions in chapter 18. While able to take quite a bit of cold, these vary in hardiness. See chapter 4 for a discussion of zones. For a map, see the color insert.

Allium flowering onion (true bulb)

> Needs: sun or part shade, well-drained, not too rich soil, regular water while leaves are growing, can take drought later
>
> Character: small flowers are clustered together in heads that drift above grassy or straplike foliage. Many species available are 1 to 2 feet tall, with small heads that look good in masses, including:
>
> > *A. cernuum* Pacific Northwest native, lavender pink flowers
> >
> > *A. moly* yellow flowers, easy and spreads well
> >
> > *A. roseum* light pink flowers, will grow almost anywhere
> >
> > *A. sphaerocephalum* rose-purple flowers
>
> Others have huge globular heads that tower 3–5 feet, specimens that should be planted in groups of at least three, including:
>
> > *A.* 'Globemaster' lavender balls, to 10 inches across
> >
> > *A. giganteum* lilac clusters on tall stems
> >
> > *A. aflatunense* looks like a smaller *giganteum*
>
> Season of bloom: late spring, early summer
>
> Hardiness: zones vary from 4–9 for *A. moly* and *A. giganteum*

One of the easiest bulbs to grow in average soil, alliums rarely smell oniony unless the leaves are crushed. If you're bothered by deer and other wildlife eating your plants, these are for you. Nothing bothers them.

Colchicum autumn crocus (corm)

> Needs: sun or light shade, good, well-drained soil, average water
>
> Character: lilac-pink vaselike flowers, similar to large crocus, some varieties double or semidouble
>
> Season of bloom: late summer, fall
>
> Hardiness: zones 5–10
>
> Possible drawbacks: poisonous, flowers may flop

Not true fall-blooming crocus, but with a similar shape, colchicums may begin blooming before you get the large corms in the ground. Plan for the large, straplike leaves that appear in spring then wither, leaving empty spots in the bed. Great in ground covers, which help to hold the large flowers up after a rain.

*Autumn crocus (Colchi-
cum) will surprise you in
August or September with
its large, pink crocuslike
blooms.*

Crocus crocus (corm)

> Needs: sun to part shade, open, well-drained soil, average water during growth

> Character: chalicelike blooms in shades of purple, lavender, white, and gold, some striped, up to 3 inches in Dutch hybrids, smaller in species crocus, with grassy, inconspicuous leaves

> Season of bloom: early spring or fall for species crocus, midspring for Dutch hybrids

> Hardiness: zones 4–8

> Possible drawbacks: needs cool winters to naturalize

Popular, inexpensive flowers that are most effective as pools of color, so use lots of them among shrubs and around perennials.

Gladiolus communis ssp. byzantinus hardy gladiolus (corm)

> Needs: sun, good soil, average water
>
> Character: smaller, more open spikes of flowers than common gladiolus, in shades of pink and maroon, about 2 feet high, narrow leaves
>
> Season of bloom: late spring
>
> Hardiness: zones 5–8

Informal and unusual, good mixed with perennials, and excellent cut flowers. These have an air of simplicity that makes them appropriate for mixing with wildflowers.

Hyacinthoides hispanica Spanish bluebell (bulb)

> Needs: sun to shade, any soil if well-drained, water when blooming
>
> Character: foot-high spikes of soft blue flowers over straplike leaves
>
> Season of bloom: late spring
>
> Hardiness: zones 4–8
>
> Possible drawbacks: spreads so easily that it can become a charming nuisance, fresh bulbs are poisonous

Just try to keep this one from colonizing your yard! Tough, bountiful, and handsome, bluebells grow almost anywhere. If you think you have a black thumb that kills everything, try this.

English bluebells, *H. non-scripta*, are closely related, somewhat more dainty, hardy in zones 5–7.

Floral Lore

The juice of the English bluebell was thought to be the best starch for stiff Elizabethan ruffs. It has also been used to fix feathers on arrows and covers on books.

Hyacinthus hyacinth (bulb)

> Needs: sun, rich soil, average water
>
> Character: rather massive, dense stalks of fragrant flowers in blues, purples, and pinks, substantial linear leaves
>
> Season of bloom: spring
>
> Hardiness: zones 4–8

Classic, richly scented, but not graceful, these plants have been used to color formal gardens more often than to mix with other flowers. Try them in clusters around taller plants such as iris surrounded by a frothy groundcover such as sweet woodruff if you want them to look more relaxed.

Ipheion uniflorum 'Wisley Blue' spring starflower (bulb)

> Needs: sun to part shade, well-drained soil, regular water while growing, little water in summer
>
> Character: blue, starlike blossoms, lighter at the center
>
> Season of bloom: spring
>
> Hardiness: zones 5–9

Long blooming and resistant to pests, this Argentine native is another bulb to naturalize in masses around shrubs and trees. Smells of onions if crushed, but the flowers have a pleasant fragrance. One of the easiest to grow.

Leucojum aestivum summer snowflake (bulb)

> Needs: sun or part shade, average soil, water during growth, plant 4 inches deep
>
> Character: 18-inch stems among straplike leaves carry 3 to 5 white, bell-shaped flowers
>
> Season of bloom: spring
>
> Hardiness: zones 3–9

An easy bulb that likes to stay in one place, untroubled by frequent dividing and transplanting. It looks wonderful at the edge of a pond or small stream. Mixes well with wildflowers and shrubs.

Lilium true lilies (bulb)

> Needs: sun (part shade in hottest areas) though they like shade over the roots, average well-drained to good soil, regular water

> Character: a thousand shades in many forms, from spires of small hanging bell-like flowers, to huge trumpets and flat upward-facing stars, all on strong stems from 2–8 feet tall, wind-resistant

> There are hundreds of species of lilies scattered all over the world. Hybridizers have crossed many of them, resulting in groups of hybrids that fall into a few large categories, each with its own character:

> > Asiatic hybrids—easiest, May to early July, zones 3–10, usually upward-facing, little or light fragrance

> > Trumpets and aurelians—July, zones 7–10, large, dropping trumpets, better in hot weather than Oriental hybrids, fragrant

> > Oriental hybrids—July to August, zones 5–9, ruffled, banded, or spotted blossoms, spicy fragrance, best in cool summers or with part shade

> Possible drawbacks: not for the desert Southwest, staking needed if grown with too much shade or for heavy-headed trumpets

Lilies are so elegantly good-looking that most people assume they are difficult to grow. Not at all. Modern lily growers have created strong, disease-resistant varieties that just get larger and have more flowers each year. If you want to start off with some reliable varieties, try the old fashioned regal lily, *Lilium regale*, the Asiatic hybrids, or a tough Oriental hybrid called 'Black Beauty'.

Lycoris squamigera autumn amaryllis (bulb)

> Needs: full or light sun, good soil, water when leave are growing, dry soil from early summer to blossoming, cover bulbs with 5 inchs of soil (6 inches in coldest regions)

> Season of bloom: late summer

> Hardiness: zones 5–10

> Possible drawbacks: large leaves wither in June, leaving gaps in plantings

Sometimes called magic lily because the flowering stalk appears so suddenly and unexpectedly in August. Don't disturb or divide until plantings are really crowded. They bloom best when cramped.

Muscari grape hyacinth (bulb)

> Needs: sun or part shade, average soil, average to occasional watering
>
> Character: small, tight clusters of blue or white flowers, 6–8 inches high, fall-sprouting, grasslike leaves
>
> Season of bloom: spring
>
> Hardiness: zones 4–8

Gratifyingly easy to grow, spreading quickly, and popping up in off corners from seed. A few are insignificant; plant dozens.

Narcissus daffodils (bulb)

> Needs: sun to part shade, average soil, average to occasional watering
>
> Character: usually yellow, white, or bicolor, with a cup or trumpet on a star-shaped saucer, above narrow leaves. Groups include:
>
>> *Cyclamineus*—flared back petals, most are shade- and moisture-tolerant
>>
>> *Jonquilla*—likes hot summers, good for Southern gardens, hardy to zone 4
>>
>> *Miniatures*—dainty, often multiflowered, many hardy only to zone 5
>>
>> *Tazetta*—many small flowers on a stem, good for Southern states, hardy to zone 5
>
> Season of bloom: early to late spring, depending on variety
>
> Hardiness: zones vary, many to zone 3, including the classic trumpet type

One of the definitions of spring, daffodils have a graceful presence that makes them equally welcome in both formal and informal gardens. If you acquire a taste for them, you can have them in miniatures and giants, for as long as five months. And if you are troubled by deer and rabbits, you can smile as you plant. Daffodils are invulnerable.

Floral Lore

Wordsworth's "host of golden daffodils" were Lent lilies, *Narcissus pseudonarcissus*, native all over Europe.

Ornithogalum umbellatum star-of-Bethlehem (bulb)

> Needs: sun or light shade, average to poor soil, regular to light watering

> Character: flat clusters of inch-wide white blooms on 6-inch stalks, grassy foliage

> Season of bloom: late spring

> Hardiness: zones 4–10

> Possible drawbacks: on the weed list in some places, leaves flop before blooming

A master colonizer, this is one of the best to grow in a lawn. The flowers are large and numerous enough to make a show without drawing too much attention to themselves. Makes a good background.

Puschkinia scilloides striped squill (bulb)

> Needs: sun or part shade, light soil, water during growth, little in summer, plant 3–4 inches deep

> Character: dainty white flowers with light blue stripe, up to 6-inch stems among substantial leaves

> Season of bloom: early spring

> Hardiness: zones 4–8

> Possible drawbacks: may need protection from wind

A neat, gratifying little bulb, these are best with winter freezing. They dislike being moved so settle them in a bed unlikely to be rearranged.

Scilla siberica 'Spring Beauty' Siberian squill (bulb)

> Needs: sun to part shade

> Character: vivid, intense blue in neat clusters of downward-facing blossoms on 4–6-inch plants

> Season of bloom: spring

> Hardiness: zones 2–8

Easy, and quick to increase, these are a must. Spread them around generously, beneath trees and shrubs and as an accompaniment to daffodils.

Tulipa tulip (bulb)

Needs: sun, excellent soil with good drainage, water during growth, plant very deep, 10–12 inches

Character: many types, from species a few inches high to tall cutting beauties of almost 2 feet. Taller ones have the classic chalicelike shape, smaller ones tend be to more open, almost flat.

Season of bloom: mid to late spring

Hardiness: zones 3–7 or 8

Tulips are spring standards, but frustratingly short-lived under many conditions. If you want dependable bloom try these groups:

Greigii tulips—mottled or striped leaves, flowers that tend to be red or gold with some coral and pink varieties

Kaufmanniana tulips—flowers open like water lilies, often red or rose with yellow or cream

Species tulips—many colors and forms available, usually under a foot high, hardiness varies

Though tulips have often been treated as formal beauty queens, they look more at home in a flower border if planted in groups of five or seven and surrounded by forget-me-nots and primroses.

Look in chapter 16 for a discussion of the larger types, most of which last no more than a few years.

Garden Talk

A species is a subdivision of a genus. Tulips are all members of the genus *Tulipa* but there are many different species. Species tulips refers to those that are close to the wild types, quite different from those that hybridizers have created with their breeding programs.

A Bouquet of Half-hardy Bulbs

If you live in zones 6, 7, or 8, you have enough winter chill to satisfy a wealth of hardy bulbs but may also be able to add the riches listed below. If in doubt, mulch heavily in winter. Often listed in catalogs with the tender bulbs, these will probably surprise your neighbors.

Allium neapolitanum Naples onion (bulb)

Needs: sun, average soil, water during growth

Character: loose white clusters of flowers with a pleasant (not oniony) fragrance on 1-foot stems, 1-inch-wide leaves

Season of bloom: spring

Hardiness: zones 7–10

Grown commercially as cut flowers, these are excellent mixed with other bulbs and perennials, especially in masses.

Canna canna (tuberous root)

Needs: sun, average soil, regular to much water during growth, warmth

Character: showy flowers in yellow, pink, orange, and red on 2–6-foot stalks, depending on variety, large oblong leaves

Season of bloom: summer, fall

Hardiness: zones 7–10

Want a tropical touch in your garden? This plant has leaves reminiscent of the banana plant and flowers that flaunt their colors boldly. Used as an accent among more finely textured plants, this can make a garden memorable. Best in warm or hot summer areas.

Gladiolus callianthus Abyssinian sword lily (corm)

Needs: sun, good soil, average water

Character: fragrant, 2–3-inch cream-colored flowers with chocolate markings, in sprays of up to 10 blooms on 2–3-foot stems

Season of bloom: late summer or fall if planted in spring

Hardiness: zones 7–10

A good mixer with perennials, sword lilies are courtly and graceful without dominating. Best in clumps

Iris Dutch hybrids iris (bulb)

Needs: full sun, average soil, water during growth, dry period following, plant bulbs 4 inches deep

Character: graceful, 3–4-inch flowers in blue, purple, white, yellow, and bicolors on 18-inch stems among narrow linear leaves

Season of bloom: late spring

Hardiness: zones 7–9

These are rather stiff singly, but impressive in clumps, especially with trailing ground covers that soften the upright stems. Intense colors make these conspicuous enough to stand out as a focal point in a bed.

Lycoris spider lily (bulb)

Needs: sun to light shade, good soil, regular water

Character: flowers with narrow petals and long stamens make these look like clusters of spiders above strap-shaped leaves:

L. radiata—warm red flowers, tolerates some shade, 18 inches

L. sanguinea—orange-red flowers, 2 feet

L. sprengeri—cool pink flowers, 2 feet

Season of bloom: late summer, fall

Hardiness: zones 7–10

These are the more tender relatives of the resurrection lily, *Lycoris squamigera*, and well worth growing where hardy. They also do well in pots. Don't transplant them frequently as they bloom best if their roots are crowded.

Narcissus 'Paperwhite' paperwhite daffodil (bulb)

Needs: sun to part shade, average soil, water when growing

Character: many small, white, fragrant flat-faced flowers in clusters on 1-foot stems

Season of bloom: spring

Hardiness: zones 8–10

Often grown indoors and especially suited for southern gardens, these are worthy trying in more northern areas. If in doubt about their hardiness, mulch heavily. They may surprise you. Or set bulbs on pebbles in a bowl, pour water in up to the base and set in a cool, dark place. As they grow, bring them out onto a table or windowsill for a sweet-scented treat.

Tigridia pavonia Mexican shell flower, tiger flower (bulb)

Needs: sun (some shade in hot areas), good soil, water during growth

Character: large, three-cornered blooms in vivid colors, often splotched with a darker color, swordlike leaves, $1^1/_2$ to $2^1/_2$ feet tall

Season of bloom: summer

Hardiness: zones 8–10

Possible drawbacks: blooms last only one day, plants bloom only for a month

If you want your garden to attract attention, plant these. Strong shades of orange, pink, red, and yellow make these look like a flock of gaudy butterflies.

Zantedeschia aethiopica common calla lily (rhizome)

> Needs: sun or part shade, average soil, average to lots of water

> Character: 18-inch arrowhead-shaped leaves surround large, white cuplike flowers

> Season of bloom: early summer

> Hardiness: zones 8–10

This plant has an exotic, rather tropical appearance, an excellent companion for more delicately textured meadow rue (*Thalictrum*) and columbine (*Aquilegia*).

Zephyranthes atamasca zephyr flower, fairy lily (bulb)

> Needs: sun, average soil, average water

> Character: white, fragrant, crocuslike blossoms with grassy foliage

> Season of bloom: spring

> Hardiness: zones 8–10

Easy to care for, these dainty flowers do especially well in the southeastern United States, where they are native.

The Least You Need to Know

➤ When you cut a bulb in half you can see the embryonic plant at the base, surrounded by thick, protecting layers of leaves.

➤ Corms are a like the base of the onion, but larger and able to store more food. The bud is at the top, exposed, not surrounded by puffy layers.

➤ A tuber is an enlarged stem base. Rather than one point at which roots emerge and one at which another stem grows, the whole lower surface may sprout roots and a number of shoots may grow from the top.

➤ Rhizomes are thickened stems that grow underground.

➤ Tuberous roots are enlargements of a section of root rather than stem.

Chapter 13

IS IT SPRING YET?

Encore Performers: Perennials

In This Chapter

➤ What do you mean by perennial?

➤ Planting tips

➤ Plan for permanence

➤ A bouquet of hardy perennials

➤ A bouquet of half-hardy perennials

➤ A bouquet of tender perennials

Picture a garden of pale yellow hollyhocks towering over white daisies, coral daylilies, a few purple iris and a cloud of baby's breath. Sounds like something out of a romantic novel, doesn't it? Something almost too good to be true, something that must take a lot of work to maintain.

Not at all. This, in fact, is one of the easiest pictures to create in a garden. Welcome to the world of perennials!

Perennials are Long-lived

These are plants that spring back to life every year, bigger and more vigorous than ever. A shrub may have a skeleton of branches visible through the winter, but a perennial is gone, leaving nothing visible above ground but inconspicuous buds.

This has some distinct advantages. One, you don't need to plant a replacement every year. Two, a perennial increases in size and therefore garden potential. Three, it can usually be split into a few smaller plants the second or third year. Sold yet?

What about disadvantages? Well, though some bloom for two or three months, even more, most are good for a month of flowers and then you're left with foliage. Handsome foliage, perhaps, but still just green. And some may not make much of a show the first year. Your patience is exercised a bit more with perennials.

In spite of these shortcomings, these plants are obviously the mainstays of a flower garden. Yes, you have to plan for entrances and exits throughout the growing season, but this also allows for freshness and variety, constant surprises.

Planting Perennials

Each perennial planted is an investment in the future, in flowers two, five, or even ten years from now. Consequently, any extra effort you put into soil preparation will pay off in faster growth and more blooms for a much longer time than if you're planting one-season annuals.

Loosen the soil deeply, especially if yours happens to be heavy, high in clay, or compressed by walking or heavy equipment. Aeration helps roots as much as fertilizer.

Green Tip

If your soil is very compacted, consider planting a crop of winter rye, a grain that has extraordinary root growth, and let its roots dig the soil for you. When the leaves are a foot high, turn it under with a shovel and sow again. The roots will penetrate farther and farther into the soil while you wait.

Add a layer of steer manure, compost, or other organic matter, top with bonemeal (a slow-release fertilizer) and mix with your soil. How deep a layer? That depends on your soil and the plants you want to grow there. Sandy and clay soils need the most. Plants listed in chapter 16, the rich feeders, need more than those listed in this one. Average soil and adaptable plants would probably do well with two inches of organic matter added and an even dusting of bonemeal.

How Deeply Should You Mix Your Amendments?

As deep as possible. Perennial roots can go three feet down or even more. If you can simply dig it into the top foot of soil, great. If you're up for some exercise, try this.

Shovel out a trench at one end of the bed, removing the top foot of soil. Now mix some organic matter in with the next foot. Top that trench with soil from a another dug next to it, mix your amendments with the bottom of that one, and repeat all the way down the bed. In practice, the slop of one layer into the next distributes the organic matter to the top foot of soil also.

Not All Plants Need This Care

Do all perennials need this kind of heroic effort to succeed? Not at all. Most are quite willing to grow with less than ideal conditions, especially if they like your climate. Experiment with a selection of the following plants and remember, not all will succeed, no matter how carefully you choose them for your site. You will have failures, as do all gardeners. But you will also have successes, plants that seem to think your garden is the best they've ever seen and are quite willing to make it theirs.

Plan for Permanence

Since plants that return every year have less need to reproduce themselves, to create seeds, they often flower for a shorter period of time. Many are in bloom for a month or six weeks. When you plan a garden, you need build around their comings and goings.

Create a Strong Skeleton

A flower bed doesn't have to be restricted to annuals and perennials. A few shrubs placed carefully to complement the shape and size of the bed add height and winter interest. They can act as mediators between a wall and your flowers, too.

Don't settle for dullness in winter. Just as the branching pattern of trees and shrubs is more apparent when leaves are gone, the lines of your garden at more obvious. If they are strong, creative and harmonious, you will enjoy looking at them in January.

Green Tip

Some shrubs and trees that look attractive in winter include dogwood (*Cornus*) for its branching pattern, wild roses (*Rosa*) for the purplish stems, and witch hazel (*Hamamelis*) for its small yellow flowers.

Foliage Is Just as Important as Flowers

When you start thinking of your flower bed as an artistic composition rather than a place to paint solid swathes of color, the textures of leaves become as much a part of the work of art as the blossoms.

Big, round hollyhock foliage combined with airy meadow rue and long, narrow Siberian iris leaves make a satisfying picture even before flowers appear. Add some purple-leaved heuchera, three to seven of them scattered beneath the taller plants and no one will pass without admiring your design, flowering or not.

Fill in Long-term Bloom

To provide continuity, choose a few annuals and perennials that have color for three or four months, or more. These may need deadheading, cutting off of old flowers, to

Green Tip

Long-blooming perennials include coreopsis, feverfew (*Tanacetum parthenium*), geum, linaria, *Rudbeckia* 'Goldsturm,' and many tender perennials often grown as annuals.

continue their show but will keep the border looking bright when the short-term stars are offstage.

White alyssum, for instance, makes a fragrant, frothy ground cover above which others can shine. Pale yellow marigolds or calendulas and *Coreopsis* 'Moonbeam' also combine well with many different plants. *Nepeta mussinii* is a cloud of lavender for months that can tie together taller, more flamboyant plants.

Now, a Roll-call of Main Characters

Here are the plants themselves, as varied a group as you'll find on any stage. These, in general, will grow with average soil, average water, and an open, sunny spot. Be sure to look at chapter 17, Sun's Abundant, Rain's Not, for a listing of the really tough ones that can take drought and poor soil. You'll find shade-lovers in chapters 18 and 19. And if you're ambitious or have rich, deep soil, try chapter 16, Enough of Everything.

A Bouquet of Hardy Perennials

For a discussion of hardiness and hardiness zones, see chapter 4. For a map, see the color insert.

Alcea hollyhock

> Needs: sun to part shade, average water, less if fully established, average soil
>
> Character: tall spires with large, flat flowers in pink, yellow, white, apricot, as well as a fine black-red, large, round leaves
>
> Season of bloom: summer
>
> Hardiness: zones 3–7
>
> Possible drawbacks: rust (remove any affected leaves, even if this bares the lower stalk), may need staking, often short-lived but seeds freely

Old-fashioned, but still the favorite of many, as striking and complement-attracting as ever. Available in doubles, but the singles seem to get more notice. Needs less sun to bloom than many people realize.

Anthemis tinctoria golden marguerite

> Needs: regular to occasional watering, good drainage

> Character: strong erect stems, 2–3 feet, with ferny, aromatic leaves, bears gold daisylike flowers

> Season of bloom: early summer through fall

> Hardiness: zones 3–10

> Possible drawbacks: long bloom season may exhaust plants, making them short-lived. Replant frequently from divisions or seeds.

Cheerful and content in most gardens, this is one of the best to try if you're unsure of your gardening ability. Good with *Crocosmia* 'Lucifer' and other orange or scarlet flowers.

Aquilegia columbine

> Needs: sun to part shade, average water, average well-drained soil

> Character: graceful, nodding, spurred flowers top ferny foliage, plants 2–3 feet high; many colors available

> Season of bloom: spring, early summer

> Hardiness: zones 3–9

> Possible drawbacks: leaf miners disfigure foliage in late summer but plants recover quickly when leaves are removed; self-seeds so freely it may become a weed

One of the best perennials for lacy texture, easy to grow and adaptable. The flowers are such an unusual shape that they gather attention from most visitors. Be sure to introduce only those colors and shapes you really like into your garden. They'll hybridize and come up forever in variations on these themes.

Floral Lore

The name *columbine* comes from the Latin word for dove, *columba*, because of the fancied resemblance of the flowers to a flock of doves.

Campanula bellflower

> Needs: sun to light shade, neutral to slightly alkaline soil (though many don't seem to mind some acidity), average water

> Character: blooms generally cup-shaped, sometimes like stars or flattened, lavender blue, height depends on variety

> Many kinds available, including:

> *C. glomerata* (clustered bellflower)—clusters of flowers at top of 1–2-foot stems in summer

> *C. persicifolia* (peach-leaved bellflower)—2–3 feet high with white or blue spikes of flowers in summer

> *C. poscharskyana* (Siberian bellflower)—sprawling ground cover with starlike flowers, late spring or early summer, vigorous

> *C. rotundifolia* (harebell)—1¹/₂–2 feet with delicate bells on thin stems in summer

> Hardiness: zones 3–7

> Possible drawbacks: taller kinds may need staking

Though they also come in white, these plants usually have flowers of a shade instantly recognizable as bellflower blue, some lighter, some darker, all somewhat purplish. It combines well with other colors. While most are easy given their basic requirements, Siberian bellflower is especially lenient, even tolerant of dry soil.

Centaurea montana mountain bluet

> Needs: sun to light shade, average soil, regular watering

> Character: flowers made up of tiny florets, lavender-blue with a touch of pink at the center, blue-green leaves making 1–2-foot clumps

> Season of bloom: early summer

> Hardiness: zones 3–8

> Possible drawbacks: may spread too enthusiastically for some

A relative of the cornflower, long-blooming and generously spreading, this is a good filler among more rigid plants. It's particularly good with lavender-pink flowers that match the shading at the center of the clusters.

Echinacea purpurea purple coneflower

> Needs: sun, average soil, modest amounts of water
>
> Character: flowers look like drooping, purplish daisies with a brownish disk, up to 6 inches wide, on strong 2–5-foot stems above hairy dark green leaves
>
> Season of bloom: summer, early fall
>
> Hardiness: zones 3–9
>
> Possible drawbacks: may mildew in humid weather

One of the garden standards, combining well with more relaxed, somewhat sprawling plants such as daylilies, evening primroses (*Oenothera*) and cranesbills (*Geranium*). 'White Swan' is a variety with white rays around a gold disk.

Geranium cranesbill, hardy geranium

> Needs: sun to light shade
>
> Character: round, flat flowers in shade of pink to blue-violet, this has mounding clumps of round, divided leaves
>
> Season of bloom: summer
>
> Hardiness: zones 4 or 5–7, depending on variety

Not the common scarlet-flowered geranium often grown as a pot plant (but scientifically a *Pelargonium*), this is one botanists have christened with the same name, a worthy flower on in its own right. It looks best in large groups or interwoven with iris and other narrow-leaved plants.

Geum avens

> Needs: sun or part shade, good soil, good drainage, regular water
>
> Character: red, orange, or yellow flowers above handsome lobed leaves, 1–2 feet
>
> Season of bloom: summer, long season
>
> Hardiness: zones 5–9

This is another one to plant in colonies. Not dramatic enough for an accent, it still is an excellent choice for supporting roles, particularly in warm-toned gardens.

Gypsophila paniculata baby's breath

> Needs: sun, average soil, good drainage, regular to occasional watering
>
> Character: tiny white or pink flowers in cloudlike sprays of up to 1,000 flowers, mounding over narrow blue-green leaves clustered at the base, 2–3 feet
>
> Season of bloom: summer
>
> Hardiness: zones 3–9

Late sprouting, but an excellent filler once it appears, baby's breath is hard to misuse. Its height gives it a substantial presence, but its delicacy makes it welcome anywhere. *Gypsophila* means lime-lover and it certainly does well in somewhat alkaline soils. Though not absolutely necessary, a bit of lime is appreciated.

Hemerocallis daylily

> Needs: sun, part shade, good drainage, most soils, best in good soil with regular water
>
> Character: strong clumps of arching leaves with lilylike flowers many shades of yellow, red, purple, almost anything but blue, many with contrasting colors at the throat, 1–4 feet
>
> Season of bloom: late spring through early fall, depending on variety
>
> Hardiness: zones 3–9

Daylilies deserve all the praise they receive, being easy to care for, long-lived, and dense enough to curb weeds. Hybridizers are continually presenting us with luscious blends of yellow, pink, and purple, so there's no chance of getting bored with this plant. The newest ones can be expensive, but favorites such as 'Stella d'Oro' are rewardingly tough as well as affordable.

Hesperis matronalis dame's rocket, sweet rocket

> Needs: sun or part shade, most soils including slightly alkaline types, average to modest amounts of water
>
> Character: small purple or white fragrant flowers on 1–3-foot plants with pointed oblong leaves
>
> Season of bloom: spring, summer
>
> Hardiness: zones 3–9

An old-fashioned plant, easy to grow in almost any situation. Will seed itself into odd corners, becoming a pleasant weed.

Iris sibirica Siberian iris

> Needs: sun or part shade, many soils, regular water in spring, can dry out some in summer
>
> Character: graceful purple, blue, or white flowers above attractive narrow linear leaves, 3 feet
>
> Season of bloom: early summer
>
> Hardiness: zones 3–9

A reliable plant that blends well with other flowers, Siberian iris blooms are reminiscent of Japanese paintings, though the classic iris of Japan, *Iris kaempheri*, needs more moisture. It would be hard to find a situation this wouldn't improve. The leaves provide one of the more useful swordlike textures even when out of bloom.

Leucanthemum* × *superbum Shasta daisy

> Needs: sun to part shade, average water
>
> Character: long-stalked classic daisy flowers above substantial oblong leaves, from 2–4 feet tall depending on variety
>
> Season of bloom: summer
>
> Hardiness: zones 4–10
>
> Possible drawbacks: taller varieties need staking

Easy and rewarding for summer bloom, forming large clumps quickly. Unless you need height for the back of a border, you're better off buying compact varieties that don't flop if you forget to stake them.

Linaria purpurea purple toadflax

> Needs: sun to light shade, most soils, good drainage, regular water
>
> Character: tiny lavender flowers in graceful spikes, 3 feet
>
> Season of bloom: summer
>
> Hardiness: zones 4–9
>
> Possible drawbacks: may seed too freely, becoming a lovely weed

A long blooming, easy-to-grow perennial that should be more widely known. Its delicate texture and soft color combine well with most other plants. 'Canon J. Went' is a form with light pink flowers.

Macleaya cordata plume poppy

> Needs: sun or part shade
>
> Character: feathery heads of tiny white flowers above large lobed leaves on strong stems, up to 8 feet tall
>
> Season of bloom: summer
>
> Hardiness: zones 4–9
>
> Possible drawbacks: can overwhelm small gardens—it's a rampant spreader

A dramatic, stately plant if you have the room, this is a back-of-the-border specimen that never needs staking despite its height.

Papaver nudicaule Iceland poppy

> Needs: sun, good soil, good drainage, regular watering
>
> Character: silky petaled, cup-shaped flowers in soft pastels as well as orange and red above clusters of light green lobed leaves
>
> Season of bloom: early summer
>
> Hardiness: zones 3–9
>
> Possible drawbacks: sometimes short-lived

Few flowers have such delicate beauty. The crepe-textured petals seem to glow in the sun, making the best colors of these medium-size perennials worth searching out. Often grown as annuals since they bloom the first year from seed.

Papaver orientale Oriental poppy

> Needs: sun, good soil, good drainage, best in cool summer areas
>
> Character: bold orange-scarlet, cup-shaped flowers 4–5 inches across above hairy pointed leaves, 2 feet high
>
> Season of bloom: late spring, early summer
>
> Hardiness: zones 3–9
>
> Possible drawbacks: leaves die back by midsummer

The pink and salmon varieties of this perennial are easier to work into the average border, but if you want to draw attention to your yard, this will do it. The gap left when leaves disappear can be filled by annuals or later-developing perennials such as baby's breath.

Penstemon beardtongue

> Needs: sun, average soil, good drainage, average to modest amounts of water, no fertilizer, will take alkaline soil

> Character: open, tubular, red or pink flowers in long-blooming spikes above glossy narrow leaves, from 1–3 feet, depending on variety

> Season of bloom: summer, fall

> Hardiness: zones 4–8

> Possible drawbacks: may be short-lived

Penstemons seem to be easy and permanent for some, an annual treat for others. Try some of the varieties such as 'Elfin Pink', about a foot tall, or 'Prairie Fire', up to 2$\frac{1}{2}$ feet. A neat, handsome plant that is also deer-resistant.

Physostegia virginiana false dragonhead, obedient plant

> Needs: sun or part shade, average soil, regular water

> Character: purple-pink or white flowers packed closely into spikes, 2–3 feet

> Season of bloom: late summer, fall

> Hardiness: zones 2–9

> Possible drawbacks: may spread too quickly in rich moist soil

An easy plant if given enough water, this combines well with asters, which like the same conditions. They bloom late in the year, when they're particularly welcome as a new face in the border.

Platycodon balloon flower

> Needs: sun or part shade, average soil, average to modest amounts of water

> Character: blue, star- or cup-shaped flowers, some varieties white, on upright stems 2–3 feet tall

> Season of bloom: summer

> Hardiness: zones 3–9

> Possible drawbacks: dislikes very mild, warm areas, sprouts late in the year and can be dug accidentally by forgetful gardeners

This plant is compact, easy, and attractive, with flowers somewhat like bellflowers, of the same lavender-blue, but larger. The clumps don't spread, but new plants can be grown from seed.

Rheum × rhabarbarum garden rhubarb

> Needs: sun, good soil, regular watering during growth
>
> Character: tiny white blossoms in a plumy cluster on a stalk up to 6 feet tall, very large, crinkled leaves, often with red stems and veins, to $2^1/_2$ feet
>
> Season of bloom: early summer
>
> Hardiness: zone 3
>
> Possible drawbacks: stalks are edible, but leaf blades are poisonous

Plant rhubarb in the flower garden? Why not? The leaves are amazingly attractive and the creamy white blossom clusters are large and showy. And you can cook the stalks for pies.

Don't relegate rhubarb (Rheum × rhabarbarum) to the vegetable garden. Show it off with your perennials.

Rudbeckia fulgida 'Goldsturm' black-eyed Susan

> Needs: sun to part shade, any soil, average water
>
> Character: gold flowers with dark centers on 2–3-foot plants, thick and tidy-looking
>
> Season of bloom: summer to fall
>
> Hardiness: zones 3–9

Easy in all but wet ground, this late-summer standard has more attractive foliage than *R. hirta*, a compact, easy to work with habit of growth, and a willingness to spread at a relaxed pace.

Rudbeckia hirta black-eyed Susan

> Needs: sun, any soil, average to occasional watering
>
> Character: broad, orange-gold to mahogany daisies with a dark center on 3–4-foot stems with hairy leaves
>
> Season of bloom: late summer, fall
>
> Hardiness: zones 3–10

Coarser than 'Goldsturm', this black-eyed Susan is often grown as an annual because it blooms so quickly from seed sown in early spring. It is best toward the back of a flower bed because of its height and will self-sow in most gardens.

Salvia azurea ssp. ***pitcheri*** var, ***grandiflora*** meadow sage

> Needs: sun, average soil, average to occasional watering, takes heat and humidity well
>
> Character: small, intensely blue flowers in spikes above narrow foliage, to 5 feet
>
> Season of bloom: summer, fall
>
> Hardiness: zones 4–9
>
> Possible drawbacks: can be leggy and sprawling, cut back in April to force branching

A real find if you love blue flowers, especially appreciated in fall.

Salvia × ***superba*** purple flowering sage

> Needs: sun, average to good soil, good drainage, regular to modest amounts of water

> Character: many spikes of tiny purple flowers over neat clumps of gray-green leaves, 2 feet

> Season of bloom: summer

> Hardiness: zones 5–8

One of the best sources of purple flowers in a summer garden, this plant mixes well with almost any other, from pale pinks to orange and scarlet. If cut back before completely finished flowering, it will send out more stalks for a second show. May self-sow.

Scabiosa caucasica pincushion flower

> Needs: sun, nearly neutral to somewhat alkaline soil with a light texture, average to modest amounts of water, good drainage in winter

> Character: flat heads of blue or white flowers, up to $2^1/_2$ feet

> Season of bloom: summer

> Hardiness: zones 3–7

> Possible drawbacks: dislikes hot, humid climates

Easy to grow and especially useful in desert climates, which tend to have slightly alkaline soil. Its long bloom time can give it a major role in the garden. Available in white also.

Sidalcea checker mallow

> Needs: sun to light shade, good deep soil, average water

> Character: looks like a small hollyhock, with 1-inch flowers in shades of pink, $2^1/_2$ to 4 feet

> Season of bloom: summer

> Hardiness: zones 5–7

Best in groups, this is great for added height in smaller beds, perhaps in a burst of flowers at the front entry.

Solidago goldenrod

> Needs: sun to light shade, average soil, average water
>
> Character: yellow to gold plumes of flowers
>
> Season of bloom: midsummer to fall
>
> Hardiness: zones 3–10

Sometimes avoided because of the fear of hay fever, this is not the culprit responsible. Instead, it is an underused wildflower that will grow in almost any soil. As an addition to the fall garden, it combines well with asters and chrysanthemums.

Stokesia Stokes' aster

> Needs: sun to part shade, well-drained soil, average watering
>
> Character: blue, purple, or white asterlike daisies
>
> Season of bloom: summer, early fall
>
> Hardiness: zones 5–9

Another tough, adaptable wildflower that has been welcomed into cultivation, this one especially useful in its native southeastern states.

Tanacetum parthenium feverfew

> Needs: sun to part shade, average to modest watering, not fussy about soil
>
> Character: head of small, white daisy flowers above bright green leaves, 1–2 feet high
>
> Season of bloom: summer, early fall
>
> Hardiness: zones 4–10
>
> Possible drawbacks: colonizes all empty corners

Few problems bother this plant. It keeps on blooming and spreading in any weather. If you still think you can't grow flowers, try this one. Neglectable.

Thalictrum aquilegifolium meadow rue

Needs: sun or part shade, ordinary soil, average to modest amounts of water

Character: purple clouds of puffy blossoms on 4-foot stems with delicate, rounded leaflets

Season of bloom: summer

Hardiness: zones 4–8

Possible drawbacks: may need staking

No other plant looks quite like this one, both airy and conspicuous. It's one of the useful group of plants that seem to go well anywhere, with anything.

Tradescantia virginiana spiderwort

Needs: sun or shade, any soil, much to occasional watering

Character: triangular, 1-inch flowers in blues, purples, and pinks on 2–3-foot stem with long, narrow leaves

Season of bloom: late spring, summer

Hardiness: zones 5–10

Possible drawbacks: may need staking

You'd have to look far before finding a garden this one won't grow in. The flowers last only a day, but come in many-budded clusters that are constantly opening new ones. Starve to prevent too-expansive growth.

Valeriana officinalis garden heliotrope, common valerian

Needs: sun or part shade, average soil, good drainage, average water

Character: clusters of fragrant pinkish flowers above large, glossy, divided leaves, 2–5 feet

Season of bloom: summer

Hardiness: zone 5

Possible drawbacks: may need to be staked

Now more commonly found in herb gardens, this easy-to-grow ornamental spreads freely and will soon populate a garden without overwhelming others. When bruised, as attractive to cats as catnip.

Floral Lore

Valerian has an effect on cats similar to catnip. They may destroy a plant whose scent has been released by bruising. Rats find it equally attractive and it has been used to bait traps.

Veronica speedwell

> Needs: sun or part shade, average soil, regular watering

> Character: tiny flowers in long, dense spikes, blue, pink, or white, small leaves

> Season of bloom: late spring to early fall depending on variety

> Hardiness: zones 3–8

Speedwells are useful plants in most situations, somewhat sprawling but willing to fill in spaces between others without complaint. Their blues are clear and refreshing.

A Bouquet of Half-hardy Perennials

Agapanthus lily of the Nile

> Needs: full sun to part shade, some shelter if light is intense

> Character: tubular flowers in shades of blue or white in clusters at the top of strong stalks that rarely need staking, straplike leaves

> Season of bloom: summer

> Hardiness: zones 6–10

Few plants have more class than this one. The leaves are thick and substantial; the flowers clusters are large and produced in abundance. Excellent in pots. Some varieties evergreen, but the hardier ones are deciduous. Divide infrequently and deadhead for more bloom. They are not troubled by pests or diseases.

Alstroemeria alstroemeria, Peruvian lily

> Needs: sandy but fertile soil, deep and cool (mulch well), a bit of shade in hot areas, regular water
>
> Character: elegant, exotic tubular flowers, often speckled with darker colors, on leafy 2–5-foot stems
>
> Season of bloom: early summer
>
> Hardiness: zones 7 or 8–10
>
> Possible drawbacks: can cause dermatitis in some people, stalks often dry up after flowering, leaving a gap in the garden

These are native to South America. *A. aurantiaca* is the hardiest, but is only for lovers of gold and orange. Ligtu hybrids are almost as hardy, with a wider variety of colors, including red, pink, and white.

Erigeron fleabane

> Needs: sun to light shade, average to sandy soil, average watering
>
> Character: pink, violet, and purple flowers
>
> Season of bloom: early summer
>
> Hardiness: zones 4–9 depending on species
>
> Possible drawbacks: may need some light support, best in cool summer regions

If you see what looks like an aster in summer, not fall, it's probably this look-alike. Easy to grow if given protection from too much heat.

Erysimum cheiri English wallflower

> Needs: sun, good soil, good drainage, regular watering
>
> Character: clusters of fragrant yellow, orange, or burgundy flowers on compact plants with narrow leaves
>
> Season of bloom: spring
>
> Hardiness: zones 8–10
>
> Possible drawbacks: may be short-lived

Popular in Europe for planting with bulbs, these are not as common as they should be. The fragrance is delightful. They'll self-sow in favorable situations, usually a cool, moist climate.

Gerbera jamesonii Gerber daisy

> Needs: sun to light shade, good soil, good drainage, average watering
>
> Character: elegant, glowing daisies in shades of pink, yellow, and orange on $1^1/_2$–2-foot stalks above large, lobed leaves
>
> Season of bloom: spring, summer depending on climate
>
> Hardiness: zones 8–10
>
> Possible drawbacks: resent having their roots disturbed

These make any bed a display garden, needing only a few supporting players in contrasting textures, perhaps some daylilies and sweet alyssum. Often sold as annual pot plants.

Mirabilis jalapa four-o'clocks, marvel of Peru

> Needs: sun to part shade, average soil, good drainage, average water
>
> Character: 1-foot, fragrant, trumpetlike flowers, in pink, red, and yellow, on fast-growing bushy plants up to 3 feet tall
>
> Season of bloom: summer
>
> Hardiness: zones 8–10

Easy to grow, you can plant seeds after last frost. They may self-sow, but if not, dig out the tuberous roots and store over winter. Flowers open in late afternoon.

Osteospermum fruticosum trailing African daisy

> Needs: sun, good drainage, average soil, drought-tolerant but more attractive with some water
>
> Character: masses of 2-inch, daisylike flowers with purple centers on sprawling branches
>
> Season of bloom: summer
>
> Hardiness: zones 8–10

One of the nicest of the multitude of daisylike plants, these are pale lilac fading to white with deeper lilac on the reverse side of the petals. Excellent in planters and hanging baskets because of their tolerance for neglect.

Penstemon gloxinioides border penstemon

> Needs: sun, well drained soil, average to occasional watering
>
> Character: tubular flowers in shades of pink to purple, in short spikes above stems with narrow, glossy leaves
>
> Season of bloom: summer
>
> Hardiness: zones 4–10
>
> Possible drawbacks: may be short-lived

Border penstemons are a group of hybrids, some with straight stems to 3 feet, others with sprawling branches no more than 2 feet. Hardiness may vary as significantly, so don't be afraid to try them in slightly colder areas. They give such a good show that even one year's bloom would be rewarding.

Schizostylus coccinea kaffir lily, crimson flag

> Needs: sun to light shade, average soil, regular water
>
> Character: watermelon-red lilylike flowers, 2 inches, above long, narrow leaves, 1–2 feet
>
> Season of bloom: late summer, fall
>
> Hardiness: zones 6–9

A truly delightful addition to the fall garden, sometimes blooming into November. The varieties 'Mrs. Hegarty', pale pink, and 'Viscountess Byng', soft pink, are especially attractive.

Viola tricolor pansy

> Needs: sun to light shade, good soil, average water
>
> Character: broad, facelike blooms in many colors and bicolors on sprawling plants up to 1 foot
>
> Season of bloom: most seasons, depending on when planted, climate
>
> Hardiness: zones 4–10

Didn't know this was a perennial, did you? Acres are planted as annuals, but mild climates can have them year-round. Small-flowered varieties are often sold as winter pansies in fall, larger-flowered ones either in fall or spring. All need occasional cutting back when they get leggy.

Floral Lore

The word *pansy* comes from the French *penses*, or thoughts. Other names for this old favorite include heartsease, Johnny-jump-up, pink-eyed-John, and bonewort.

A Bouquet of Tender Perennials

Argyranthemum frutescens marguerite daisy

Needs: sun, good soil, good drainage, regular water, some fertilizer

Character: neat, somewhat shrubby plants covered with white or yellow daisies, $1^1/_2$–$2^1/_2$ feet

Season of bloom: spring or summer, depending on climate

Hardiness: zones 9–10

If you like daisies, you'll find these much more rewarding than Shastas, being both longer-blooming and bushier.

Felicia amelloides blue marguerite

Needs: sun, average soil, average to occasional water

Character: small blue daisies, 1–$1^1/_4$ inches, on 18-inch mounded plants with small hairy leaves

Season of bloom: spring to fall

Hardiness: zones 9–10

This is an excellent plant for warm, dry summers, draping over raised beds or neatly covering flat, sunny spots. Long blooming, but may need a shearing in late summer to continue though fall

Gazania rigens treasure flower

> Needs: sun, average soil, good drainage
>
> Character: elegant daisylike flowers, gleaming colors, often shades of gold, bronze, and rose with shiny, lance-shaped leaves, 6–8 inches tall
>
> Season of bloom: late summer, fall as an annual, earlier in mild areas
>
> Hardiness: zones 9–10
>
> Possible drawbacks: flowers tend to close on cloudy days

Few daisies come in pinks as well as gold and bronze. This one does, most flowers having circles of darker shades near the center. Definitely worthy of a display bed.

Heliotropium arborescens heliotrope, cherry pie

> Needs: sun to part shade, good soil, regular water
>
> Character: attractive veined leaves on sturdy stems bear fragrant purple clusters of flowers
>
> Season of bloom: summer
>
> Hardiness: zones 9–10
>
> Possible drawbacks: poisonous if eaten

A common annual in northern states, this is well known as an old-fashioned flower, one of grandmother's favorites. The richly colored flowers and deep green veined leaves make it useful as a contrast to flowers in pale pink and yellow.

Pelargonium × ***hortorum*** geranium

> Needs: sun to part shade, good soil, average water, best with cool nights
>
> Character: clusters of scarlet, salmon, white, or pink flowers above soft, round leaves
>
> Season of bloom: summer
>
> Hardiness: zones 9–10
>
> Possible drawbacks: the scent of the leaves and flowers is disliked by some

An old standard, probably grown by someone on every block in every town in the United States, with good reason. These are easy and bright. The common scarlet variety looks particularly good with brick and black ironwork.

Pelargonium peltatum ivy geranium

> Needs: sun to part shade, good soil, average water
>
> Character: clusters of soft pink to rose flowers on somewhat trailing stems with shiny, ivy-shaped leaves
>
> Season of bloom: summer
>
> Hardiness: zones 9–10

A lovely low plant for borders or hanging baskets that seems to take heat better than the common geranium. Excellent in hanging baskets and window boxes.

Salvia patens gentian sage

> Needs: sun to part shade, average soil, average to occasional water
>
> Character: intense, sky-blue tubular flowers, 2 inches long, on plants with hairy leaves, 1–2 feet
>
> Season of bloom: summer, fall
>
> Hardiness: zones 9–10

Unusual and striking, this is an attention-getter. It likes warmth, but seems to succeed well in cooler areas also. Worth experimenting with.

Sutera cordata bacopa

> Needs: sun or part shade, most soils, average water
>
> Character: tiny white flowers cover 4–6-inch plants that spread quickly
>
> Season of bloom: almost all year
>
> Hardiness: zones 9–10

This charmer is just coming into the nursery trade and if you see it, buy it. Neat and constantly blooming, it makes an excellent edging for containers or borders, suitable for the most elegant setting.

The Least You Need to Know

➤ Not all perennials need rich soil. Find the ones that match your site.

➤ Perennials will be with you a long time, so loosen the soil well and add any amendments you want before you plant.

➤ Easy perennials include: golden marguerite (*Anthemis tinctoria*), feverfew (*Tanacetum parthenium*), echinacea, coreopsis, linaria, sweet rocket (*Hesperis*), and daylilies (*Hemerocallis*).

Chapter 14

Social Climbers: Vines

In This Chapter

➤ What do you mean by vines?

➤ Where and when to use vines

➤ Caring for vines

➤ A bouquet of annual vines

➤ A bouquet of hardy vines

➤ A bouquet of half-hardy vines

➤ A bouquet of tender vines

We tend to think of flower beds as flat, as color-filled shapes laid out on the ground. But some resourceful plants put color at eye level and above it, scrambling through trees, draping walls, and spilling over balconies.

From roses blossoming at the ends of fifteen-foot branches to dainty clematis over an arbor, these are plants that make good use of space. Welcome to the world of vines!

What Are Vines?

Imagine a shrub with extra-long flexible branches, able to extend its reach upward ten, twenty feet or more. Or sideways. Or even down a bank. That's a vine.

The branches may be as thin as wires, but they're still branches. These are plants that have given up sturdy independence for the advantages of being spread out; able to cover large distances quickly.

Most have developed clever techniques such as twining tendrils or small, suckerlike disks known as holdfasts to grab onto nearby trees or branches. All need support to become something more than sprawling ground covers.

Consider the Advantages of Vines

First, they take up very little space on the ground. A garden crowded with trees, shrubs, and flowers still has room for one or two vines. A strip only a few feet wide between a path and a fence has room for vines as well as some perennials at its base.

Second, they cover large areas quickly. Have a fence that's less than beautiful? Conceal it with a vine. Need something to screen the neighbor's windows? Set up some netting or a trellis and plant a vine.

Third, they are willing to adapt to your creative plans. You can train them around a window or over a trellis. You can emphasize an arch or a pillar. You can even guide them into circles and loops. They may send out shoots in all directions, but they never question your leadership.

Choosing Vines

To have a healthy vine covered with blossoms you need to make sure your yard suits its requirements, the sun-soil-water-air combination covered in chapter 4. This is crucial to the success of your planting. Give your vine what it likes and it will give you all the growth you want without coddling.

Next, know the purposes you want it to serve. Is it purely decorative, just for its flowers? Or do you need the quick disguise of an unsightly view? Is it for clambering through a tree or covering a porch railing? The qualities that make a vine great for one situation may disqualify it for another. A vine whose stems can twist around wire or string, for instance, would need to be tied every few feet to cover a solid wall. And a climbing hydrangea that sends out tiny root-like projections to cling to a wall would never attach itself to a netting.

Different Ways of Climbing

Each vine has a preferred method of keeping itself upright. Work with it and you'll spend less time on chores such as tying and training.

Twining vines. A new shoot grows in a spiral, twisting itself around any small object it meets, even its own stems. It will usually need a thinning every few years to prevent the branches from becoming a solid, unwieldy mass.

It can't encompass posts and other large objects, so your best bet is to use cord or wire to guide it in the direction you prefer. If you want it to grow along a solid surface such as a wall, have the lines at least five or six inches away so the branchlets can move in and out, winding around them.

Vines with tendrils. The same wires work well for vines whose small offshoots or leaf bases do the work of anchoring branches. They can be set nearer a wall, since the tendrils need less room to turn.

If you have a surface that will need repainting, put the lines on a framework that can be pulled away a few feet or laid down.

These are a bit more work to thin, since the twisting shoots grab more tightly, becoming somewhat like wire springs. They are, however, easier to guide, more likely to find their way around every narrow object in their path.

Clinging vines. If you have a flat surface to cover, these are your workmen. Whether they have tiny roots that find every crevice, clawlike tendrils, or suction cups, these are masters at anchoring themselves firmly. Your work is minimal since they rarely need thinning or guidance.

Be sure, however, that the surface they are covering can survive a permanent screening. Rock, brick and tree bark are fine. Painted wood is not, unless you don't mind some rot caused by constant moisture.

Vines with trailing stems. These don't seem to care whether or not they grow as ground covers or wall plants, sending out 10- or 20-foot branches in all directions. It's your choice and your tying that keeps them upright.

Caring for Vines

Sometimes, but not always, vines ask more care than a shrub with the equivalent mass of flowers. For instance, vines with trailing stems need tying up and pruning unless they have a tree to clamber through without restraint. Almost all need an occasional thinning.

Roots. Though the runners take up vertical space, the roots need some horizontal room to spread. Will they interfere with other plants? Probably not. Most vines interplant well, but don't expect to be able to dig and move flowers around the base without cutting off some vine roots.

If in a strip bed next to a wall, will they be too cramped? Most vines are excellent choices for small beds, but be sure that you mix extra organic matter with the soil and fertilize regularly.

Many vines grow well with their roots in the shade if the leaves get plenty of sun. After all, stretching toward the light is their greatest talent. Some, like clematis, even require it. If your summers are hot, consider giving any vine a bush or a cover of perennials to shadow the root system. You'll get two flower shows for the price of one.

Pruning. As mentioned, many vines need thinning. The success of your next season's bloom may depend, however, on when you prune. If you cut off growth at the wrong time, you'll lose the embryonic buds in storage for next year.

Take Care!

Always cut a branch back to a bud. If you leave a bare stalk, it will die back to the nearest bud anyway, and possibly farther. The cut has difficulty healing and disease may get started.

A safe bet is to prune right after flowering. If your clematis blooms in spring (on growth from last year), the new shoots that come after your thinning have time to set buds.

If it blooms in summer (on new branches), your cuts will force out extra growth for blossoms in July. Spring pruning often works best in cold areas where new growth in fall may freeze back.

A Bouquet of Annual Vines

Many tender perennials will grow quick enough from seed to flower the first year and are often sold as annuals. Consider cathedral bells (*Cobaèa scandens*), chickabiddy (*Asarina*), morning glory (*Ipomoea tricolor*), and moonflower (*Ipomoea alba*), all listed as tender vines.

Ipomoea quamoclit cypress vine

> Method of climbing: twining stems
>
> Needs: sun, average soil, average to occasional watering
>
> Character: tubular red flowers like miniature, star-shaped morning glories, $1^1/_2$ inches wide, on quick-growing stems up to 20 feet with threadlike leaves
>
> Season of bloom: summer

A tropical relative of the moonflower and morning glory, this also likes warmth; don't plant them until night temperatures are above 50 degrees. Soak the hard seeds overnight then sow them in their permanent sites. They dislike transplanting.

Tropaeolum peregrinum canary creeper

> Method of climbing: twining leaf stalks
>
> Needs: light shade, average soil, average watering
>
> Character: feathery yellow flowers, 1 inch wide, on vines 10–15 feet' with lobed leaves
>
> Season of bloom: summer

These flowers are so airy they seem far removed from their close cousins, the nasturtiums, though this asks for slightly richer, more moist conditions, Use it for quick, light cover in part shade, though it can take sun in cool summer areas.

Tropaeolum nasturtium

> Method of climbing: twining leaf stalks
>
> Needs: sun to part shade, ordinary soil without fertilizer, regular to occasional watering
>
> Character: open, tubular flowers in maroon, red, orange, gold, or yellow, 1 inch, on stems with round leaves
>
> Season of bloom: summer
>
> Possible drawbacks: may be attacked by aphids

A cheerful vine for summer screening. Leaves, flowers, and unripe seeds are all edible, tasting slightly peppery.

A Bouquet of Hardy Vines

Remember to check your hardiness zone. For a discussion of zones and hardiness, check chapter 4. For a map, see page 341.

Aristolochia macrophylla Dutchman's pipe

> Method of climbing: twining stems
>
> Needs: sun to full shade, any soil, average or extra water
>
> Character: large, heart-shaped leaves with $1^1/_2$-inch purplish brown flowers shaped like an old-fashioned pipe
>
> Season of bloom: late spring or early summer
>
> Hardiness: zones 4–10

A vigorous vine whose leaves are excellent for screening, useful in moist or shady situations where few other vines flourish. Deciduous.

Campsis radicans trumpet vine, trumpet creeper

> Method of climbing: clinging
>
> Needs: sun or part shade, most soils, regular or modest amounts of water
>
> Character: sprays of 3-inch orange tubular flowers on vigorous stems with divided leaves
>
> Season of bloom: summer, early fall
>
> Hardiness: zones 5–9
>
> Possible drawbacks: spreads by suckers, any piece of root will grow a new plant, may become so heavy that it pulls away from support

An easy to grow standard, never bothered by insects, this is practically fail-safe. 'Flava' is a golden yellow variety equally attractive to hummingbirds. Deciduous.

Campsis × *tagliabuana* 'Mme Galen'

Method of climbing: clinging

Needs: sun to part shade, ordinary soil, regular or modest amounts of water

Character: apricot-orange flowers up to 3 inches long with dark green leaves

Season of bloom: all summer, on current year's growth

Hardiness: zones 5–9

A hybrid between *C. radicans* and an Asian relative, this variety may not be quite as vigorous, but that's still energetic enough for most gardens. Beautiful and generous with its flowers. Deciduous.

Clematis hybrids large-flowered hybrid clematis

Method of climbing: tendrillike leaf bases

Needs: sun on leaves, shade on roots (stones work well), average water, good soil

Character: 4–8-inch blossoms in vivid or pastel pink, lavender, purple, and white, on 10-foot vines

Season of bloom: summer

Hardiness: zones 3–9, some varieties 4–10

A summer conversation piece, excellent in entries and by patios. Will cover an apple tree with blossoms in summer if you plant it at the base. If it doesn't freeze to the ground, don't feel that you need to cut it back so severely yourself. Just thin the stems and allow it to climb higher. Deciduous.

Clematis paniculata sweet autumn clematis

Method of climbing: tendrillike leaf bases

Needs: sun, average soil, average water

Character: irrepressible growth to 30 feet, masses of 1-inch fragrant white flowers followed by feathery silver seed heads

Season of bloom: late summer, fall, on current year's growth

Hardiness: zones 4–9

Possible drawbacks: self-seeds freely, grows too vigorously for some gardens

One of a number of almost indistinguishable species called sweet autumn clematis, all excellent for covering almost anything with fragrance and frothy swells of white blossoms. To keep under control, prune the branches that have just flowered back to a few buds. Deciduous.

Lonicera periclymenum woodbine honeysuckle

> Method of climbing: twining stems

> Needs: part shade or sun, average soil, average water

> Character: 2-inch white to yellow fragrant flowers, sometimes flushed with purple are followed by red berries, evergreen leaves in mild areas

> Season of bloom: summer

> Hardiness: zones 4–9

This resembles the weedy, invasive Japanese honeysuckle but is a much superior garden plant, easy to grow without running over everything else. A must for those who love fragrant flowers. Semievergreen.

Floral Lore

The herbalist John Gerard said that the seed of woodbine "gathered and dried in the shadow and drunk for four days together, doth waste and consume away the hardness of the spleen and removeth wearisomeness."

Lonicera sempervirens trumpet honeysuckle

> Method of climbing: twining stems

> Needs: sun to part shade, average soil, average water

> Character: orange to scarlet tubular, $1^1/_2$-inch flowers in clusters, unscented, followed by red fruit

> Season of bloom: late spring through summer, on current year's growth

> Hardiness: zones 3–9

Vivid color makes up for the lack of fragrance in these beautiful flowers. The plant's as easy to grow as any, with few pest problems. Loved by hummingbirds. Deciduous.

Polygonum aubertii silver lace vine

> Method of climbing: twining stems
>
> Needs: sun, any soil, regular to little water
>
> Character: foamy sprays of tiny white flowers nearly covering the heart-shaped leaves
>
> Season of bloom: midsummer to fall
>
> Hardiness: zones 4–9
>
> Possible drawbacks: doesn't know when to stop growing!

If you want to cover 100 square feet in a single season, this is the vine for you. It will want an equal amount next year, however. To balk its tendency to smother anything in its path, prune it firmly, even cutting it down to the ground each year. This delays the flowers but keeps it from crawling in the windows. Deciduous in colder areas

Wisteria floribunda Japanese wisteria

> Method of climbing: twining stems
>
> Needs: sun to light shade, average soil, average to little water
>
> Character: fragrant cascades of lavender or white flowers, opening slowly from top to bottom, on solid, woody branches with divided leaves
>
> Season of bloom: late spring
>
> Hardiness: zones 4–10
>
> Possible drawbacks: heavy enough to crush light trelliswork

Nothing else can drape a wall with such magnificent color. A giant of a vine, easily climbing tall trees. Around patios, give it stalwart support and a yearly lopping back. *W. sinensis*, Chinese wisteria, has shorter clusters that bloom all at once and is hardy in zones 5–9. Deciduous.

A Bouquet of Half-hardy Vines

Actinidia deliciosa kiwi, Chinese gooseberry

> Method of climbing: twining stems
>
> Needs: Sun or part shade, rich soil, regular or modest amounts of water, strong support

Character: creamy, 1^1/$_2$-inch fragrant flowers, darkening to beige as they age, on vigorous branches to 30 feet, the new growth attractively covered with red hairs

Season of bloom: late spring

Hardiness: zones 7–10

Possible drawbacks: needs frequent pruning and tying unless it has a large area to expand across, sends up shoots yards from the base

A beautiful vine if you have the room. A 50-foot trellis would be just right. As a plus, if you have both a male and a female you'll get the egg-shaped fruit common in grocery stores. Another species, *A. arguta*, is hardier, to zone 4, but has inconspicuous flowers. Deciduous.

Akebia quinata five-leaf akebia

Method of climbing: twining stems

Needs: sun or shade, average soil, regular water

Character: delicate, 5-part leaves on 20–40-foot stems, evergreen in mild areas, with clusters of purple flowers, sometimes followed by sausagelike purple fruit, 2^1/$_4$ feet long

Season of bloom: spring

Hardiness: zones 4–9

Possible drawbacks: can become unruly, sending out runners from the base

One of the best vines for screening because of its lacy effect. The clusters of flowers are attractive and unusual in spite of their somewhat dull texture. Best if thinned every year to prevent the stems from clumping. Deciduous.

Bignonia capreolata crossvine

Method of climbing: both tendrils and holdfasts

Needs: sun or part shade, average to poor soil, regular water

Character: Reddish or orangish trumpet flowers, divided leaves, rapid growth to 30 feet or more

Season of bloom: spring

Hardiness: zones 6–10

Useful for covering large areas such as fences and unsightly buildings, especially where an evergreen vine is needed. 'Tangerine Beauty' has peach-apricot-colored flowers. Evergreen or semievergreen.

Floral Lore

The name *crossvine* comes from the fact that a cross section of the stem shows the unmistake-able shape of a cross.

Clematis armandii evergreen clematis

> Type: vine with tendrillike leaf bases
>
> Needs: sun or part shade, good soil, regular water
>
> Character: leathery evergreen leaves, 4–5 inches long, are borne on somewhat brittle stems up to 30 feet, white, 1-inch flowers in masses
>
> Season of bloom: spring
>
> Hardiness: zones 7–9

Though often slow for a year or two after planting, this vine grows quickly and vigorously when it settles in, soon becoming dense enough to need thinning. Coarse textured but spectacular in bloom, its evergreen leaves make it valuable as a screen.

Clematis montana anemone clematis

> Method of climbing: tendrillike leaf bases
>
> Needs: sun, some shade on roots, average water, average soil
>
> Character: 2-inch pink flowers with the scent of vanilla in drifts on a vigorous vine to 20 feet or more
>
> Season of bloom: spring
>
> Hardiness: zones 6–9
>
> Possible drawbacks: may outgrow small areas

One of the easiest to grow vines, with magnanimous flower displays for little work. Just thin occasionally and help it spread outward. The variety *rubens* has darker flowers with reddish purple new stems and leaves, extremely attractive even when out of bloom. Deciduous.

Gelsemium sempervirens Carolina jessamine

> Method of climbing: twining
>
> Needs: sun to shade, average soil, regular water
>
> Character: tubular 1–1^1/$_2$-inch yellow flowers, fragrant, on long graceful branches, grows to 10–20 feet
>
> Season of bloom: late winter, early spring
>
> Hardiness: zones 7–9
>
> Possible drawbacks: poisonous

Excellent for screening or growing up small trees, this vine is vigorous but not to the point of making a nuisance of itself. Evergreen.

Jasminum grandiflorum Spanish jasmine

> Method of climbing: trailing stems, semievergreen to deciduous
>
> Needs: sun to part shade, good soil, regular watering
>
> Character: clusters of fragrant, 1^1/$_2$-inch white flowers, divided leaves, stems up to 15 feet
>
> Season of bloom: summer
>
> Hardiness: zones 7–10

This is one of the hardiest of fragrant jasmines; the perfume is almost irresistible. An open airy vine, it's excellent for training up a post or along a fence. *J. officinale*, poet's jasmine, is very similar but will cover a larger area and is slightly less hardy.

Passiflora × **alato-caerulea** passionflower vine

> Method of climbing: tendrils
>
> Needs: sun, average soil, average to modest amounts of water, warmth
>
> Character: unusual 3–4-inch flowers, white shaded to pink and lavender with purple at the center, on strong-growing vine with lobed leaves
>
> Season of bloom: summer
>
> Hardiness: zones 8–10
>
> Possible drawbacks: needs thinning frequently

One of the hardiest of the passion vines, this is a conversation piece with finely detailed flowers. Does well in containers. Evergreen in mild areas.

Phaseolus coccineus scarlet runner bean

> Method of climbing: twining stems
>
> Needs: sun to light shade, good soil, average watering
>
> Character: sprays of bright red flowers on 10–20-foot stems, leaves divided into 3 rounded leaflets
>
> Season of bloom: summer
>
> Hardiness: zones 8–10

You'll often find this listed with the vegetables since the pods make excellent cooked string beans, but the flowers make this quite respectable as an ornamental.

A Bouquet of Tender Vines

Asarina antirrhinifolia chickabiddy, climbing snapdragon

> Method of climbing: trailing stems
>
> Needs: sun to part shade, average soil, cool roots, regular watering
>
> Character: lavender to purple trumpetlike flowers similar to snapdragons, on stems with arrowhead-shaped leaves
>
> Season of bloom: summer
>
> Hardiness: zones 9–10

Fast growing enough to be a rewarding annual in northern areas, this is also a good pot plant. It likes crowded roots, so don't repot too often.

Bougainvillea spectabilis bougainvillea

> Method of climbing: trailing stems
>
> Needs: sun, average soil, regular to modest amounts of water
>
> Character: vibrantly colored bracts in many shades surround insignificant flowers, strong thorny stems
>
> Season of bloom: summer
>
> Hardiness: zone 10

A fine pot plant in colder areas that blooms and grows quickly in warm weather. Few other plants equal the intensity of its color. Watch out for the wickedly strong thorns. Roots are fragile and may break apart. Set the container in your planting hole and cut it away with tin snips, then pack soil carefully around the root ball. Evergreen.

Cobaea scandens cup-and-saucer vine (tender perennial)

> Method of climbing: tendrils
>
> Needs: sun to part shade, average soil, good drainage average water
>
> Character: 2-inch long bell-shaped flowers with green bracts at the base are borne on vines up to 20 feet
>
> Season of bloom: late summer to frost
>
> Hardiness: zones 9–10

Quick to grow and bloom, this is suitable for annual screening in northern areas.

Ipomoea alba moonflower (tender perennial)

> Method of climbing: Twining stems
>
> Needs: sun, average soil, good drainage, average watering
>
> Character: tubular buds open to flat, white fragrant blossoms, on 10-foot stems with heart-shaped leaves. Flowers open at night and last a single day.
>
> Hardiness: zones 9–10

Pale and delicate, useful for patios and other places where you can enjoy the scent in the evening. Likes heat.

Ipomoea tricolor morning glory (tender perennial)

> Method of climbing: twining stems
>
> Needs: sun, average soil, good drainage, average water
>
> Character: a fast-growing climber to 8 feet or more with blue flowers that open in early morning and last one day
>
> Hardiness: zones 9–10

This may reseed in favorable climates and can be grown as a houseplant if given four hours of sun every day. 'Heavenly Blue' is a popular form with true-blue flowers. Likes heat.

Ipomoeas, including morning glories and moonflowers, need long warm summers to come to their full glory.

Jasminum nitidum shining jasmine, angelwing jasmine

> Method of climbing: trailing stems
>
> Needs: sun to part shade, good soil, regular watering
>
> Character: clusters of 1-inch, very fragrant white flowers, purple-tinged beneath, glossy leaves, stems up to 20 feet; evergreen to semievergreen
>
> Season of bloom: late spring, summer
>
> Hardiness: zones 9–10, not below 25 degrees

The fragrance of this plant rewards every effort to grow it. It needs warmth and a long growing season to bloom, but makes a good container plant. Shelter it in a greenhouse if you need to.

Lablab purpureus hyacinth bean (tender perennial)

> Method of climbing: twining stems

> Needs: sun, average soil, good drainage, average water, warmth

> Character: scented pink-purple or white pealike flowers are borne in clusters on stems 15 feet or more with 6-inch leaves and followed by fuzzy purple pods

> Season of bloom: summer

> Hardiness: zones 9–10

A lovely, unusual vine that dislikes transplanting so should be sown in place after evening temperatures reach 50 degrees.

Solanum jasminoides potato vine

> Method of climbing: trailing stems

> Needs: sun to part shade, average soil, regular water

> Character: clusters of 1-inch white flowers and purple-tinged leaves on stems up to 30 feet; evergreen in mild areas

> Season of bloom: much of the year, heaviest in spring

> Hardiness: zones 9–10

> Possible drawbacks: like many plants in the potato family, may be poisonous

A strong growing vine with showy flowers that blends well with other plants. Good in containers.

Thunbergia alata black-eyed Susan vine

> Method of climbing: twining stems

> Needs: sun to part-shade, good soil, good drainage, regular watering, warmth

> Character: tubular, 1-inch orange, yellow or white flowers with purple throats on stems up to 10 feet with triangular leaves

> Season of bloom: summer

> Hardiness: zone 10

A vine that grows and flowers fast enough from seed to be a rewarding annual, perhaps for window boxes or hanging baskets. Will also grow inside with half a day of sun.

The Least You Need to Know

➤ Use vines for quick cover where height is more important than thickness.

➤ Choose a twining vine for growing up wires. Choose a clinging vine for walls.

➤ Some vines need thinning and shaping, especially the ones that grow fastest. To keep chores to a minimum, chose a less vigorous species.

➤ Prune spring blooming vines right after flowering. Prune summer blooming vines after flowering or in early spring.

Chapter 15

Not Just Scenery: Trees and Shrubs

In This Chapter

➤ What's a shrub, anyway?

➤ Using flowering trees and shrubs

➤ Planting tips

➤ A bouquet of flowering shrubs

➤ A bouquet of flowering trees

Come November, a bed filled with annuals and perennials often looks pretty bare. By definition, these lack the woody stems and trunks that can add interest to a winter landscape. Contrast an empty flower bed with the delicate branching pattern of a dogwood silhouetted against firs. Who wouldn't take the trees?

And who wants a whole landscape of plants three feet and under, no matter how much summer color they provide? A garden needs height, a vertical dimension to balance the carefully planned ground-level design.

Though many trees and shrubs are available, those that offer the gift of showy flowers as well as attractive shape are doubly valuable. Here's an introduction to these substantial, lasting plants that offer so much more than green.

Tree or Shrub?

What's the difference between them? Often, but not always, trees are much taller. You certainly wouldn't call a 50-foot maple a shrub. On the other hand, many flowering trees are smaller, perhaps up to 20 feet, the height of a tall shrub.

The difference is often in the shape. When a woody plant has an open center with a distinct trunk divided into several main branches, with most of the smaller limbs and leaves toward the outer edges, most people would describe it as a tree.

If, however, the plant was so densely branched to the ground that its center was hidden or if the center was multitrunked with many branches sprouting in all directions, most would term it a shrub.

There are, in fact, a number of shrubs who can be carefully pruned to make handsome small trees, a useful fact to remember if you wish a flowering specimen that won't overtop your house. Simply choose one stem to become a trunk, allow it to divide into just a few branches, then keep the rest of the shoots thinned to a treelike openness. This technique works best with rounded shrubs that tend to have trunklike main stems.

Green Tip

Prune branches off at the collar where it joins the trunk. If you leave a stub, it will die back rather than healing over.

How Can You Use Them?

When in bloom, most of these are eye-catchers. Drifts of pale-pink cherry blossoms (*Prunus*), warm golden forsythia, huge cuplike magnolia flowers, and sprays of white spiraea are all center-stage attractions.

So make the most of them while they're present. Plant something with a contrasting color at the base, or repeat a similar color in a different texture, perhaps scattering clumps of rose-pink tulips beneath your cherry.

Should you plant one as a specimen or use masses? Should you have them in a prominent place or just as a background? That depends on how attractive the plant is when out of bloom. Some, like forsythia, are a bit untidy for display. Whether you plant one or five, it's best to give it an out of the way corner and other plants in front to draw attention away from it during the summer.

Some shrubs look a bit forlorn as singles. Evergreen azaleas, for instance, really need to be planted in groups, making a low thicket that might just as well be called a tall ground cover. Heaths and heathers, also, seem to need the company of their own kind to be effective.

If you have tall trees, try an understory of rhododendrons or other shade-tolerant shrubs. Many forests have this middle layer as part of their ecology and it can provide shelter for a host of wildlife.

If, on the other hand, you have a tree or shrub such as a dogwood (*Cornus*), magnolia, or crabapple (*Malus*) that can stand up to constant attention, make it one of the cornerstones of your design. You can place it at the entryway of the house or in full view of your favorite window. Or you can make an open grove of three, giving each one room to spread.

Consider its most prominent seasons. Does it have red berries or leaves that turn bright yellow in fall? If so, place it so you can appreciate the color. Does it have attractive bark? If so, place it close to the house so you'll notice this detail in winter. Are the leaves particularly good-looking? Then complement them with contrasting textures (see chapter 2) and use them as a summer backdrop.

How to Get Them Off to a Good Start

Remember that roots are the basis of good growth. A cramped, skimpy root system won't nourish a healthy plant. So care for the roots of trees and shrubs as if they were the most valuable part of the plant. They are.

Buying bareroot stock in early spring is an inexpensive way to get the plantings you need, but be sure that you buy from a reputable dealer who has cared for the vulnerable root system properly. Dryness can set back growth or even kill the tree.

Soak the roots for at least an hour before you plant. Even container-grown stock should be well watered before being put in the ground.

Make sure the roots are spread out. If they are crammed into a small hole, the mature root system may be small and unable to withstand any drought.

Loosen the soil around the hole, making it easier for the new roots to expand. Though enriching the soil isn't as important as buying plants that like its basic composition, you may want to add some extra organic matter as you fill around the roots, especially for container plants that have been grown in a rich, organic mix. If your soil is especially poor, improve an area as large as the root ball.

Take Care!

If trees and shrubs are sold bareroot in packages, you can't examine the roots before you buy. They may have been shortened to fit the bag. Pay a little more and buy a good root structure to start with.

Make sure you get rid of any air pockets around the root ball. If your soil is high in clay, press lightly. If it's loose and high in organic matter, press firmly. Water thoroughly when you're done.

Your new shrub will need extra care for a year or two, until the root system expands to its mature size. Even drought-tolerant species need extra water at first. Make sure it lacks for nothing as it becomes established, and later you'll have a healthy, independent specimen that will be able to thrive with minimum maintenance.

A Bouquet of Flowering Shrubs

Remember to check your hardiness zone. For a discussion of zones and hardiness see chapter 4. For a map, see page 341.

Abelia* × *grandiflora glossy abelia

Needs: sun to light shade, average soil, regular water

Character: small, tubular, pink flowers line the arching branches, leaves 1 inch with bronze-tinged new growth, evergreen to semievergreen

Height: 8 feet

Season of bloom: summer, early fall

Hardiness: zone 5

A graceful, fine-textured shrub for backgrounds and hedges. Prune out the oldest stems occasionally to make way for new growth from the base.

Calluna vulgaris heather

Needs: sun, good drainage, regular watering

Character: spikes of tiny white to pink or purple flowers on bushy plants, a few inches to 3 feet tall depending on variety

Garden Talk

Evergreen means that a plant keeps its leaves all year. The oldest ones, however, will be shed occasionally, often in late summer. *Deciduous* means that the plant will drop its leaves in fall, overwintering as a skeleton of bare branches.

Season of bloom: mid to late summer

Hardiness: zone 5

Possible drawbacks: does best in cool summer areas

This is the true heather, blooming much later than the heaths (see *Erica* below). Plant in quantity for pools of bloom around shrubs and trees. Keep plants dense by shearing after blossoms fade.

Chimonanthus praecox wintersweet

Needs: sun or light shade, good drainage, occasional watering

Character: 1-inch pale yellow blossoms before leaves emerge on open bush up to 10 feet high

Season of bloom: late winter or early spring

Hardiness: zone 7

Plant this near a doorway so you'll enjoy its spicy scent even when the weather's poor. To keep it head height, remove some of the oldest stems after they have finished blooming.

Chionanthus virginicus fringe tree

> Needs: sun to shade
>
> Character: feathery clusters of fragrant white flowers on large, multistemmed shrub or small tree, deciduous, to 20 feet
>
> Season of bloom: early summer
>
> Hardiness: zones 5–9

A good choice for multiseason interest, with gold fall color as well as blue fruits on female trees.

Cornus mas cornelian cherry

> Needs: sun or light shade, regular to occasional watering
>
> Character: masses of small yellow blossoms open before leaves, bright red edible fruits in fall, deciduous, to 20 feet
>
> Season of bloom: late winter or early spring
>
> Hardiness: zone 4

An open, twiggy shrub or small tree, cornelian cherry is a dogwood without the white, petallike bracts that make a dogwood flower showy. The fruit is often used to make jam or jelly. The attractive flaky bark provides winter interest.

Deutzia gracilis slender deutzia

> Needs: sun to light shade, regular watering
>
> Character: clusters of white flowers on arching branches, deciduous, to 6 feet
>
> Season of bloom: spring
>
> Hardiness: zone 5
>
> Possible drawbacks: dull when out of bloom, place in background

Adds height to spring displays of tulips and iris, and lightens plantings of evergreens. Delicate and attractive in bloom.

Erica carnea heath

Needs: sun, regular watering, good drainage, acid soil

Character: tiny flowers in spikes on bushy plants, evergreen, usually 6–18 inches

Season of bloom: spring or summer

Hardiness: zone 5

Take Care!

Heather may be invaded by nearby grass. Once the grass roots are intertwined with the shrub roots, they're difficult to remove. Place a barrier or narrow trench between your lawn and patches of heather.

A good plant in masses, especially with bold-textured perennials and shrubs. Shear after blooming to keep the plants dense.

Forsythia × intermedia forsythia

Needs: sun, regular to occasional watering

Character: sunny yellow blossoms line willowy branches on a sprawling deciduous bush up to 10 feet

Season of bloom: early spring

Hardiness: zone 4

Not only cheery color for gray spring day, forsythia branches are easy to force indoors. Just cut, place in water, and wait. In a few days you'll have extra early flowers to brighten a room. Forsythia may not be the most beautiful bush when out of bloom, but it blends in with most others, becoming a green backdrop for showier plants.

Hibiscus syriacus rose of Sharon

Needs: sun, regular water to occasional watering, likes hot summers

Character: hollyhocklike blossoms, single or double, in shades of white, pink, lavender, and purple, on large, deciduous bush, to 10 feet

Season of bloom: midsummer to fall

Hardiness: zone 4

This is an easy to grow relative of the tropical hibiscus (*H. rosa-sinensis*) with smaller flowers but a tougher disposition. Good for late summer blahs.

Hydrangea quercifolia oak-leaf hydrangea

Needs: sun to part shade, regular to occasional watering

Character: clusters of white flowers fading to pink set off by large, lobed leaves with red fall color, deciduous, to 6 feet

Season of bloom: spring, early summer

Hardiness: zone 5

A bold textured hydrangea for sunnier, drier sites than the common blue one will accept, this can also be grown as a container specimen. Easy and quick to fill in.

Kerria japonica Japanese rose

Needs: sun to light shade, regular to occasional watering

Character: single or double gold flowers on green stems, yellow fall color, deciduous, to 6 feet

Season of bloom: spring

Hardiness: zone 4

Possible drawbacks: suckers may increase one plant to a thicket

An arching shrub whose green stems provide a bright contrast to winter grays and browns. A good companion to other warm-colored spring flowers such as those of the flowering quince (*Chaenomeles*, see chapter 17).

Kolkwitzia amabilis beauty bush

Needs: sun to part shade, most soils, regular watering

Character: clusters of pink blossoms cover the arching bush, followed by red-brown seed heads, deciduous, up to 10 feet

Season of bloom: early to midspring

Hardiness: zone 4

A heavy blooming, graceful shrub for spring color. If you want it to stay small, cut it to the ground after bloom, or take out the oldest stems.

Philadelphus coronarius mock orange

Needs: sun to part shade, good drainage, regular to occasional watering

Character: fragrant white flowers in clusters on a vigorous bush, deciduous, to 12 feet

Season of bloom: late spring to early summer

Hardiness: zone 4

An old standard, mock orange will grow almost anywhere. If the quality of the fragrance is important, buy one in bloom so you can test different varieties.

Rhododendron azalea, rhododendron

> Needs: part shade, good loose, acid soil, regular watering
>
> Character: tubular to flat blossoms in many colors and shades, large or small leaves, some with attractive felty undersides, from 1–20 feet, depending on variety, evergreen or deciduous
>
> Season of bloom: spring to early summer
>
> Hardiness: varies by species and variety
>
> Possible drawbacks: leaves are poisonous

Few groups of plants have as much variety as this one. From flame-colored deciduous azaleas to low, dwarf, and treelike Himalayan species with huge leaves, there's one here for every garden. They do look best in groups, or with other woodlanders, however.

Rhododendrons and azaleas flower lavishly in part shade. Often considered to be mild-climate shrubs, some species and varieties are hardy to -35 degrees.

Monk's Hood *(Aconitum nepellus)*

Saucer Magnolia *(Magnolia soulangiana)*

Painted Tongue *(Salpiglossus)*

Love-in-a-Mist *(Nigella)*

New England Aster *(Aster novae-angliae)*

Siberian Iris *(Iris siberica)*

Hollyhock Mallow *(Malva alcea fastgiata)*

Cornflower *(Centaurea cyanus)*

Cardinal Flower *(Lobelia cardinalis)*

Guara *(Guara)*

Turkestan Rose *(Rosa rugosa)*

Rocket Larkspur *(Consulida ambigua)*

Mimosa *(Albizia julibrissin)*

Crocosmia *(Crocosmia)*

Pot Merigold *(Calendula officinalis)*

Autumn Crocus *(Culchicum autumnall)*

Yellow Corydalis *(Corydalis lutea)*

Nasturtium *(Tropaeoleum)*

Sweet Pea
(Lathyrus odoratus)

Yarrow *(Achillea)*

Columbine *(Aquilegia)*

Star Magnolia *(Magnolia stellata)*

Zinnia *(Zinnia elegans)*

Gooseneck Loosestrife *(Lysimachia clethroides)*

Clematis *(Clematic henryi)*

Asiatic Lilies *(Lilium)*

Tickseed *(Coreopsis verticillata)*

Snapdragons *(Antirrhinum majus)*

Sambucus canadensis American elderberry

> Needs: sun or part shade, regular watering

> Character: large, flat clusters of tiny white flowers followed by edible purplish black berries, leaves divided into segments up to 6 inches long, to 8 feet

> Season of bloom: early summer

> Hardiness: zone 3

> Possible drawbacks: may sucker into larger clumps than you wished

The large leaves give this an almost tropical appearance, making it a good shrub to use for texture contrast. The flower clusters are showy, as are the clusters of berries. You can find varieties selected for their taste and others for golden or finely cut leaves. The European elder (*Sambucus nigra*) is less hardy, with less flavorful berries, but grows taller, making a small tree 20–30 feet high. There is a purple-leaved variety whose effect is stunning among other shrubs.

Rosa hybrids and species rose

Most commonly grown roses belong in the high-maintenance category (see chapter 16), needing rich soil and regular pruning, feeding and insect and disease control. Some species, however, such as *Rosa rugosa*, are as tough as any shrub grown. There are also hybrids that have been chosen for disease resistance and ease of care. Ask local experts which are best for your area.

Floral Lore

It was once the custom in England to hang a rose over the dinner table as a sign that all secrets told were to be held sacred.

Spiraea prunifolia bridal wreath

> Needs: sun to light shade, most soils, regular to occasional watering

> Character: cascades of tiny white flowers in clusters on arching branches, deciduous, to 6 feet

> Season of bloom: spring

> Hardiness: zone 4

This plant is so tough and easy it's become a standard in cold-winter areas. The fountain-shaped bush has dark green leaves that show some purplish fall color.

Syringa vulgaris common lilac

> Needs: sun, well-drained soil, regular to occasional watering
>
> Character: dense, elongated clusters of fragrant lavender to purple flowers, sometimes pink or white, on a vigorous, suckering bush, deciduous, to 15 feet
>
> Season of bloom: spring
>
> Hardiness: zone 3
>
> Possible drawbacks: subject to some pests and diseases

Another standard, loved both for its fragrance and for its easy, generous disposition. Plant one and in five years you'll have a thicket. If you don't want it to spread, dig up all the suckers and give them to a plant sale. Grafted varieties need suckers removed so the rootstock doesn't take over from the more ornamental top.

Viburnum viburnum, snowball

> Needs: sun to part shade, regular watering
>
> Character: clusters of white (sometimes pink) flowers, often fragrant, size and shape depending on species:
>
> *V. × carlcephalum* fragrant snowball
>
> dense round clusters, 4–5 inches wide, on a 6–8-foot bush, deciduous, zone 5
>
> *V. davidii*
>
> flat loose clusters followed by metallic blue berries, attractively veined evergreen leaves, 3–4 feet high, zone 7
>
> *V. opulus* cranberry bush
>
> lace-cap flowers (tiny ones surrounded by a row of larger ones) followed by red berries; maplelike leaves have good fall color, yellow, red to purplish; takes boggy soils; deciduous, to 15 feet high, zone 3
>
> *V. plicatum tomentosum* doublefile viburnum
>
> lace-cap flowers above strongly veined leaves, tiered branching pattern, occasional fruit, purplish-red fall color, to 15 feet, zone 4

V. tinus laurestinus

pink buds opening to loose flat clusters of small flowers, metallic blue berries, dense branching pattern, good for screens and hedges, to 10 feet, zone 7 or 8

Season of bloom: spring, except for *V. tinus*, fall through spring

Viburnums are some of the most attractive, versatile shrubs available. They mix well with rhododendrons and azaleas, as well as more sun-tolerant shrubs.

Weigela florida weigela

Needs: sun to part shade, regular watering

Character: tubular pink to rose colored flowers on arching branches, deciduous, to 10 feet

Season of bloom: spring

Hardiness: zone 5

Lovely shrubs in bloom, a bit stiff and dull the rest of the rest of the year, so give them an out-of-the-way corner. Hummingbirds love them.

A Bouquet of Flowering Trees

Aesculus × carnea red horse chestnut

Needs: sun, average soil, regular water

Character: 8-inch spikes of deep pink flowers, deciduous dark green leaves, to 40 feet

Season of bloom: spring

Hardiness: zone 3

Possible drawbacks: dislikes hot humid summers, glossy seeds are somewhat toxic

A dense, round-headed tree that casts deep shade, this horse chestnut is good for screening unsightly views.

Albizia julibrissin silk tree

> Needs: sun to part shade, regular water, likes heat
>
> Character: pink powder-puff blossoms over fine-textured leaves, to 40 feet
>
> Season of bloom: summer
>
> Hardiness: zone 7
>
> Possible drawbacks: may get a wilt disease in some areas

Few other trees have such a delicate, light appearance in the garden. Can be a showy presence at an entryway or an airy contrast to a fir or pine.

Amelanchier** × **grandiflora apple serviceberry

> Needs: sun to part shade, average soil, regular to occasional watering
>
> Character: clusters of white flowers followed by edible fruit, deciduous, to 25 feet
>
> Season of bloom: spring
>
> Hardiness: zone 4
>
> Possible drawbacks: blossoms may be short-lived in warm weather

This is a graceful tree with berries that taste somewhat like blueberries and great fall color, particularly suited to informal plantings.

Catalpa speciosa catalpa

> Needs: sun to part shade, any soil, regular to occasional watering
>
> Character: clusters of 2-inch trumpet-shaped flowers, white with yellow and brown markings, followed by beanlike pods, large heart-shaped leaves, deciduous, to 50 feet
>
> Season of bloom: late spring, summer
>
> Hardiness: zone 4
>
> Possible drawbacks: litter of flowers and pods may annoy some gardeners

Unbothered by heat or cold, a catalpa can be a showy specimen that rivals subtropical trees when in bloom. Its bold texture and light green leaves are attention-getters; contrast with darker, more delicate plants.

Cercis canadensis Eastern redbud

Needs: sun to light shade, regular watering

Character: tiny purplish pink pealike blossoms in profuse clusters followed by beanlike pods, rounded form with heart-shaped leaves, deciduous, to 25 feet

Season of bloom: spring

Hardiness: zone 4

A good tree for natural settings, in groups or as a specimen. Some varieties have pure pink or white flowers, some have purple leaves. All have good fall color. *C. occidentalis* is a more drought-tolerant species native to western North America.

Crataegus laevigata English hawthorn

Needs: sun, well-drained soil, occasional watering

Character: clusters of tiny, white to rose-colored flowers outline branches, small lobed leaves without fall color, bright red fruit, thorny branches, deciduous, to 25 feet

Season of bloom: spring

Hardiness: zone 4

Possible drawbacks: subject to pests and diseases, does poorly in hot, humid summers

A pretty, fine-textured tree, but tenacious under its preferred conditions. Will often self-sow.

Floral Lore

Did you know that hawthorn is called May tree in Britain? Often planted near holy wells, it is also called quickset because it makes a good quick (living) hedge.

Laburnum anagyroides golden chain

> Needs: sun or light shade, well-drained soil, regular watering
>
> Character: long clusters of yellow pealike flowers, similar to wisteria, cloverlike leaves, bright green bark, deciduous, to 30 feet
>
> Season of bloom: spring
>
> Hardiness: zone 5
>
> Possible drawbacks: not for southern states, seedpods are poisonous

An easy to grow tree that may seed itself around the garden, especially useful against a dark background that allows the green bark and golden flowers to draw attention.

Malus flowering crab apple

> Needs: sun, regular to occasional watering
>
> Character: white to rose flowers, single or double, followed by small red to yellow apples
>
> Season of bloom: spring
>
> Hardiness: zones vary, usually 3 or 4
>
> Possible drawbacks: subject to a number of diseases

Somewhat tolerant of damp soils, crabapple also do well in other less-than-ideal situations, including gravelly and slightly alkaline soils. Many named varieties are available, some with more disease resistance than others, some with larger fruit that can be used for making jelly.

Prunus × blireana, P. cerasifera varieties flowering plum

> Needs: sun, good soil, regular watering
>
> Character: masses of cool pink single or double flowers line the branches, leaves are often purplish, deciduous, to 12–30 feet, depending on variety
>
> Season of bloom: spring
>
> Hardiness: zone 6

This is a more adaptable flowering tree than the flowering cherry, a little less graceful perhaps, but deservedly popular. Needs little pruning except to keep excess twiggy growth and suckers out of the center of the tree.

Prunus serrulata varieties Japanese flowering cherry

> Needs: sun, excellent drainage, regular watering
>
> Character: white or pink blossoms in airy or dense clusters on graceful branches, deciduous, various heights
>
> Season of bloom: early to late spring
>
> Hardiness: zone 6
>
> Possible drawbacks: subject to root rot in poorly drained soils

Few flowering trees have the graceful presence of flowering cherries, an elegance that makes them an essential for Japanese gardens. Their noncompetitive roots and light shade make them good trees to garden beneath. Depending on the species and variety, flowering cherries may be spreading or upright, early or late blooming.

Prunus subhirtella 'Autumnalis' autumn cherry

> Needs: sun, excellent drainage, regular watering
>
> Character: pale pink double blossoms on graceful branches, deciduous, various heights
>
> Season of bloom: early spring, some blossoms opening in autumn and winter
>
> Hardiness: zone 5
>
> Possible drawbacks: subject to root rot in poorly drained soils

This provides much-appreciated flowers when the weather is still gray and cold. Its slender, horizontal branches seem perfect for its delicate flowers. Another variety, *P. s.* 'Whitcombii,' has somewhat larger, deeper pink flowers but rarely opens before late winter.

The Least You Need to Know

➤ Trees and shrubs add height and strength to a garden.

➤ Large shrubs can often be turned into small trees by training to a single trunk with a few main branches.

➤ Healthy roots will give you a healthy tree. Take the time to care for them.

➤ Easy flowering shrubs: bridal wreath (*Spiraea*), mock orange (*Philadelphus*), cornelian cherry (*Cornus*).

➤ Easy flowering trees: catalpa, golden chain (*Laburnum*), flowering crab apple (*Malus*).

Part 3
Matching Place and Plant

If you've ever had a plant refuse to grow, you probably blamed yourself for its failure. You didn't do this right, or that, or another thing. Most likely, though, the plant needed a different environment than the one you provided.

With one simple step—pairing plants with the conditions they like—you can eliminate most problems and leave the work of growing to the specialists: the plants themselves. Here's a look at the most common environments you'll encounter.

Enough of Everything

Maybe you moved into a house previously owned by a gardening addict. Maybe you decided to spend your exercise time in the garden digging in organic matter instead of going to the gym. However it happened, here you are with the kind of soil every gardener dreams of, rich, well-drained, and eager to grow plants. And there's no need to be stingy with the water. These plants will lack for nothing.

What Does This Garden Look Like?

From a plant's point of view, the soil is the main attraction. Dark, loose, and with good drainage but enough organic matter to hold moisture. It's at least a foot deep, giving encouragement to far-ranging roots. Rich soils are usually slightly acid to neutral because of the acidifying action of the decaying organic matter, but most plants grow well in this pH range.

What does the best texture look like? Cut a chunk of sod out of a lawn and notice the crumbly, grainy texture of the dirt around the roots. That's what you're looking for, granular, rough, and full of spaces for air and water.

The water supply is even, without sudden droughts or constant flooding. Nothing checks the growth of new sprouts and flowers. If you're supplying the water yourself, soak when the top inch or two of soil is dry, then let it dry out again. A mulch helps keep the moisture even and the soil cool in summer heat. If dry periods are a problem, see chapter 17.

In this chapter, we'll look at plants that need sun, with perhaps some light shade for part of the day. If you have a shady area to landscape, see chapters 18 and 19.

Climate Is Your Limiting Factor

Almost anything will do well for you, assuming it can take your patterns of heat and cold. It may be obvious that a plant at home in Florida may freeze out in Illinois, but not so obvious that another will fail in North Carolina because of the summer heat and humidity no matter how cold hardy. Others will thrive in heat but languish in cool coastal settings. So, before you plant, find out if your intended purchase likes your climate.

Even drought-resistant plants will grow well with a little pampering, as long as the drainage is good. You'll get quick growth, sometimes a little too rampant. You may have to prune long shoots back to get a compact well-shaped plant.

Green Tip

You can help plants prepare for winter by watering less and leaving flowers to form seeds. If you've been removing all the roses before they form seedpods (also known as hips), for instance, let most of them stay on the branches beginning in September. This will send a signal to the bush that winter's coming.

Can Anything Go Wrong?

Some plants may mildew with the frequent overhead watering. To avoid this, water early in the day so leaves can dry out by evening or use a drip irrigation system.

A few flowers, such as nasturtiums (*Tropaeolum*) put out lots of leaves in good soil but few flowers. They need a lean diet in ground others would disdain. You may also have this problem if you use a high nitrogen fertilizer too often. All the growth is channeled into green shoots, not flowers.

Shrubs and trees that have regular water late in the summer may not harden off for winter as well as those who have been allowed to dry out. One of the advantages of a shrubbery bed separate from the annuals and perennials is that you can cut down on water when they need a rest.

Now let's look at some of the beauties you can grow that will bring sighs of envy from your friends. Be sure to look at chapter 20, also. Most plants that tolerate wet conditions will grow perfectly well here.

Annuals and Tender Perennials Grown as Annuals

Antirrhinum snapdragon

> Needs: sun, some shade in hot areas, good soil (best in neutral to slightly alkaline soils), regular water

> Character: from dwarfs a foot high to giants 3 feet or more, snapdragons have velvety, bright-colored, tubular flowers in solid spikes, all colors but blue, some bicolors

> Season of bloom: winter and spring in mild areas, summer when grown as an annual

> Hardiness: zone 8

> Possible drawbacks: taller kinds may need staking

Snapdragons are garden classics, and their popularity is well deserved. Their rich colors, unusually shaped flowers and vertical form are useful in both formal and informal compositions.

Callistephus chinensis annual aster, China aster

> Needs: sun, good drainage, light, rich soil, regular water

> Character: asterlike flowers in many colors and forms, 1–3 feet high

> Possible drawbacks: subject to disease, look for resistant varieties, and grow in a different location each year

Excellent cut flowers and bright, attractive bedding plants when grown without lack of water or nutrients. They have difficulty recovering from setbacks, so give them extra attention.

Consolida ambigua larkspur, annual delphinium

> Needs: sun, rich soil, regular watering

> Character: tall spikes of blue, lavender, white, or rose-colored flowers, finely cut leaves, 1–5 feet high, hardy annual

> Possible drawbacks: poisonous

The blue shades are classic, glorious sky-colored blue, but the other varieties are handsome, too. Best in cool weather, though some varieties are heat-tolerant. Larkspur dislikes transplanting so seed it in place in early spring.

Lathyrus odoratus sweet pea

> Needs: sun, rich, cool, neutral pH soil, regular watering
>
> Character: fragrant pealike blossoms in rose, white, blue, purple, and red on vining (5-foot) or bushy (1-foot) plants, hardy annual

Old-fashioned favorites, sweet peas need constant moisture and a mulch to keep the soil cool. Any extra work is amply repaid by the fragrance and bright color you gain. Best sown where they are to grow.

Lobelia erinus lobelia

> Needs: sun to part shade, moist, rich soil, regular watering
>
> Character: small blue, purple-blue, or white tubular flowers on low plants, some varieties with trailing stems, to 6 inches

Lobelia is one of the most popular bedding annuals, complementing almost anything. Though hanging baskets benefit from the trailing kinds, these also go well in casual beds and borders. The clumping varieties tend to be more formal, better for close-packed edging and outlining.

Phlox drummondii annual phlox

> Needs: sun, good drainage, rich soil, regular watering
>
> Character: heads of simple rounded flowers in all colors but orange and blue, to $1^1/_2$ feet tall, half-hardy annual
>
> Possible drawbacks: needs deadheading for longest bloom

Showy and attractive in mixed borders, phlox comes in both dwarf and tall strains. Can be sown in fall in mild climates.

Reseda odorata mignonette

> Needs: sun to part shade, rich soil, regular watering
>
> Character: copper-tinged green flowers in pyramidal clusters on a sprawling plant to $1^1/_2$ feet high, hardy annual

Not showy, but deservedly loved for its spicy fragrance. Mix a few with more colorful flowers for a bed that appeals to both eye and nose.

Salpiglossis sinuata *painted tongue*

> Needs: sun, good drainage, regular watering

> Character: petunialike flowers in a tapestry of color, purple, orange, yellow, and pink, veined and shaded with contrasting hues, 2–3 feet tall

> Possible drawbacks: may need staking, deadheading

This is the plant for those who want to surprise their friends. The richly hued blossoms always attract attention and a few of these in a bed will assure your reputation as an excellent gardener.

Bulbs

Dahlia hybrids dahlia

> Needs: sun to light shade, rich soil, regular watering

> Character: single, daisylike, double to many-petaled blooms in a wide variety of colors and sizes, dwarfs to 5-foot-tall giants

> Season of bloom: summer

> Hardiness: zone 9

> Possible drawbacks: tall varieties need staking, tubers need to be dug and stored in colder areas

Dahlias have a richness and intensity that delights those with a passion for concentrated color, though pastels are also available. They tend toward the formal and precise in appearance, looking most at home in cutting gardens and geometric borders. Their roots need careful handling to avoid breaking the narrow-necked tubers and new shoots.

Fritillaria imperialis crown imperial

> Needs: sun, loose soil enriched with humus, regular watering

> Character: 3–4 feet tall, with bare stems topped by a tuft of leaves and large bell-like red, orange, or yellow flowers

> Season of bloom: spring

> Hardiness: zone 5

Garden Talk

Humus is the end production of decomposition, the dark brown, gummy substance that leaves, wood, and animal matter becomes. It's excellent for holding water and nutrients. What most people call humus, however, is the partially decayed product, still fibrous and good for aerating the soil.

Possible drawbacks: has an odor unpleasant to some, bulbs may skip a year's growth after flowering or planting

An unusual attention-getter, crown imperials are impressive in a perennial border. If they grow well for you, plant large clumps.

Gladiolus gladiolus

Needs: sun, rich loose soil, regular watering

Character: large blooms in tall spikes, many shades available, $1^{1}/_{2}$–4 feet

Season of bloom: early summer to fall, depending on planting time

Hardiness: zone 9

Possible drawbacks: needs staking

Excellent cut flower and vertical accent in a border. The wide range of colors and ease of planting makes them popular in areas where they need to be dug and stored over winter. Many small corms form at the base of the original one, each needing only a year or two of growth to bloom themselves.

Take Care!

Put stakes in the ground at the same time you plant the bulbs. This reduces the risk of spearing a bulb later on.

Gladiolus callianthus Abyssinian sword lily

Needs: sun, rich soil, regular watering

Character: large fragrant white flowers blotched with brown, 3–6 on each 3-foot stem

Season of bloom: late summer or fall

Hardiness: zone 9

Possible drawbacks: flowers better if divided each year

An elegant addition to a flower or shrub border, these should be grown more often. Plant five or ten corms in a clump for best effect.

Hyacinthus orientalis common hyacinth

Needs: sun or light shade, rich soil, regular watering during growth

Character: fat spikes of fragrant tubular flowers, white, lavender-blue, purple, or pink, straplike leaves, to 1 foot

Season of bloom: spring

Hardiness: zone 4

Possible drawbacks: need winter chill

Graceful they're not, but hyacinths still charm with fragrance and color, especially when clustered and mixed with more willowy blossoms. They do well in containers, even blooming with no more than water and pebbles. Keep them in a dark, cold place until well rooted, then bring into a warm room. Roman or French Roman hyacinths (*H. o. albulus*) are better adapted to mild-winter areas and may even naturalize.

Lilium true lilies

Needs: sun (part shade in hottest areas) though they like shade over the roots, average well-drained to good soil, regular water

Character: a thousand shades in many forms, from spires of small, hanging bell-like flowers, to huge trumpets and flat, upward-facing stars, all on strong stems from 2–8 feet tall, wind-resistant

Some hybrids are as follows:

Asiatic hybrids—easiest, May to early July, zone 3, usually upward-facing, little or light fragrance

Trumpets and aurelians—July, zone 7, large, dropping trumpets, better in hot weather than Oriental hybrids, fragrant

Oriental hybrids—July to August, zone 5, ruffled, banded, or spotted blossoms, spicy fragrance, best in cool summers or with part shade

Possible drawbacks: not for the desert Southwest, staking needed if grown with too much shade or for heavy-headed trumpets

Lilies are so elegantly good-looking that most people assume they are difficult to grow. Not at all. Modern lily growers have created strong, disease-resistant varieties that just grow taller and have more flowers each year. If you want to start off with some reliable varieties, try the old-fashioned regal lily, *Lilium regale*, the Asiatic hybrids, or a tough Oriental hybrid called 'Black Beauty'.

Ranunculus asiaticus Persian buttercup

Needs: sun, excellent drainage, and regular watering

Character: double roselike blooms in many shades of pink and yellow to red and orange, tuberous roots, bright green cut leaves

Season of bloom: spring

Hardiness: zone 8

Possible drawbacks: best if dug each year even where hardy

These are often seen as potted plants in spring, their clear colors especially appreciated during gray, wet weather. Their many-petaled blossoms are neat and well organized, suitable for formal gardens.

Tulipa tulip

> Needs: sun or light shade in hot areas, rich soil with extra fertilizer, regular watering when growing

> Character: cup-shaped blossoms, some varieties with twisted or wide-spreading petals, some with double or multicolored petals, on stiff stems, many colors available, 6 inches to 2¹/₂ feet tall

> Season of bloom: early to late spring depending on variety

> Hardiness: zone 3

> Possible drawbacks: most varieties need winter chill

From small wild species tulips to elegant hybrids, tulips are one of the most popular bulbs grown. The Greigii and Kaufmanniana varieties are the most permanent, though some species tulips, such as tiny *T. tarda* will also naturalize. Deep planting may help hybrids rebloom each year, though many gardeners treat them as annuals.

Perennials for Repeat Performances

Aconitum monkshood

> Needs: Moist to damp, cool, rich soil, sun to partial shade

> Character: flowers in a shade of blue or purple, depending on the species, borne in spikes 2–5 feet tall

> Season of bloom: summer

> Hardiness: zone 2

> Possible drawbacks: very poisonous! Keep away from children, far from vegetable gardens; not for hot, humid summer areas.

Excellent rich color from plants that are easy to grow, given the right conditions. They can substitute for delphiniums in slightly shady areas.

Floral Lore

Monkshood was said by the Greeks to be the invention of Hecate, the goddess of ghosts and witches, from the foam of Cerberus, the guardian of Hades. It was one of the poisons used by elderly men on the island of Ceos who were condemned to death when they became too weak to be of use to the State.

Aster hybrids Michaelmas daisies

> Needs: sun, rich soil, regular watering
>
> Character: blue-violet to purple, pink, or white daisylike blossoms on well-branched willowy plants, 1–4 feet
>
> Season of bloom: late summer, fall
>
> Hardiness: zone 3
>
> Possible drawbacks: may need staking

These are best for the back of a fall focal point, tall enough to make a grand show, but a bit sparse at the base. Few plants, however, equal their liberality with their flowers.

Chrysanthenum × *morifolium* florist's chrysanthemum

> Needs: sun, rich, well-drained soil, regular watering
>
> Character: many flower forms, from single daisies to many-petaled doubles, petals sometimes narrow, spiderlike or spooned, in yellow, gold, and bronze, sometimes pink and burgundy, 1–3 feet depending on variety
>
> Season of bloom: late summer, fall
>
> Hardiness: zone 5
>
> Possible drawbacks: many varieties need pinching to bush out, some need staking

Mums seem the perfect autumn flower, their rich tints echoing the fall leaves. If you choose dwarf varieties and give them plenty of nutrients, you'll find them easy and undemanding.

Cosmos atrosanguineus chocolate cosmos

> Needs: sun, rich well-drained soil, regular to occasional watering
>
> Character: red-brown single flowers with the scent of chocolate, deeply cut foliage, tuberous roots, 2—2$^1/_2$ feet
>
> Season of bloom: late summer, fall
>
> Hardiness: zone 8, 7, with a heavy mulch

Hard to believe as it is, this really does smell like chocolate! If in doubt about its hardiness, treat like a dahlia. Dig the roots in fall, store in a cool place over winter, and replant in spring.

Delphinium species and hybrids delphinium

> Needs: sun, rich well-drained soil, regular watering
>
> Character: tall spikes of flowers, usually blue to purple but also in pink, lavender, and white, large lobed or cut leaves, 1–8 inches depending on species and variety
>
> Season of bloom: early summer
>
> Hardiness: zones 2–3
>
> Possible drawbacks: taller kinds require staking

One of the best sources of true blue in the garden, large enough to stand out clearly. The types with largest flowers and tallest spikes are often more trouble to grow and shorter-lived than shorter kinds.

Delphiniums need deep, rich soil and plenty of water, but compensate you for the extra work with dignified spires of white, clear blue, or purple.

Dianthus plumarius cottage pink

> Needs: sun, light but rich soil (neutral pH is best), good drainage, even moisture without overwatering
>
> Character: very fragrant, double pink, white, or rose flowers, blue-green linear leaves, about 1 foot
>
> Season of bloom: summer, fall
>
> Hardiness: zone 4
>
> Possible drawbacks: needs deadheading to bloom longest

Yes, pinks are beautiful but their greatest charm is in their spicy fragrance. Nothing else is quite like it except the closely related carnation. This is sweeter, though, and more intense.

Iris bearded hybrids

> Needs: sun, good soil (though clay is all right), regular to occasional watering
>
> Character: large blooms, available in many shades, above swordlike leaves, 8 inches to 4 feet, depending on variety
>
> Season of bloom: summer
>
> Hardiness: zone 4
>
> Possible drawbacks: subject to leaf spot in wet weather, rhizome rot in poorly drained soil, iris borer in some areas

These showy blossoms are summer favorites, often ruffled and shaded with contrasting colors. They make large clumps that can hold their own among substantial shrubs. Divide the rhizomes after bloom.

Lupinus Russell hybrids

> Needs: sun, well-drained slightly acid soil, regular watering
>
> Character: tight spikes of pealike blossoms in many colors, leaves divided into fingerlike segments, $1^1/_2$–4 feet, depending on variety
>
> Season of bloom: late spring, early summer
>
> Hardiness: zone 4
>
> Possible drawbacks: best in cool summer areas, may be short-lived

Richly colored, hybrid lupines make large specimen plants that contrast well with more spreading perennials. Dwarfs can be used in masses. May self-sow, but seedlings may revert to resemble less showy parents.

Paeonia peony

Needs: sun, rich, deep, well-drained soil, regular watering, winter cold

Character: huge blooms, up to 10 inches across, usually double, in white, pink, or red, 3–4 feet

Season of bloom: spring

Take Care!

Don't spread diseases. Put all infected leaves in the garbage can, not the compost pile.

Hardiness: zone 3

Possible drawbacks: may get botrytis (a fungus disease), heavy flowers need support

Peonies are lush, beautiful, and long-lived. If they do well for you, you may pass them on to your grandchildren. Remember that when you want to skimp on soil preparation. As with most plants, some people find themselves constantly fighting disease, others have no trouble at all.

Papaver nudicaule Iceland poppy

Needs: sun, good soil, good drainage, regular watering

Character: silky-petaled, cup-shaped flowers in soft pastels as well as orange and red above clusters of light green lobed leaves

Season of bloom: early summer

Hardiness: zones 3–9

Possible drawbacks: sometimes short-lived

Few flowers have such delicate beauty. The crepe-textured petals seem to glow in the sun, making the best colors of these medium-size perennials worth searching out. Often grown as annuals since they bloom the first year from seed.

Schizostylus coccinea Kaffir lily, crimson flag

Needs: sun to light shade, average soil, regular water

Character: watermelon-red lilylike flowers, 2 inches, above long, narrow leaves, 1–2 feet

Season of bloom: late summer, fall

Hardiness: zones 6–9

A truly delightful addition to the fall garden, sometimes blooming into November. The varieties 'Mrs. Hegarty,' pale pink, and 'Viscountess Byng,' soft pink, are especially attractive.

Vines for Vertical Color

Actinidia deliciosa kiwi, Chinese gooseberry

> Method of climbing: twining stems
>
> Needs: sun or part shade, rich soil, regular or modest amounts of water, strong support
>
> Character: creamy, $1^1/_2$-inch fragrant flowers, darkening to beige as they age, on vigorous branches to 30 feet, the new growth attractively covered with red hairs
>
> Season of bloom: late spring
>
> Hardiness: zone 7
>
> Possible drawbacks: needs frequent pruning and tying unless it has a large area to expand across, sends up shoots yards from the base

A beautiful vine if you have the room. A 50-foot trellis would be just right. As a plus, if you have both a male and a female you'll get the egg-shaped fruit common in grocery stores. Another species, *A. arguta*, is hardier, to zone 4, but has inconspicuous flowers. Deciduous.

Clematis hybrids large-flowered hybrid clematis

> Method of climbing: tendrillike leaf bases
>
> Needs: sun on leaves, shade on roots (stones work well), average water, good soil
>
> Character: 4–8-inch blossoms in vivid or pastel pink, lavender, purple, and white, on 10-foot vines
>
> Season of bloom: summer
>
> Hardiness: zone 3, some varieties zone 4

A summer conversation piece, excellent in entries and by patios. If it doesn't freeze to the ground, don't feel that you need to cut it back so severely yourself. Just thin the stems and allow it to climb higher. Deciduous.

Green Tip

Clematis can be planted at the base of an apple or other fruit tree, covering the tree with large blossoms for a showy summer display.

Clematis armandii evergreen clematis

> Type: vine with tendrillike leaf bases
>
> Needs: sun or part shade, good soil, regular water
>
> Character: leathery evergreen leaves, 4–5 inches long, are borne on somewhat brittle stems up to 30 feet, white, 1-inch flowers in masses
>
> Season of bloom: spring
>
> Hardiness: zone 7

Though often slow for a year or two after planting, this vine grows quickly and vigorously when it settles in, soon becoming dense enough to need thinning. Coarse textured but spectacular in bloom, its evergreen leaves make it valuable as a screen.

Phaseolus coccineus scarlet runner bean

> Method of climbing: twining stems
>
> Needs: sun to light shade, good soil, average watering
>
> Character: sprays of bright red flowers on 10–20-foot stems, leaves divided into 3 rounded leaflets
>
> Season of bloom: summer
>
> Hardiness: zone 8

You'll often find this listed with the vegetables since the pods make excellent cooked string beans, but the flowers make this quite respectable as an ornamental.

Thunbergia alata black-eyed Susan vine

> Method of climbing: twining stems
>
> Needs: sun to part shade, good soil, good drainage, regular watering, warmth
>
> Character: tubular, 1-inch orange, yellow, or white flowers with purple throats on stems up to 10 feet with triangular leaves
>
> Season of bloom: summer
>
> Hardiness: zone 10

Another vine that grows and flowers fast enough from seed to be rewarding annual, perhaps for window boxes or hanging baskets. Will also grow inside with half a day of sun.

Shrubs

Daphne × ***burkwoodii*** burkwood daphne

> Needs: sun or light shade, good drainage, cool soil, regular to occasional watering

> Character: clusters of small fragrant flowers, white to pink, at the branch ends, evergreen to deciduous, to 5 feet tall

> Season of bloom: late spring, often repeated in late summer

> Hardiness: zone 5

> Possible drawbacks: poisonous

A rounded, bushy shrub that blends well with others in a border or at the edge of a woodland. The scent is truly amazing.

Gardenia jasminoides gardenia

> Needs: sun to light shade, good, well-draining soil, regular watering, warmth

> Character: double, white, intensely fragrant blossom set off by glossy green leaves, evergreen, height varies by variety

> Season of bloom: spring or summer

> Hardiness: zone 8

A prize, often grown indoors but suitable for mild warm-summer climates. Every effort to grow this beauty is rewarded by the fragrance.

Magnolia × ***soulangiana*** saucer magnolia

> Needs: sun to part shade, good soil, regular water

> Character: large, purple-pink tulip-shaped flowers among coarse, light green leaves, spreading branches, deciduous, slow growing to 15 feet

> Season of bloom: spring

> Hardiness: zone 5

> Possible drawbacks: first flowers may be damaged by frost

Is this a tree or a shrub? A little of both. Can be a dense multistemmed shrub, or a small, spreading, single-trunk tree. The flowers are as eye-catching as huge tulips and combine well with fine-textured ground covers such as sweet woodruff (*Galium odoratum*). Magnolias dislike root disturbance so plant where it can settle in.

Magnolia stellata star magnolia

> Needs: sun to part shade, good soil, regular water
>
> Character: a profusion of medium-size white flowers with narrow petals covers the slow-growing bush, deciduous, to 6 feet
>
> Season of bloom: early spring
>
> Hardiness: zone 5

A beauty, delicate and serene, smaller in all its proportions than the saucer magnolia. Use in entryways and among choice perennials. A few varieties are fragrant.

Floral Lore

Did you know that the Romans cultivated roses? To bring them to bloom as early as possible, they dug ditches around the plants just as the buds formed then poured warm water into the ditches.

Rosa rose

> Needs: sun to very light shade, good soil plus extra fertilizer for most hybrids, good drainage, regular water (some species tolerate less)
>
> Character: single to double and many-petaled varieties, all colors but blue, on deciduous bushes, 1–20 feet, depending on variety
>
> Season of bloom: early summer, many varieties continuing until frost
>
> Hardiness: zones vary, some species are hardy to zone 2 but most of the modern hybrids need winter protection where temperature drop below 10 degrees
>
> Possible drawbacks: subject to disease and insect pests if poorly adapted varieties planted, some varieties more disease-resistant than others

The Queen of Flowers is a title that could well be applied to roses. Few plants have inspired such affection over the centuries, a fondness that continues to spur gardeners to buy them in quantities each year. And few plants have such a diversity of forms and characters to offer.

Here are a few:

Hybrid teas—the classic florist's rose, popular and widely grown. Bushes may be 2–6 feet tall.

Grandifloras—extra vigorous, with one or several flowers to a stem. Up to 10 feet.

Floribundas—smaller flowers but more of them, well-branched, bushy plants, lots of vigor.

Miniature roses—everything reduced in size on plants up to 2 feet. Dainty and more cold-tolerant than hybrid teas.

Climbing roses—long branches can be tied up to fences, posts, and walls, giving a vertical display of large flowers above your head.

Shrub roses—a category containing a wide variety of plants, usually ever blooming, with a large, bushy form that blends into a landscape better than hybrid teas.

Old roses—hybrids developed before the mid-1800s, some dating from medieval selections.

Species roses—a huge category of wild and semiwild plants, including some excellent landscaping specimens. Some need rich soil and care, many others do not. See chapter 17 for low-maintenance types.

When planting roses, be especially careful to research the best kinds for your area. A star on one coast may bomb on the other. And pay attention to soil preparation. Healthy root systems make for disease-resistant plants.

The Least You Need to Know

➤ These are good gardening conditions, rich well–drained soil and even moisture, never too dry or too wet. Almost anything will grow well here.

➤ Some plants dislike heat and high humidity. Others don't thrive until the thermometer reaches 80 degrees. Suit the plants to your climate as well as your soil.

➤ Easy annuals for enough of everything: snapdragons, lobelia, and phlox.

➤ Easy bulbs for enough of everything: dahlias, gladiolus, hyacinths, lilies.

➤ Easy perennials for enough of everything: chrysanthemums, bearded iris, kaffir lily.

➤ Easy vines and shrubs for enough of everything: kiwi, clematis, roses.

Chapter 17

Sun's Abundant, Rain's Not

In This Chapter

➤ What kind of place is this?

➤ Colorful annuals

➤ Dependable bulbs

➤ Lasting perennials

➤ Vivid vines

➤ Good-looking trees and shrubs

One of the facts of gardening life is that many plants available have been selected for what is usually called good gardening conditions. This includes moisture-retentive soil, regular watering in most areas of the country, and occasional fertilizing.

What if your schedule doesn't allow you much time to improve the soil, keep track of whether or not the asters need water, and when to apply the next box of fertilizer? What if you'd rather become a gourmet cook than a gardening fanatic?

Here are tips on growing plants whose needs are far less demanding than the average garden specimen. After an initial settling-in period, you can practically ignore them. Does this sound like your kind of garden? Then read on!

What Does This Garden Look Like?

In some ways, this is a gardener's dream, an open, sunny, well-drained site that just asks a few flowers for color and interest. It may be by the seashore, swept by winds and salt spray, or on a rocky slope. It may be simply a bright backyard you don't want to bother watering.

For water is the key here. There isn't enough natural rainfall to meet the needs of many common plants. And you yourself would rather save tap water than pamper thirsty plants.

Are you limiting yourself too much? Well, some plants will have to be crossed off your list, but there are so many others you may not miss them. These are just as beautiful as any you'll find in well-watered gardens, and just as willing to settle in and grow.

What Is Drought Tolerance?

Drought tolerance is the ability to thrive on less than even moisture, certainly, but how much less depends as much on your climate as on the plant. For instance, a potentilla planted in full sun in Arizona will need more water than one planted in light shade in Seattle. Water will evaporate through the leaves much more quickly in the sun and dry desert air.

Take Care!

When you water, soak the ground thoroughly. Frequent light applications of water will cause roots to stay in the upper layers of soil, becoming more vulnerable to drought.

Natural rainfall patterns, too, mean that drought in Arizona has a different definition than drought in Washington State. Many plants that would take a dry Seattle summer in stride would need supplemental water during July in Arizona.

You can often get hints on the level of drought tolerance from knowing a plant's native area. Those from the Mediterranean, for instance, are often good bets. Naturally adapted to dry, hot summers, they'll welcome the same conditions in your garden.

Wait to Withdraw the Water

A newly transplanted root system may take several years to gain the ability to support the leafy top during dry spells. Full drought tolerance may take as long as four or five years. So treat small plants gently. Give them enough water now and they'll grow quickly into self-reliant specimens.

Soil Preparation Is Important

Deep roots are more important in dry spells than ever, so loosen the soil well. If your climate is extra dry or if you can't give much supplemental water, be sure to dig in lots of organic matter. Whether it's well-aged manure, rotted sawdust, compost, or dried leaves, any organic matter increases the water holding capacity of the soil.

Drainage Is Important

Tolerance to drought often means intolerance of wet feet. There are exceptions, of course, but if you have a dampish area either turn to chapter 20 or try raised beds to elevate the roots.

Green Tip

Use a garden fork to loosen the ground before you mix in organic matter. It's easier to push into compacted soil. Once broken up, you can put a layer of organic matter on top, then turn it under with a shovel.

But what if I love dahlias, or roses? Plant them, by all means. But cluster your thirsty favorites in one bed close to the hose. You'll be able to suit the watering to each plants needs if they're grouped with others of the same disposition.

Too Much Sun?

Are there any problems with too much sunlight? Yes. Leaves exposed to strong sunlight without becoming accustomed to it may burn, turning yellow and brown in patches. This may happen when plants are moved from shady areas to sunny ones. Annuals that have been started indoors, for instance, often need a few days of gradually increasing periods of exposure to intense sunlight before they can safely be planted in permanent places.

Occasionally, shrubs or other plants placed against a south or west wall may burn because of strong reflected light. If this happens, simply move the plant farther out, leaving a protective gap of two to three feet.

Annuals and Tender Perennials Grown as Annuals

Argemone platyceras prickly poppy

> Needs: sun, good drainage, occasional to little watering

> Character: big white flowers on spiny-leaved and stemmed plants, to 3 feet

Native to desert areas, this is a fully drought-tolerant flower whose blossoms are showy enough for display. A relative, *A. mexicana*, has yellow or orange flowers.

Calendula pot marigold

> Needs: good drainage, any soil, modest amounts of water

> Character: large, yellow to orange daisylike flowers on plants up to $2^1/_2$ feet with medium-size, light green oval leaves

> Possible drawbacks: seeds prolifically, may sprawl, older varieties not resistant to heat

This plant may be found in named varieties from a soft primrose yellow through bright orange. Its big seeds and quick growth make it a good choice for children's gardens. Colonies will bloom through light frosts and begin again early in spring.

Centaurea cyanus cornflower, bachelor's buttons

> Needs: average soil, sun, average or light amounts of water

> Character: somewhat stiff stems to 3 feet with bluish green leaves topped by blue, white, pink, or rose flowers, about 1 inch across

Grow these and you'll understand why cornflower blue is a synonym for clear, vivid sky-blue, these are especially striking with California poppies. 'Jubilee Gem' is an excellent dwarf strain. Cornflowers may self-sow, but not so prolifically as to overwhelm other plants.

Floral Lore

Cornflower got its name from its habit of growing in fields of wheat, called corn before the name was applied to the New World grain. Its tough stems also earned it the name hurt sickle.

Cynoglossum amabile Chinese forget-me-not

> Needs: sun, semishade in hot areas, average to less water, not for humid summer areas

> Character: clear blue, fragrant flowers, about $1/_4$ inch across, in loose clusters on foot-high plants with bluish leaves, effective in masses

Reminiscent of true forget-me-nots but with deeper blue flowers and with more sun and drought tolerance. An excellent filler to sow among stouter plants.

Dimorphotheca hybrids African daisy

> Needs: sun, light soil, good drainage, occasional watering

> Character: daisylike flowers, orange, yellow, salmon, or white petals, dark centers, bushy plants to 1¹/₂ feet

> Possible drawbacks: flowers close at night and on cloudy days

Cheerful and tough, these annuals are good in large groups or mixed with other flowers.

Eschscholzia californica California poppy

> Needs: sun, good drainage, especially in humid, hot summers, any soil, little to average water

> Character: gold to orange flowers with fine bluish foliage

These are wildflowers quite willing to take over the cultivated world as well. They look best mixed with gold, scarlet, and purple. If orange isn't your favorite color, look for 'Mission Bells', a strain with shades of cream, pink, and rose. There's also a delicate pink variety, not quite as vigorous, but an elegant charmer.

Gaillardia blanketflower

> Needs: sun, average soil, average to little water, tolerant of heat

> Character: large, daisylike blooms in bright, warm colors on 1–2-foot plants with grayish leaves

Here's another cheerful daisy, almost as good as sunflowers for raising your spirits. Best if sown in place.

Gomphrenia globosa globe amaranth

> Needs: sun to part shade, average soil, good drainage, occasional watering

> Character: round flower heads that look somewhat like clover, long-lasting, in purple to pink and white bloom on plants up to 1¹/₂ feet

Garden Talk

Everlastings are plants whose flowers tend to be drier than most. Their petals keep their shape and sometimes much of their color even after the plant has wilted.

One of the group known as everlastings with papery heads that dry quickly for winter bouquets.

Gypsophila elegans annual baby's breath

> Needs: sun, average soil, good drainage, regular to little water

> Character: frothy sprays of white or pink flowers mound to 2 feet accompanied by narrow, grayish leaves

Few plants are as dainty as this one. Use as a florist would in a bouquet, to fill in space between larger plants and add a sense of unity to a composition.

Helichrysum bracteatum strawflower

> Needs: sun, average soil, good drainage, regular to little water

> Character: shiny, papery blossoms in many colors on bushy plants with narrow leaves

Another everlasting often seen in commercial dried arrangements. The colors are clear and bright and the flowers continue to look like true blossoms even when dried.

Lavatera trimestris annual mallow

> Needs: sun, average soil, average to little water, best with cool summers

> Character: hollyhocklike with flat satiny blossoms, pink or rose, on stalks 2–5 feet (depending on variety) with soft lobed leaves

An easy plant for substantial summer color, this can be helpful in filling bare new gardens. It's worth a place of honor in mature gardens, too.

Limonium sinuatum statice

> Needs: sun, good drainage, most soils, occasional water once established

> Character: flowers in blue, lavender, or shades of rose in sprays at the end of winged stems, lobed leaves, 1–2 feet

One of the most common flowers found in dried bouquets, this is also lovely mixed with helichrysum. Often self-sows.

Linum grandiflorum 'Rubrum' flowering flax

> Needs: sun, light soil, good drainage, occasional watering

> Character: single rose-red blossoms on upright stems with narrow leaves, 1–1$^1/_2$ feet

A lovely fine-textured plant for filling between larger specimens. It often reseeds, but without becoming a nuisance.

Bulbs

Allium caeruleum blue allium

Needs: sun, good drainage, enough water during growth

Character: tight, 2-inch heads of true blue flowers on foot-high stems

Season of bloom: late spring

Hardiness: zone 2 or 3

This is a good plant for areas with spring rains but summer dry spells, taking a good parching after it dies down. Excellent cut flower or dried. Native to Siberia.

Amaryllis belladonna belladonna lily, naked lady

Needs: sun, good drainage, regular watering while leaves are growing, best with warm, dry summers, winter rains

Character: pink fragrant trumpets at the top of naked stalks (hence the name naked lady), big, bold leaves in fall and winter

Season of bloom: late summer

Hardiness: zone 8

Potential drawbacks: bulbs are poisonous

Similar to the plant commonly called amaryllis (*Hippeastrum*), a stand of these makes a spectacular show in dry borders. If your summers are cool, try putting these at the base of a stone wall for the reflected heat. Native to South Africa.

Camassia quamash camas

Needs: sun, regular watering during growth

Character: spikes of deep blue flowers, long, narrow leaves, to 1 foot

Season of bloom: spring

Hardiness: zone 5

Another plant for winter wet/summer dry areas, can even take standing water in spring yet dry out completely in summer. It has an airy quality that blends well with most plants, yet is colorful enough for flower borders.

Floral Lore

Camas was a staple starchy food for native peoples of the Pacific northwest. If you end up with too many bulbs, you can eat them!

Iris reticulata

Needs: sun, well-drained soil, water during fall to spring

Character: fragrant, blue-purple flowers, angular narrow leaves, 6–8 inches

Season of bloom: early spring

Hardiness: zone 5

Possible drawbacks: dislikes summer moisture

This one's a charmer, a dwarf iris with the delicacy of a wildflower and the presence of a prized garden rarity. Closely related species include bright yellow–flowered *I. danfordiae* and pale blue *I. histrio*. Hybrids are available in various shades of blue and purple. Native to the Caucasus.

Narcissus daffodils

Needs: sun to part shade, average soil, average to occasional watering

Character: usually yellow, white, or bicolor, with a cup or trumpet on a star-shaped saucer above narrow leaves

Season of bloom: early to late spring, depending on variety

Hardiness: zones vary, many to zone 3, including the classic trumpet type

Possible drawbacks: poisonous

Many, but not all, daffodils are quite drought-tolerant. Some of the best varieties for dry areas will be found under the category of for naturalizing. See chapter 12 for more details on varieties available.

Nerine sarniensis Guernsey lily

> Needs: sun to part shade, average soil, regular watering during winter and spring

> Character: clusters of large, funnel-shaped red flowers on 2-foot stems above strap-shaped leaves

> Season of bloom: late summer or fall

> Hardiness: zone 9

In mild area where this is hardy, look for pink, salmon, orange, and white varieties. Dislikes disturbance, so don't divide until overcrowded. Native to South Africa.

Triteleia 'Queen Fabiola'

> Needs: sun, good drainage, water during active growth

> Character: clusters of deep purple-blue, tubular flowers on 2-foot stalks, grasslike leaves

> Season of bloom: late spring

> Hardiness: zone 6

As much at home in the dry border as in a wildflower meadow, this flower should be grown in groups of five or more. Good cut for indoor arrangements.

Perennials

Achillea yarrow

> Needs: sun, occasional watering

> Character: flat heads of blossoms in white, yellow, or pastels, most have ferny foliage, several inches to 3 feet, depending on species

> Season of bloom: summer

> Hardiness: zones vary by species, some down to zone 2

One of the easiest plants to grow. Some are mat-forming ground covers, some are tall and bold. All are good for cutting and drying.

Floral Lore

Common yarrow, *Achillea millefolium*, has been used for many centuries to stop bleeding, earning itself the name soldier's wound wort and knight's milfoil. It is also said to be the herb with which Achilles staunched the wounds of his soldiers, hence the name *Achillea*.

Agapanthus Headbourne hybrids lily of the Nile

> Needs: sun to part shade, regular to occasional watering
>
> Character: heads of large, blue, tubular flowers on 2^1/$_2$-foot stems, straplike leaves
>
> Season of bloom: summer
>
> Hardiness: zone 6

These hybrids are the hardiest varieties available of this elegantly sculptural plant. Many others are sold for warmer areas. Good in pots and containers, especially as an accent on patios.

Amsonia amsonia

> Needs: sun to part shade, regular to occasional water, average soil
>
> Character: clusters of blue flowers on plants 1–3 feet high depending on the species; full, almost rigid, clumps
>
> Season of bloom: early summer
>
> Hardiness: zone 3

A milkweed relative native to eastern states, this has excellent yellow fall color as a bonus. Native to southern United States.

Anaphalis margaritacea pearly everlasting

> Needs: good drainage, sun
>
> Character: heads of white flowers dot 1–3-foot plants with grayish, linear leaves
>
> Season of bloom: summer
>
> Hardiness: zone 3
>
> Possible drawbacks: may be invasive

Dependable as a background and filler between more brilliantly colored plants. Native throughout northern temperate areas.

Anchusa azurea alkanet

> Needs: sun, average soil, regular to occasional watering
>
> Character: brilliant, true blue flowers in one-sided cluster, coarse hairy leaves, 3 feet
>
> Season of bloom: early summer
>
> Hardiness: zone 3
>
> Possible drawbacks: may be short-lived

Most valuable for their excellent blue color, these can be a bit sprawling. Varieties are available in different shades of blue and with shorter, more compact form.

Armeria maritima thrift, sea pink

> Needs: good drainage, full sun
>
> Character: small balls of pink flowers up to a foot high stand above clumps of grassy leaves
>
> Season of bloom: spring, early summer; in mild areas into fall
>
> Hardiness: zone 3

Many varieties available, from miniatures to giants several feet tall, from white through deep rose. Exceptionally good for crevices in rocks and seashore gardens. Native to Iceland, Greenland, and northern Europe.

Asclepias tuberosa butterfly flower

> Needs: sun and well-drained soil, little water
>
> Character: flat orange heads of flowers top stiff stems with narrow leaves. Seed heads are ornamental.
>
> Season of bloom: mid to late summer
>
> Hardiness: zones 3–9
>
> Possible drawbacks: shows up late in spring; mark its place so you don't dig it up accidentally, doesn't like transplanting, poisonous

Other colors are available in selected strains. Best used in masses.

Catananche caerulea Cupid's dart

>   Needs: sun, good drainage, modest amounts of water

>   Character: 2-inch-wide flowers, somewhat like graceful lavender-blue daisies, slender, gray-green leaves making a tidy 2-foot clump

>   Season of bloom: summer, early fall

>   Hardiness: zone 4

A grand plant for most gardens, especially if planted in groups of at least five. Mix with other delicate perennials like *Coreopsis verticillata* 'Moonbeam' and thrift (*Armeria*) and arrange in a bed close enough to admire details of the blossoms. Native to southern Europe.

Echinops globe thistle

>   Needs: sun, good drainage, regular to occasional watering

>   Character: round, blue heads of spiky flowers, large, deeply cut prickly leaves, to 4 feet

>   Season of bloom: midsummer, fall

>   Hardiness: zone 3–10

A decorative thistle most would welcome into their gardens, this blends well with baby's breath and California poppies (Eschscholzia).

Erysimum 'Bowles Mauve' mauve wallflower

>   Needs: sun, good drainage, occasional to little watering

>   Character: violet flowers in spikes above gray-green foliage, to 3 feet

>   Season of bloom: spring to fall

>   Hardiness: zone 6

Almost constantly in bloom, this wallflower combines well with purple-leaved sage and many types of yarrow (*Achillea*).

Gaura lindheimeri gaura

Needs: well-drained soil, regular to little water, tolerant of heat and high humidity

Character: delicate, airy plant with white to pink blossoms, 2–4 feet high

Take Care!

Plants that bloom profusely for long periods of time, such as mauve wallflower, may exhaust themselves, living only a few years. Cut off all blossoms and newly formed seed heads occasionally to give the plant a rest.

Season of bloom: summer through fall

Hardiness: zone 3

Possible drawbacks: may self-sow too enthusiastically

Few gardens would not be improved by this adaptable plant, whose lovely flowers blend well with most others. Native to Texas and Louisana.

Hylotelephiium spectabile showy stonecrop

Needs: sun to part shade, average to poor soil, good drainage, little water

Character: tiny pink flowers in flat heads up to 5 inches across, pale green rounded leaves, $1\frac{1}{2}$–2 feet high

Season of bloom: late summer, early fall

Hardiness: zone 3

Possible drawbacks: may need staking in good soil

Sedums, common drought-tolerant succulents, come in all sizes, this being one of the largest. It has ornamental seed heads that can be left for winter interest.

Liatris spicata blazing star, gayfeather

Needs: sun, good to sandy soil, average to little water

Character: purple spikes of flowers to $2\frac{1}{2}$ inches

Season of bloom: late summer, fall

Hardiness: zone 3

Possible drawbacks: may need staking in fertile soil

These are some of the most rugged plants available, enduring poor soil, heat, cold and drought well. Their upright habits makes a nice contrast to more spreading plants. Native to central and eastern United States.

Limonium perezii sea lavender

Needs: sun, good drainage, occasional watering

Character: small, papery flowers on branched stems, deep green 1-foot leaves, to 3 feet

Season of bloom: spring, summer

Hardiness: zone 9

A great plant for seashore planting. Likes heat and is resistant to wind damage.

Oenothera fruticosa sundrops, evening primrose

> Needs: sun to light shade, average soil, occasional watering

> Character: bright yellow cup-shaped flowers, reddish stems, to 2 feet

> Season of bloom: summer

> Hardiness: zone 4

This should be in every garden for its carefree nature and willingness to spread without overwhelming everything. Another species, *O. speciosa*, hardy to zone 5, has pink flowers and a more invasive disposition. *O. missouriensis*, zone 6, has larger yellow flowers on trailing stems. These are all native to North America.

Origanum vulgare oregano, wild marjoram

> Needs: sun, average to poor soil, good drainage, regular to little water

> Character: heads of pink flowers above round, medium green leaves

> Season of bloom: summer, early fall

> Hardiness: zone 3

Plant oregano in the flower garden? Why not? Its heads of pinkish flowers make a nice show and it can even be a drought-tolerant flowering ground cover. The variety 'Herrenhausen' has deeper pink flowers and purple-edged, deep green leaves. Native to southern Europe.

Oregano is a spreading herb that can be a pink-flowering ground cover in dry gardens.

Solidago goldenrod

> Needs: sun or part shade, ordinary soil, occasional watering
>
> Character: tiny yellow flowers on clusters that branch into feathery plumes, arching stems, 3–5 feet, depending on species
>
> Season of bloom: late summer, fall
>
> Hardiness: zones 3 or 4, depending on species

Goldenrods are wonderful gold accents to add to fall borders. They're tough, easy to grow, and carefree. Don't be afraid of hay fever. The blame for its attack at that time of the year should be laid on other plants.

Verbena bonariensis Brazilian verbena

> Needs: sun, good drainage, occasional watering
>
> Character: tiny violet flowers in clusters at the top of 3–6-foot stems
>
> Season of bloom: summer
>
> Hardiness: zone 8, self-sowing annual in zone 4
>
> Possible drawbacks: self-seeds freely

An airy, easy to use plant that adds vertical interest to dry borders. Native to South America.

Verbena canadensis 'Homestead Purple'

> Needs: sun, good drainage
>
> Character: bright purple flowers on an 8-inch-tall spreading plant, to 3 feet wide
>
> Season of bloom: summer, fall
>
> Hardiness: zone 6

Vivid flowers, neat leaves, and a quick-spreading disposition make this an excellent choice for filling in space between taller plants. The species is native from Virginia to Colorado and south.

213

Easy Vines

Lathyrus latifolius perennial sweet pea

> Method of climbing: tendrils
>
> Needs: sun, occasional watering
>
> Character: purplish pink clusters of flowers on plants that sprawl to 9 feet
>
> Season of bloom: summer
>
> Hardiness: zone 3

These are as easy to grow as annual sweet peas are demanding, often naturalizing along roadsides. Varieties with white or pale pink flowers are available. Native to southern Europe.

Polygonum aubertii silver lace vine

> Needs: sun, occasional watering
>
> Character: tiny flowers in airy masses, heart-shaped leaves, may cover 100 square feet in one year
>
> Season of bloom: late spring to fall
>
> Hardiness: zone 4
>
> Possible drawbacks: too vigorous for some areas

Think twice before you plant this one. Tough and beautiful it is, shy it is not. It will be all over everything nearby before you can get out the pruning shears. If quick cover is what you want, go ahead. Just be prepared for an annual pruning or an annual leap forward. Native to western China.

Wisteria species wisteria

> Needs: sun to part shade, ordinary soil, regular watering when young, occasional watering thereafter
>
> Character: long clusters of white or lavender-blue flowers hang from stout vines with pale green leaves divided into many leaflets
>
> Season of bloom: early summer
>
> Hardiness: zone 4 (*W. floribunda*), 5 (*W. sinensis*)
>
> Possible drawbacks: needs annual pruning to control size

Another tough vine, so large you need a stout framework to support it. Or a nearby tree. The stems become so thick that you can grow this vine as a tree or shrub by supporting them with a stake until they harden. The long clusters of lavender-blue or white flowers are showy without being flamboyant. *W. floribunda*, Japanese wisteria, has longer flower clusters than *W. sinensis*, Chinese wisteria, but the individual blooms open successively, making less of an immediate show than the other.

Trees and Shrubs

Green Tip

Wisteria occasionally refuses to bloom. Try root pruning it, making cuts with a spade 2 or 3 feet from the stem. Severe treatment may cause its survival instinct to push it into bloom.

Buddleia davidii butterfly bush

> Needs: sun to light shade, average to poor soil, good drainage, regular to occasional watering
>
> Character: arching spikes of lavender, white, pink, or purple flowers at the ends of upright branches, 4–8-inch leaves with white undersides; deciduous or semi-evergreen
>
> Season of bloom: summer
>
> Height: 3–6 feet if cut to ground in winter, up to 15 feet otherwise
>
> Hardiness: zone 5
>
> Possible drawbacks: may seed where it's not wanted

This is a great shrub, graceful and showy, loved by birds and butterflies and a quick, strong grower. Will regrow from the roots if stems are killed. May seed in odd corners. Native to China.

Caragana arborescens Siberian peashrub

> Needs: sun, occasional to little water
>
> Character: yellow, sweet-pealike blossoms, deciduous, fast growth to 20 feet, deciduous
>
> Season of bloom: spring
>
> Hardiness: zone 2

Almost indestructible. Train as a shrub or small tree, then forget it. Native to Siberia and Manchuria.

Caryopteris* × *clandonensis bluebeard

> Needs: sun, good drainage, occasional watering

> Character: clusters of small, cool blue flowers at the base of leaves, to 2 feet; deciduous

> Season of bloom: late summer, fall

> Hardiness: zone 5

Best if cut to the ground every winter, even if it hasn't frozen back. This will give it a bushy, flowery character instead of the straggly shrub it would otherwise become. Useful in masses. It is a hybrid of parents native to Asia.

Ceanothus thyrsiflorus ceanothus, blue blossom, wild lilac

> Needs: sun, good drainage, occasional watering

> Character: puffy clusters of tiny blue flowers, glossy, deep green leaves, to 20 feet in warm areas; evergreen

> Season of bloom: spring

> Hardiness: zone 8

Heat- and wind-tolerant, rarely bothered by pests and diseases, this is tough customer that asks only minimal care to get started. After it gets a good start all you have to do is enjoy the blossoms. Native to the western United States.

Chaenomeles speciosa flowering quince

> Needs: sun, good drainage, occasional watering

> Character: flowers often orange-pink but varieties are available with white, pink, and coral blossoms, bright green leaves on thorny branches, sometimes small fruit, to 6 feet; deciduous

> Season of bloom: early spring

> Hardiness: zone 4

Just try to kill this one with neglect! It may not be the most beautiful bush after blooming, but it is one of the most permanent. And the blossoms are really lovely, like small single roses. Take the time to search out a variety with a color you really love. Native to China.

Cistus hybridus rock rose

> Needs: sun, good drainage, occasional to little watering
>
> Character: white or pink single blossoms like huge wild roses, dense, well-branched shape, to 6 feet; evergreen
>
> Season of bloom: spring
>
> Hardiness: zone 8, some species may be hardier

This is good plant for hedges, needing no shearing to become bushy. It takes poor soil and drought without seeming to notice any lack. Native to the Mediterranean and North Africa.

Cotinus coggygria smoke tree

> Needs: sun, good drainage, occasional watering once established
>
> Character: insignificant blossoms that become puffy masses of smoke as they fade, rounded leaves, often purple, with excellent fall color, to 15 feet or more; decidous
>
> Season of bloom: summer
>
> Hardiness: zone 4

This is a tree that should be challenged with poor soil or drought to show its best character. Though young plants need regular watering, once they have a good start you can forget them. Often can't make up its mind whether to be a shrub or tree; encourage it by pruning to a single stem. Native from southern Europe to Asia.

Cytisus broom

> Needs: sun, good drainage, occasional to little watering
>
> Character: pealike blossoms, pale yellow, gold, pink, or red, on dense, nearly leafless, branchlets, to 8 feet
>
> Season of bloom: spring
>
> Hardiness: vary from zone 5–9, depending on species
>
> Possible drawbacks: species such as *C. scoparius* may be invasive, look for varieties that behave themselves

Brooms are excellent drought-tolerant shrubs that have much more to offer than often supposed. They accept poor, rocky soil and can be found in subtle attractive colors. Native to Europe.

Lantana hybrids lantana

> Needs: sun, average to poor soil, occasional watering
>
> Character: bright clusters of tiny blossoms, yellow, pink, purple, cream, orange, or red on a sprawling plant, 2–4 feet
>
> Season of bloom: all year in frost-free areas
>
> Hardiness: zone 8
>
> Possible drawbacks: fruits are poisonous

Few plants give as much color for as little effort as this. Far from demanding rich soil, it will withhold its blossoms if either fertilizer or water are too plentiful. Many varieties available, multicolored or single-hued. Its long bloom season and quick growth makes it valuable as an annual in cold-winter areas.

Lavandula angustifolia lavender

> Needs: sun, good drainage, occasional watering
>
> Character: spikes of small, fragrant, lavender to purple flowers, gray-green narrow leaves, 1 to 3 feet, depending on variety; evergreen
>
> Season of bloom: late spring, summer
>
> Hardiness: zone 4
>
> Possible drawbacks: often needs shearing to stay dense

One lavender is lovely but twenty is breathtaking. Both leaves and flowers have a delicious scent that perfumes the air on warm days. Many varieties are available with blossoms of different shades, foliage of different heights. Good cut flower. Native to the Mediterranean.

Lavatera thuringiaca 'Barnsley' tree mallow

> Needs: sun to light shade, well-drained soil, regular to occasional watering
>
> Character: pale pink 3-inch flowers with white center, much like small, single hollyhock blossoms, loose, open branches, to 8 feet; evergreen
>
> Season of bloom: all summer
>
> Hardiness: zone 4

An easy to grow recent introduction that deserves wide popularity. Few visitors can resist its generous display.

Nerium oleander oleander

> Needs: sun, good drainage, occasional to little watering
>
> Character: single or double flowers, 2–3 inches, available in many colors, glossy narrow leaves, 8–12 feet; evergreen
>
> Season of bloom: spring to fall
>
> Hardiness: zone 8
>
> Possible drawbacks: poisonous

These are landscaping standards in warm winter areas, deserving their popularity for both color and neatness of habit. Native to the Mediterranean.

Potentilla fruticosa bush cinquefoil

> Needs: sun, good drainage, occasional watering
>
> Character: small, single roselike blooms, usually yellow but sometimes cream or orange, small leaves, 2–4 feet; deciduous
>
> Season of bloom: summer to fall
>
> Hardiness: zone 2

This is a cheerful little shrub, not fussy about growing conditions, usually disease- and insect-free, and available in many varieties, some with grayish leaves, some with bright green ones. Native to most northern areas.

Rosa rugosa and hybrids rugosa roses, sea tomato

> Needs: sun, good drainage, occasional to little watering
>
> Character: large, single, bright lavender-pink blossoms, dense, thorny branches, to 8 feet; deciduous
>
> Season of bloom: spring, scattered blooms summer, fall
>
> Hardiness: zone 2

These are some of the toughest roses you can grow, able to take intense cold, heat, drought and seaside conditions. While the magenta blossoms are not for every garden, there are varieties available with white flowers and hybrids that extend the range to yellow and pale pink. The large red hips add color to the fall garden and make good jelly. Native to Asia.

Rosmarinus officinalis rosemary

> Needs: sun, good drainage, occasional watering
>
> Character: small, lavender-blue flowers, narrow aromatic leaves, to 4 feet, taller in warm climates; evergreen
>
> Season of bloom: winter, spring
>
> Hardiness: zone 6

This shrub offers color, year-around foliage, scent, and culinary value. Some varieties have deeper blue flowers. If you need a ground cover, there are prostrate forms available. Native to southern Europe and Asia Minor.

The Least You Need to Know

➤ Drought-tolerant plants need good drainage and extra organic matter added to the soil.

➤ Water regularly the first few years to foster a good, deep root system. Then gradually withdraw the extra water.

➤ Group your plants according to their watering needs. Your favorite high-maintenance plants should be placed near the faucet. Those you plan to leave to their own devices can be planted at the back of the yard.

➤ Easy annuals for lots of sun and low water: California poppy (*Eschscholzia*), pot marigold (*Calendula*), cornflower (*Centaurea*).

➤ Easy bulbs for lots of sun and low water: most bulbs will take a dry period during dormancy, but crocus, daffodils (*Narcissus*), and flowering onions (*Allium*) are the easiest.

➤ Easy perennials for lots of sun and low water: yarrow (*Achillea*), gaura, evening primrose (*Oenothera*).

➤ Easy vines and shrubs for lots of sun and low water: perennial sweet pea (*Lathyrus*), silver lace vine (*Polygonum*), butterfly bush (*Buddleia*), flowering quince (*Chaenomeles*), bush cinquefoil (*Potentilla*).

Less Sun, Enough Water

Shade, a lack of direct light because of overhanging branches, close-set walls or competition from other plants, can bring some flowers to full glory, or it can cause others to languish.

Different plants have different tolerances for shade, from growth and bloom without any direct sun at all, to sparse bloom if they get less than eight hours of strong sunlight.

Whether your garden is a cool, calm oasis filled with flowers, or a dark corner depends on how shade-smart you become. Here's tips for using dim areas to the best advantage.

What Does This Garden Look Like?

Shady areas have more variety than any others. Some may have rainfall blocked by eaves or dense branches, giving a natural dryness that needs frequent watering to bring many plants to full growth. Others have fierce competition from roots of thirsty plants such as willows, giving the same effect. If you'd rather not provide supplementary water, see chapter 19 for ideas.

The quality of shade can be light and airy underneath high-branching, small-leafed such as Japanese maples (*Acer palmatum*). Or it can be dense and dark beneath large-leafed, well-branched trees such as horse chestnut (*Aesculus*).

If it is open to the sky, on the north side of a building, for instance, a gray, cloudy day may actually give the plants more useable light than a sunny one would. This is because the available light is diffused, bounced through the clouds in all directions.

Perhaps the most difficult areas to garden in occur in corridors between buildings. No direct sunlight reaches the ground and the buildings themselves block light from the sky as well.

Why Is Shade a Problem?

Plants use sunlight to produce food for their own growth. For many plants, a lack of light translates directly into a lack of growth. One of the first indications that a plant needs more light is a dearth of flowers. The leaves may be deep healthy green but buds simply refuse to form. Next, if a plant's light needs are not met, leaves may turn pale green then brown. Soon the plant may die.

Some plants, however, do quite well under low-light conditions. Many have large, light-gathering leaves. Others simply have adapted their photosynthetic processes to reduced levels of sunlight.

Many flowers will accept light shade, the shadow cast by a tree for a few hours a day, or a the shelter of a west facing wall. They may grow a little more leggy, with slightly larger leaves than those in full sun, but they'll bloom satisfactorily.

Half a day of sun will cut down on flowers for most plants, but growth may still be healthy and green. Any less direct sunlight than this will call for shade-tolerant plants exclusively.

What Are Some of the Advantages of Dark Corners?

These are often protected from wind, allowing more delicate leaves to develop without being tossed around. Humidity is often higher because of the shelter, leading to reduced evaporation through the leaves.

Some of the most beautifully textured plants grow in shade, including most varieties of ferns, many mosses, and a number of plants with large, bold leaves. Few other areas offer the same diversity of shapes and sizes of leaves. These can all contribute to an pleasing design.

Few sunny areas offer the same sense of relaxation and repose as you can find in a shady garden. There's a certain lush, luxuriant, almost tropical feel to a well-planted shadowy area that can make it a gardening treasure.

What If I Don't Have Enough Shade?

If you want to grow fuchsias, ferns, tuberous begonias and other prize shade-lovers, you can create artificial pockets of softer light by careful placement of trellises, vines, and shade cloth supported on frames. These are especially useful in hot, dry climates where some shelter from the sun is essential for all but the toughest plants.

A quick-growing deciduous vine such as grape or silver lace vine (*Polygonum aubertii*) supported by wires can give summer shade while letting in needed winter light.

Commercially available trellises made from thin strips of wood cast an evenly broken pattern of shadow and sunlight that is ideal for many shade-tolerant plants.

Garden Talk

Shade cloth is a loosely woven synthetic fabric used by many greenhouses to cut the level of light over seedlings of impatiens, begonias, and perennials such as bleeding heart (*Dicentra*). You could use it to cover a patio during the summer or tack it to a frame to protect plants during hottest weather. Try ordering it through your local nursery.

What's the Soil Like?

In general, shade-loving plants tend toward an appetite for high organic soils with even moisture. Many of these plants come from wooded areas where leaves falling from the surrounding trees creates a rich, crumbly soil that offers little resistance to fine roots.

If you have only enough time and energy to improve the soil in one bed, make it this one. Whether your basic soil is sandy or clayey, abundant quantities of organic matter will improve both its texture and its water-holding qualities.

Many woodland soils are acid, and many acid loving plants do well in these conditions. There are exceptions. Christmas rose (*Helleborus niger*), for instance, prefers neutral or slightly alkaline soil.

Now, let's look at some of the best plants for stocking shadowy nooks, patios and flower beds. Some will take sun in cooler areas, but are listed here because they reach their best development with some shade.

Be sure to look for more plants in chapter 20. Most of those that tolerate wet soil grow well in regularly watered part shade.

Annuals, Biennials, and Tender Perennials Usually Grown as Annuals

Begonia × ***semperflorens-cultorum*** fibrous begonia, wax begonia

> Needs: part shade, sun in cool areas, rich well-drained soil, regular watering

> Character: small, single flowers, white, pink, or red, round, green or bronze leaves, 6–12 inches, depending on variety

Compact and floriferous, these are excellent pot plants and fillers among ferns and other fine-textured plants. They make fine houseplants, too.

Clarkia amoena godetia, farewell to spring

> Needs: shade, sun in cool areas, ordinary soil, regular watering

> Character: cup-shaped 2-inch flowers in white, pink, red, or lavender, blotched with darker shades, 10 inches–3 feet, depending on variety

Usually sold in mixed colors, godetia can fill in bare areas between shrubs or trees. Closely related to *C. elegans*, it should also be sown in place in unfertilized soil.

Clarkia elegans clarkia, mountain garland

> Needs: shade, sun in cool areas, ordinary soil, regular watering

> Character: single or double flowers in every color except blue, upright stems, 1–3 feet

Sow these in place; they don't transplant well. They do, however, reseed themselves into perpetually renewing colonies, a boon to busy gardeners. There's no need for extra fertilizer.

Dianthus barbatus sweet William

> Needs: part shade, sun in cool areas, rich, well-drained soil, regular watering

> Character: tight clusters of pink to rose, white, or purple flowers, shiny, dark green leaves to $1^1/_2$ feet high

> Hardiness: zone 4

Sweet William suggests cottages and cozy fires. Who could hold on to a bad mood in its presence?

Impatiens walleriana impatiens, busy Lizzie

> Needs: part to full shade, good, well-drained soil, regular watering

> Character: single or double flowers in many shades, but no blues or yellows, from 6 inches–2 feet tall, depending on variety

> Hardiness: zone 10

Quick-growing and useful for masses of color. Excellent dug up and potted for winter flowers.

Myosotis sylvatica annual forget-me-not

> Needs: part shade, average soil, regular to extra water

> Character: clouds of small blue flowers with a white eye, mildly hairy leaves on plants up to 1 foot

This seeds in such profusion that it provides a fine backdrop for spring bulbs and primroses. Two dwarf, more compact varieties are 'Blue Ball' and 'Royal Blue Improved'. In warmer areas may act as a biennial in zones 5 to 6, its clumps of leaves lasting over winter to bloom early in spring.

Nicotiana alata flowering tobacco

> Needs: part shade, sun in cool areas, regular watering

> Character: star-shaped fragrant flowers with tubular throats, white, lime-green, pink, or red, large, soft leaves, 1–4 feet, depending on variety.

> Hardiness: zone 9

Flowering tobacco is one of the best flowers for including in a shady border, both for its large leaves and its height. These combine well with impatiens, ferns, and perennials. One of the most fragrant cultivars is 'Grandiflora.' *N. sylvestris* is the most fragrant of all, but may reach 5 feet in height.

Pericallis × ***hybrida*** cineraria

> Needs: part shade, average soil, average water

> Character: broad clusters of daisies in blue, pink, and white on compact plants, 1 foot

Often sold potted in florist shops, cineraria does best in cool spring weather, or similar conditions. May reseed where especially contented.

Primula malacoides fairy primrose

> Needs: part shade
>
> Character: small white, pink, or lavender flowers in clusters above lobed, hairy leaves
>
> Season of bloom: spring
>
> Hardiness: zone 8

Often grown as an annual pot plant, Fairy primrose is delicate and sweet. Best used in quantity.

Schizanthus pinnatus poor man's orchid, butterfly flower

> Needs: part shade, good soil, and regular watering
>
> Character: quantities of small lilac to rose pink, purple, or white flowers, ferny foliage, to $1^1/_2$ feet

Good in pots and likes cool conditions. Excellent for giving a frothy, overflowing-with-flowers look to window boxes and pots.

Torenia wishbone flower

> Needs: part shade, good soil, regular watering
>
> Character: blue trumpet-shaped flowers with deeper markings and yellow centers, bushy 1-foot plants

This is good in cool, moist borders and as a houseplant. Grow them in an area where the blossoms, which look like miniature gloxinias, can be seen close up.

Bulbs and Tubers

Anemone blanda

> Needs: part shade to sun, water during growth, can take some dryness later
>
> Character: delicate plants, usually less than 6 inches, with single, multipetaled flowers (a bit like a daisy) in blue, white, or pink
>
> Season of bloom: spring
>
> Hardiness: zone 6–9, farther north with a deep mulch
>
> Possible drawbacks: short-lived in warm regions, poisonous

When you buy these, you'll get shriveled-looking, dark tubers that may puzzle you. Which way is up? It doesn't matter. Just be sure to plant lots; these look best as carpets under shrubs and trees.

Begonia tuberous begonia

> Needs: part shade, rich soil, regular watering
>
> Character: large, roselike leaves in shades of pink, red, yellow, and orange, upright or trailing stems with large leaves
>
> Season of bloom: summer
>
> Hardiness: zone 9
>
> Possible drawbacks: subject to mildew, dislikes heat and low humidity

These give glorious pure color in quantity, a much-appreciated quality in shade. In colder areas, buy the tubers and start them indoors in spring, or buy small plants in bloom. Good air circulation reduces the possibility of mildew.

Chionodoxa luciliae glory of the snow

> Needs: part shade, good soil, moisture during growth
>
> Character: blue stars with whitish centers in open spikes on small plants, to 6 inches
>
> Season of bloom: early spring
>
> Hardiness: zone 3
>
> Possible drawbacks: dislikes dry areas of the Southwest

One of the best for carpeting shady areas, chionodoxa can be grown in lawns left unmown until the leaves die down or in woodland. May self-sow if conditions are favorable.

Erythronium tuolumnense 'Pagoda' yellow fawn lily

> Needs: part shade, rich loose soil, regular watering when growing
>
> Character: delicate yellow blossoms like small lilies, tongue-shaped leaves, 15 inches
>
> Season of bloom: spring
>
> Hardiness: zone 3

Wildflower dainty, these lilies deserve a place of honor. This variety is more vigorous and easier to grow than most erythroniums so don't hesitate to try it. Needs little water when dormant.

Galanthus nivalis common snowdrop

Needs: shade or sun, rich moist soil, regular watering

Character: hanging, bell-shaped white flowers, 6–9 inches

Season of bloom: earliest spring

Hardiness: zone 3

Possible drawbacks: bulbs are poisonous if eaten, best in cold climates

Classic messengers of the arrival of spring, snowdrops sometimes bloom at the edge of snowbanks. If you plant them at all, plant lots. A cluster of a few looks lonely; even a hundred seems like just a beginning.

Muscari botryoides grape hyacinth

Needs: shade or sun, regular watering when growing

Character: tiny, deep blue flowers in tight upright clusters, 6–12 inches high

Season of bloom: spring

Hardiness: zones 2–3

These are one of the easiest bulbs to grow you could ask for. Not large, they still make a fine display when planted in quantity. And they soon develop into large gatherings, increasing from offsets and seeds. *M. azureum* has sky-blue flowers, *M. armeniacum* has bright blue ones. They become such a permanent feature of the garden that it's worth searching out a type you particularly like.

Scilla siberica Siberian squill

Needs: part shade or sun, regular watering when growing

Character: intense blue flowers in loose clusters on stems up to 6 inches, straplike leaves

Season of bloom: spring

Hardiness: zone 1

These are one of the best blues to be found and easy to grow given winter chill. Though large enough to be seen easily, use it in quantities of at least five per grouping, preferably more.

Perennials

Acfaea black snakeroot

> Needs: part shade, sun if well-watered, rich, well-drained soil, regular watering
>
> Character: tall, narrow spikes of small white flowers, divided leaves, to 6 feet
>
> Season of bloom: summer to fall
>
> Hardiness: zones 2–3

These are stately plants for the back of a border or mixed with shrubs in a woodland garden. These should be allowed to spread slowly without disturbance.

Allium schoenoprasum chives

> Needs: part shade or sun, good soil, regular watering
>
> Character: purplish rose flowers in round clusters, round, grasslike leaves with onion scent and flavor, to 2 feet
>
> Season of bloom: spring
>
> Hardiness: zones 2–3

Chives in the flower garden? Why not? The flowers are certainly as ornamental as most others and you also acquire a bonus of leaves and edible blossoms for the kitchen. Another species with flat leaves and larger white clusters, *A. tuberosum*, is called Chinese chives.

Anemone* × *hybrida Japanese anemone

> Needs: part shade, sun in cooler areas, regular water
>
> Character: showy, 2-inch flowers in shades of pink and white above large, attractive lobed leaves; forms spreading clumps when established
>
> Season of bloom: late summer, fall
>
> Hardiness: zone 5
>
> Possible drawbacks: poisonous if eaten, may be slow to establish but will spread vigorously thereafter

One of the standards for a late-summer shade garden, substantial but not gaudy. Double and semidouble forms are available.

Anemone sylvestris snowdrop anemone

> Needs: partial to full shade, good drainage, regular water, humus-rich soil
>
> Character: large, white, fragrant flowers on a spreading low plant, to 1¹/₂ feet
>
> Season of bloom: spring, but may bloom again throughout summer and fall
>
> Hardiness: zone 3
>
> Possible drawbacks: poisonous if eaten

A low charmer, this one, with larger blooms than most wildflowers but the air of woods dweller, nonetheless. Makes wide mats when happy.

Aruncus dioicus goatsbeard

> Needs: partial shade, sun in cool areas, fertile soil, regular water
>
> Character: up to 6 feet tall, with branched plumes of tiny white flowers above divided leaves
>
> Season of bloom: summer
>
> Hardiness: zone 3

Many shady areas can use a plant with height and this is one that blends well with shrubs and trees but doesn't overpower more delicate plants.

Arum italicum Italian arum

> Needs: part shade, good soil, regular watering
>
> Character: white, hoodlike bract over a spike of tiny true flowers, followed by red berries, arrow-shaped leaves, to 1 foot
>
> Season of bloom: spring, early summer
>
> Hardiness: zone 6
>
> Possible drawbacks: sap is irritating when ingested, berries are poisonous

The flowers of this plant are subtle, the berries lasting, looking like small scarlet ears of corn. Grow them as a curiosity or an accent.

Italian arum is one of the few perennials to bear bright-colored berries.

Astilbe × *arendsii* astilbe

Needs: part shade, rich deep soil, regular watering

Character: feathery plumes of tiny flowers over deeply cut foliage, $1^1/_2$–3 feet, depending on variety

Season of bloom: late spring, summer

Hardiness: zone 4

Astilbes are one of the showier shade flowers, useful in masses. You can give them sun if you also give them plenty of water. They don't like constantly wet soil, however.

Bellis perennis English daisy

Needs: sun to part shade, average water, average soil

Character: small, single or double daisy flowers, white, pink, or rose, 3–6 inches

Season of bloom: spring

Hardiness: zone 5

Possible drawbacks: may seed into lawns, becoming an attractive weed

Low, neat mats of leaves topped by miniature daisies make this one of the nicest weeds you could find. Larger-flowered varieties are more showy, but less charming.

Bergenia cordifolia heartleaf bergenia

> Needs: part shade, good soil, regular watering
>
> Character: clusters of pink blossoms on stalks held above broad leaves, 1$^1/_2$ feet
>
> Season of bloom: spring
>
> Hardiness: zone 4

This is a tough plant, enduring neglect but repaying a little care with more attractive leaves. Varieties with white flowers, bronze foliage, and larger or smaller leaves are available.

Brunnera macrophylla brunnera

> Needs: part shade, good soil, regular watering
>
> Character: small blue flowers in loose clusters, heart-shaped leaves, to 1$^1/_2$ feet
>
> Season of bloom: spring
>
> Hardiness: zone 3

The flowers could pass for forget-me-nots, but the leaves are more attractive. Would make a good ground cover if planted in quantity.

Dicentra spectabilis common bleeding heart

> Needs: part shade, good soil, regular watering
>
> Character: unusually shaped pink and white blossoms hang from arching stems, fernlike leaves, to 3 feet
>
> Season of bloom: spring
>
> Hardiness: zones 2–3

A spring standard, this plant blends well with tulips and other slightly stiff plants. It will die down by midsummer, so have annuals to plant in the gaps.

Doronicum caucasium Caucasian leopard's bane

> Needs: part shade, good soil, regular watering
>
> Character: 2–3-inch yellow daisies above rounded leaves, 1$^1/_2$ feet
>
> Season of bloom: spring
>
> Hardiness: zone 4
>
> Possible drawbacks: dislike hot, humid summers

Most daisies bloom in summer or fall, but this one's an early bird, valuable for its clear yellow and neat habit. It's a good companion for primroses and forget-me-nots. Dies back by midsummer, so plant near others that can fill the gaps.

Helleborus niger Christmas rose

> Needs: part shade, rich organic neutral soil, regular watering

> Character: white, single, roselike 2-inch flowers, large glossy leaves divided into fingerlike segments, to 2 feet

> Season of bloom: late fall, winter or early spring depending on weather

> Hardiness: zone 4

> Possible drawbacks: roots and leaves are poisonous

Winter flowers are much appreciated treasures and this is one of the best. The blossoms turn to pink and rose as they fade. Transplant carefully and only if necessary. The roots are brittle and it reestablishes slowly.

Myosotis scorpioides perennial forget-me-not

> Needs: part shade, good soil, regular watering

> Character: tiny blue flowers above shiny green leaves, to 10 inches

> Season of bloom: spring

> Hardiness: zone 3

Lower growing and longer blooming than its annual relative, this forget-me-not also saves you the bother of relying on seedlings to continue colonies.

Floral Lore

The juices of forget-me-not were once thought to harden steel. In Europe, it is sometimes made into a syrup and given for lung ailments.

233

Polemonium caeruleum Jacob's ladder

> Needs: part shade, good well-drained soil, regular watering
>
> Character: clusters of lavender-blue flowers above fernlike leaves, 2 feet
>
> Season of bloom: spring
>
> Hardiness: zones 2–3

This is a good companion for shrubs, bleeding heart, and daffodils under deciduous trees. It tends to blend into the background, so plant at least three, preferably more.

Polygonatum commutatum Solomon's seal

> Needs: part shade, good soil, regular watering
>
> Character: small, bell-like white flowers hang from arching stems with paired horizontal leaves, 3–5 feet
>
> Season of bloom: spring
>
> Hardiness: zone 3

This plant has a very different appearance from any other, curving yet upright. A clump is an eye-catcher in spite of the small flowers.

Primula* × *polyantha primrose

> Needs: part shade, good soil, regular watering
>
> Character: rounded, single flowers in many colors, rounded, crinkled leaves, to 5 inches
>
> Season of bloom: early spring
>
> Hardiness: zone 3

Individually, primroses seem squat and graceless, but cluster them in masses among fine-textured leaves and they become delightful. Best in groups of single colors.

Pulmonaria saccharata Bethlehem sage

> Needs: part shade, good soil, regular watering
>
> Character: small blue flowers among white-spotted leaves, to $1^1/_2$ feet

Season of bloom: spring

Hardiness: zones 2–3

Not flashy, but with a charm that blends well with hostas, ferns, and more colorful plants. Varieties are available with pink or white blossoms and more silvery leaves. *P. angustifolia* has deeper blue flowers and unspotted leaves.

Vines

Hydrangea anomala ssp. petiolaris climbing hydrangea

Method of climbing: clinging rootlets

Needs: part shade, good soil, regular watering

Character: flat heads of white flowers, tiny ones in the middle, larger ones at the outside, round leaves; deciduous

Season of bloom: summer

Hardiness: zone 4

Few vines have the refined presence of this one. Use against walls or the trunks of large trees. May be a little slow to start, but growth should speed up in a few years.

Trachelospermum jasminoides star jasmine

Method of climbing: twining stems

Needs: part to full shade, moist, well-drained soil

Character: 1-inch fragrant white flowers in small clusters, glossy green leaves, to 20 feet; evergreen

Season of bloom: spring, early summer

Hardiness: zone 8

This versatile vine can also be trained into a shrub or allowed to sprawl into a ground cover. So attractive both in and out of bloom that it can be set in a prominent place.

Trees and Shrubs

Many of these plants are forest dwellers in the wild and seem to complement each other in gardens. Mix and match them freely.

Camellia japonica common camellia

> Needs: part shade, rich, well-drained, slightly acid soil, regular to occasional watering
>
> Character: tidy, slightly waxy, roselike flowers, usually shades of pink, single or double, glossy leaves, usually 6–12 feet, depending on variety
>
> Season of bloom: spring
>
> Hardiness: zone 7

Camellias make dense bushes that may be covered with blooms if not given too much shade. They also make excellent pot plants. Look for varieties whose blooms drop off cleanly rather than turning brown on the branch. Another species, *C. sasanqua*, blooms in late fall and early winter, has a more graceful form and small flowers. It's also slightly less hardy.

Floral Lore

Black and green teas are made from the leaves of a species of camellia, *Camellia sinensis*, and differ only in the processes that they undergo to become flavorful. The bush has white, fragrant flowers, about 1¹/₂ inches across and is a bit more hardy than the common camellia.

Cornus dogwood

> Needs: part shade, good soil, regular watering
>
> Character: white, sometimes pink, petallike bracts surrounding small true flowers, deeply veined leaves, 10–30 feet, depending on variety; deciduous
>
> Season of bloom: spring
>
> Hardiness: zone 5 (*C. kousa*), zone 4 (*C. florida*)
>
> Possible drawbacks: eastern dogwood, *C. florida*, is often attacked by an anthracnose fungus

Glorious small trees, these have attractive branching patterns and flowers that are woodland beauties. Korean dogwood, *C. kousa*, flowers late in spring, after the leaves have unfolded. Disease-resistant hybrids between the two species are available.

Halesia carolina snowdrop tree, silver bell

> Needs: part shade, deep, rich, cool soil, regular watering
>
> Character: bell-shaped, $^1/_2$-inch white flowers hang from graceful branches, to 30 feet
>
> Season of bloom: spring
>
> Hardiness: zone 5

These are also elegant woodland trees, often seen as a not-too-quick-growing understory to taller ones. They have an elegance that makes them suitable as specimen trees in shady front entries. Prune to a single trunk.

Hamamelis mollis Chinese witch hazel

> Needs: part shade or sun, good soil, regular watering
>
> Character: fragrant, yellow, 1-inch flowers with narrow, ribbonlike petals, round felted leaves, 10–15 feet; deciduous
>
> Season of bloom: late winter
>
> Hardiness: zone 5, zone 4 (*H. virginiana*)

Flowers are more welcome than ever as winter is turning toward spring and these are both dainty and durable. Tree or shrublike depending on how many trunks you leave. The native witch hazel, *H. virginiana*, has slightly smaller flowers, but is more cold-tolerant.

Hydrangea macrophylla bigleaf hydrangea

> Needs: part shade, good soil, regular watering
>
> Character: large heads of blossoms, sometimes solid, sometimes lace-cap with tiny flowers in the middle, pink, white, or blue, rounded leaves, 4–8 feet; deciduous
>
> Season of bloom: summer, fall
>
> Hardiness: zone 5

Try to get newer varieties with more intense blue or pink flowers. They're far more attractive than the grocery store standard. It's worth going to a specialty nursery to get one of the new ones.

Kalmia latifolia mountain laurel

> Needs: part shade, rich, well-drained, acid soil, regular watering
>
> Character: pointed, balloonlike buds open to rounded flowers, usually shades of pink, glossy pointed leaves, to 8 feet; evergreen
>
> Season of bloom: spring
>
> Hardiness: zone 4

These slow-growing elegant bushes blend well with azaleas and dogwoods. Native from Canada to Florida, there are many forms and varieties, some with deep pink buds that are as attractive as the flowers themselves. It's best to choose one from a similar climate zone.

Pieris japonica lily of the valley shrub

> Needs: part shade, good soil, regular watering
>
> Character: drooping clusters of urn-shaped white flowers, glossy leaves with reddish new growth, to 10 feet; evergreen
>
> Season of bloom: spring
>
> Hardiness: zone 5
>
> Possible drawbacks: leaves and nectar are poisonous

A most useful shrub, this one is attractive even when not flowering, especially when the bronzy new leaves unfold.

Rhododendron azalea, rhododendron

> Needs: part shade, good, loose, acid soil, regular watering
>
> Character: tubular to flat blossoms in many colors and shades, large or small leaves, some with attractive felty undersides, from 1–20 feet, depending on variety; evergreen or deciduous
>
> Season of bloom: spring to early summer
>
> Hardiness: zones vary by species and variety
>
> Possible drawbacks: leaves are poisonous

Few groups of plants have as much variety as this one. From flame-colored deciduous azaleas to low, dwarf, and treelike Himalayan species with huge leaves, there's one here for every garden. They do look best in groups, or with other woodlanders, however.

Stewartia pseudocamellia Japanese stewartia

> Needs: part shade, rich, organic, well-drained acid soil, regular watering

> Character: cup-shaped 2-inch white flowers, bronze to purple fall color, slow growing to 30 feet

> Season of bloom: summer

> Hardiness: zone 5

This is a tree to show off. Gracefully branching, somewhat pyramidal, it not only has exquisite camellialike flowers, but good fall color and attractively mottled bark that adds interest in winter. Slow, but worth waiting for.

The Least You Need to Know

➤ Use texture contrast to add interest to beds rather than relying exclusively on color.

➤ Most shade plants need rich, slightly acid soil with lots of organic matter.

➤ Easy annuals for low sun and enough water: fibrous begonias, impatiens, forget-me-nots (*Myosotis*).

➤ Easy perennials for low sun and enough water: bergenia, English daisies (*Bellis*), Bethlehem sage (*Pulmonaria*).

➤ Easy bulbs for low sun and enough water: glory of the snow (*Chionodoxa*), Siberian squill (*Scilla siberica*), grape hyacinth (*Muscari*).

➤ Easy trees and shrubs for low sun and enough water: camellia, hydrangea, rhododendron.

Chapter 19

Dry Shadows

In This Chapter

➤ What kind of place is this?

➤ Colorful annuals

➤ Dependable bulbs

➤ Lasting perennials

➤ Vivid vines

➤ Good-looking trees and shrubs

Less than perfect conditions exist all over the world, and dry soil combined with shade is a common challenge for many plants. Whether it's found beneath a Mediterranean oak wood or a below a stand of fir near Seattle, dry shadows are home to a number of flowering plants.

Perhaps not as many, though, as you'd find in more hospitable conditions. Don't look for large, lush blooms, or at least not as many as you'd find in well-watered areas. Wildflowers with subtle, delicate textures are your most likely candidates.

In fact, texture is your greatest ally here. Find some plants with strong bold lines, either broad or sword-shaped leaves, and complement with lacy, ferny foliage. When you find a flower that does well, plant square yards of it, broad ribbons, and pools among the green leaves. Then sit in the shade and enjoy.

What Does This Garden Look Like?

Most often, it's beneath trees. Their roots often draw moisture from the soil to leave less for other plants. The branches are designed to guide rain to the outer edges of the tree's root area. Any plant has to be tough to survive here.

Or it may be an area between tall buildings that shelter the soil from natural rainfall. Or you may live in an area where rain is scarce in summer. Perhaps this shady corner is awkward to reach with a hose and you'd like to plant things that would survive on their own.

If you're gardening beneath trees, the plus is that the ground is usually well drained. The roots have created channels through the soil that allow excess water to flow away.

Dry shade is also usually protected against strong winds. In fact, it may be sheltered enough to grow plants that would be cut down by the coldest frosts in more open areas. Overhanging branches and walls create a slightly warmer zone beneath them, a microclimate of warmth in winter and coolness in summer.

What if There is Too Much Shade?

Again, as in the garden discussed in the previous chapter, shade limits the number of flowering plants available to choose from. The less the light, the less energy available for flowering. Some plants, of course, are well adapted to low-light conditions. In general, however, you'll find larger leaves and fewer blooms the more shade you have.

If you garden under trees, you can thin the branches to allow more light to reach the ground. Start from the main trunk and remove any large unessential limbs. Often the tree's shape depends on just a few, and extras can be pruned off without changing the basic form.

Next move to the smaller branches, thinning as many as possible. Unless it's a very small tree, you may want to stop there as thinning the branchlets on a tall tree is a tedious job. By now you should have an open tree that allows a little sunlight to penetrate. You're ready to start planting.

Make the Most of the Water You Have

First, give the soil some extra organic matter. Dig in as much as you can, then mulch with more on top. Don't worry about cutting off some of the roots of your overhanging tree. It can afford to lose a few and this is one situation where soil improvement can definitely help make gardening easier, both by holding on to water as it passes through the soil and, as a mulch, by keeping it from evaporating from the surface.

Also loosen the soil as much as possible below and to the sides of your zone of organic matter. Well-aerated earth is an invitation to roots to extend their range, increasing the drought-tolerance of your shrub or perennial.

242

Give your plants the best start you can. They'll have plenty of work to do here, plenty of challenges to overcome. Make life easy for them whenever possible.

Baby Them for a Few Years

Don't expect heroism from small plants. Most need regular watering their first summer and nearly as much the second. Then you can allow them to fend for themselves, with extra in really dry periods. Remember that drought is considerably drier and hotter in the Southwest than in Maine. Adjust your expectations accordingly.

Annuals and Biennials

If your shade is light, feel free to experiment with some of the annuals listed in chapter 17. They may not flower as profusely, but, in this area, take what you can get.

Cynoglossum amabile Chinese forget-me-not

Needs: sun, semishade in hot areas, average to less water, not for humid summer areas

Character: clear blue, fragrant flowers, about $1/4$ inch across, in loose clusters on foot-high plants with bluish leaves, effective in masses

Season of bloom: summer

Reminiscent of true forget-me-nots but with deeper blue flowers and with more sun and drought tolerance. An excellent filler to sow among stouter plants.

Digitalis purpurea foxglove

Needs: part shade to sun, good drainage, regular to occasional watering

Character: tall spikes of tubular lavender-rose flowers, sometimes white, large hairy leaves, to 5 feet

Season of bloom: late spring, early summer

Hardiness: zone 5

Possible drawbacks: poisonous

Plant lots of these, especially some of the newer varieties in soft yellows and pinks. Their leaves are attractive contrasts to finer textured plants even when not blooming. They reseed well.

Floral Lore

The name *foxglove* was originally folks-glove or the glove or the fairies, the good folk. It has also been called witches' gloves, dead men's bells, bloody fingers, fairy caps, and fairy thimbles.

Lobularia maritima sweet alyssum

> Needs: sun to part shade, average soil, average water
>
> Character: tiny flowers in white to lavender-pink and purple hide the small-narrow leaves
>
> Season of bloom: spring to fall

More drought-resistant than most shade-tolerant annuals, sweet alyssum makes a fine-textured filler between larger plants.

Lunaria annua honesty, silver dollar plant

> Needs: part shade to sun, good drainage, regular to occasional watering
>
> Character: clusters of mauve flowers, followed by papery silver disks, 2 feet
>
> Season of bloom: spring
>
> Hardiness: zone 4

While usually grown for the silver dollars, this plant has attractive flowers that make a good filler under trees and in informal gardens.

Bulbs and Tubers

Convallaria majalis lily of the valley

> Needs: best in shade, most soils, regular to occasional watering
>
> Character: small, fragrant white bells above bold 6-inch leaves
>
> Season of bloom: spring
>
> Hardiness: zone 2
>
> Possible drawbacks: can invade nearby plantings, difficult to eradicate

244

When grown in dry shade, this makes a thin carpet, popping up every 6 inches or so, leaving room for other plants. Plant only where it can travel without annoying anyone.

Crocosmia masoniorum crocosmia

> Needs: part shade to sun, regular to occasional watering
>
> Character: curving stems topped with a line of orange blossoms, swordlike leaves, to 3 feet
>
> Season of bloom: summer
>
> Hardiness: zone 7

These are carefree and colorful, making large clumps in time. They're good cut flowers as well. Look also for another species *C. × crocosmiiflora*, montbretia, and hybrids between the two. One of these, 'Lucifer', is a standout, growing to 4 feet with large, flame-red flowers.

Cyclamen hederifolium dwarf cyclamen

> Needs: part shade or sun, winter and spring moisture
>
> Character: dainty pink curved flowers above marbled leaves, to 5 inches
>
> Season of bloom: late summer
>
> Hardiness: zone 5

A beauty that looks natural interplanted with shrubs and trees, or in masses at the front of the border. Leaves sprout in fall after flowering and make a dense, good-looking ground cover until the following June. Native to central and southern Europe.

Hyacinthoides hispanica Spanish bluebell

> Needs: sun to shade, any soil if well-drained, water when blooming
>
> Character: foot-high spikes of soft blue flowers over straplike leaves
>
> Season of bloom: late spring
>
> Hardiness: zone 3
>
> Possible drawbacks: spreads so easily that it can become an charming nuisance

Just try to keep this one from colonizing your yard! Tough, bountiful, and handsome, bluebells grow almost anywhere. If you think you have a black thumb that kills everything, try this.

English bluebells and *H. non-scripta* are closely related, somewhat more dainty, hardy in zone 5.

Perennials

Agapanthus   Headbourne hybrids lily of the Nile

> Needs: sun to part shade, regular to occasional watering
>
> Character: heads of large, tubular flowers on 2½-foot stems, straplike leaves
>
> Season of bloom: summer
>
> Hardiness: zone 6

Give these water until well started and as much sun as possible. Though these hybrids are hardiest, many others are sold for warmer areas.

Alchemilla mollis lady's mantle

> Needs: part to full shade, but can take sun in cool areas, little (in shade) to much water
>
> Character: plants up to 2 feet have clouds of tiny greenish yellow flowers and large, lobed leaves, softly hairy, that often hold a few drops of water after a shower
>
> Season of bloom: early summer
>
> Hardiness: zone 3
>
> Possible drawbacks: intolerant of hot, humid summers, self-sows a bit too freely for some gardeners

An excellent background for plants with more vivid flowers and a bold texture to contrast with ferns and swordlike leaves.

Floral Lore

According to some old sources, the name *alchemilla* was given to this plant because the dew that was caught by the leaves was used by alchemists in many of their potions.

Anaphalis margaritacea pearly everlasting

> Needs: part shade, regular watering

> Character: small white flowers, gray leaves, 2 feet

> Season of bloom: summer

> Hardiness: zone 3–9

This is the gray-leafed plant most tolerant of shade, even damp soil. It's useful with pinks and pale yellows and is easy to dry.

Centranthus ruber Jupiter's beard, red valerian

> Needs: sun to part shade, ordinary soil, occasional to little watering

> Character: small, warm or cool pink flowers in clusters at the end of sprawling branches, to 3 feet

> Season of bloom: late spring, early summer

> Hardiness: zone 4

This is tough as well as beautiful. Don't waste good soil on it—red valerian thrives on neglect.

Corydalis lutea golden corydalis

> Needs: part shade to heavy shade, ordinary soil, occasional to little watering

> Character: small, golden-yellow blooms on ferny gray-green foliage, to $1^1/_2$ feet

> Season of bloom: spring through fall

> Hardiness: zone 5

Never heard of this one? You will. Neat habit, excellent texture, long bloom period and ease of care make this one of the best for dry shade. It reseeds itself so you'll soon have masses.

Cymbalaria muralis Kenilworth ivy

> Needs: shade to part shade, average soil, tolerates alkaline soil, regular to little water

> Character: round, scalloped leaves are accompanied by tiny lilac flowers that look like miniature snapdragons

> Season of bloom: summer

> Hardiness: zones 3–9

A quick-growing, delicate trailer often sold as an annual for hanging baskets. Often seeds itself into cracks in walls and pavement.

Epimedium grandiflorum bishop's hat

> Needs: part shade to shade, ordinary soil, occasional watering

> Character: small spurred flowers, white, pink, or lavender above rounded leaves, to 1 foot

> Season of bloom: spring

> Hardiness: zone 3

Epimediums are among the best fillers for dry shade. The flowers are small but numerous and the leaves are handsome. It spreads slowly to form large clumps.

Helleborus orientalis Lenten rose

> Needs: part shade, good soil, regular to occasional watering

> Character: clusters of nodding flowers in cream, pale green, or purplish-rose, substantial leaves divided into fingerlike segments, to 2 feet

> Season of bloom: late winter, early spring

> Hardiness: zone 4

Lenten rose has a subtle appeal, with strong lines rather than bright color. It's a good foil for more delicate plants.

Hesperis matronalis dame's rocket, sweet rocket

> Needs: sun or part shade, most soils including slightly alkaline types, average to modest amounts of water

> Character: small, purple or white fragrant flowers on 1–3-foot plants with pointed oblong leaves

> Season of bloom: spring, summer

> Hardiness: zone 3

An old-fashioned plant, easy to grow in almost any situation. Will seed itself into odd corners, becoming a pleasant weed.

Floral Lore

In the language of flowers, dame's rocket was used to represent deceit because it scents the air in the evening, but not the day.

Hosta hybrids plantain lily, hosta

> Needs: part shade to shade, good soil, regular to occasional watering

> Character: spikes of white to lavender tubular flowers above rounded, strongly veined leaves, often splashed or streaked with white or yellow, 1–3 feet

> Season of bloom: summer

> Hardiness: zone 3

Few shade gardens would not be improved by adding hostas. Their well-defined lines balance more frothy plants. Can be planted in solid masses to make a weedproof ground cover.

Iris sibirica Siberian iris

> Needs: sun or part shade, many soils, regular water in spring, can dry out in summer

> Character: graceful, purple, blue, or white flowers above attractive, narrow, linear leaves, 3 feet

> Season of bloom: early summer

> Hardiness: zone 3

A reliable plant that blends well with other flowers, Siberian iris blooms are reminiscent of Japanese paintings. The leaves provide one of the more useful swordlike textures even when out of bloom.

Lobelia siphilitica big blue lobelia

>Needs: part shade, dry shade, moist or wet soil

>Character: lavender-blue flowers in spikes to 3 feet

>Season of bloom: late summer

>Hardiness: zone 5

>Possible drawbacks: contains poisonous alkaloids

A little shorter the its red cousin, this lobelia is a good background or large filler, being enjoyable without asking for admiration.

Meconopsis cambrica Welsh poppy

>Needs: part shade, good soil, frequent to occasional watering

>Character: large, lemon-yellow poppy flowers or soft orange above light green ferny leaves, to 2 feet

>Season of bloom: early summer

>Hardiness: zone 4

>Possible drawbacks: dislikes heat

This is one of those unusual plants that take both wet soil and dry. An easy to grow species in a genus filled with fussy flowers, this does need cool, moist summers to succeed.

Oenothera fruticosa sundrops, evening primrose

>Needs: sun to light shade, average soil, occasional watering

>Character: bright yellow cup-shaped flowers, reddish stems, to 2 feet

>Season of bloom: summer

>Hardiness: zone 4

This should be in every garden for its carefree nature and willingness to spread without overwhelming everything. Another species, *O. speciosa*, hardy to zone 5, has pink flowers and a more invasive disposition. *O. missouriensis*, zone 6, has larger yellow flowers on trailing stems. These are all native to North America.

Omphalodes verna blue-eyed Mary

> Needs: part shade, good soil, regular to occasional watering

> Character: small, sky-blue flowers with a white eye on creeping plants

> Season of bloom: spring

> Hardiness: zone 7

Few ground covers are as charming as this one or have such clear blue flowers. Spreads slowly, but will make large mats in time.

Oxalis oregana Oregon wood sorrel

> Needs: part or full shade, occasional watering

> Character: pink or white five petaled flowers, to 1 inch, above 3-part clover-shaped leaves, up to 10 inches high

> Season of bloom: spring

> Hardiness: zone 7

This looks delicate, but will spread rapidly once it gets going, even in poor soil. Both flowers and leaves are edible, tasting sour and lemony.

Wood sorrel looks like large-leafed clover, and, like these relatives, can occasionally sprout 4-part leaves.

Sedum stonecrop

> Needs: sun to part shade, ordinary, well-drained soil, occasional to little watering

> Character: flat clusters of yellow, pink, or white flowers, succulent leaves, 2 inches–2 feet

> Season of bloom: varies by species

> Hardiness: zones vary by species, some to zone 3

Sedums come in many forms, some with tiny leaves, others with broad ones. Some are prostrate, others upright. All are carefree, easy-to-grow plants that look well with rocks and driftwood.

Tradescantia virginiana spiderwort

> Needs: sun or shade, regular to occasional watering

> Character: small, 3-petaled flowers, blue, purple, or shades of pink, grasslike foliage, 1^1/$_2$–3 feet tall

> Season of bloom: spring and summer

> Hardiness: zone 4

> Possible drawbacks: may need staking in rich soil

Don't expect heroic tolerance to dry soil from this one, merely an acceptance of neglect. It's so vigorous that once started well, it simply doesn't stop. Useful for its linear foliage as well as long flowering period.

Vinca minor periwinkle

> Needs: part or full shade, most soils, regular or occasional watering

> Character: flat, single, lavender-blue flowers, glossy leaves, 6 inches; evergreen

> Season of bloom: spring

> Hardiness: zone 4

A common ground cover, periwinkle is less spreading in dry soil, still attractive in bloom. *V. major* is larger in all dimensions, more invasive and less hardy, to zone 7.

Vines

Actinidia kolomikta Arctic kiwi

> Method of climbing: twining stems
>
> Needs: part shade or sun, good soil, regular to occasional watering
>
> Character: small, fragrant white flowers, showy leaves splashed with white and pink, to 15 inches or more
>
> Season of bloom: early summer
>
> Hardiness: zone 4

A double bonus of flowers and unusually tinted leaves makes this a standout. Foliage colors best in cold climates.

Campsis radicans trumpet vine, trumpet creeper

> Method of climbing: clinging
>
> Needs: sun or part shade, most soils, regular or modest amounts of water
>
> Character: sprays of 3-inch orange tubular flowers on vigorous stems with divided leaves; deciduous
>
> Season of bloom: summer, early fall
>
> Hardiness: zone 5
>
> Possible drawbacks: spreads by suckers, any piece of root will grow a new plant, may become so heavy that it pulls away from support

An easy-to-grow standard, never bothered by insects, this is practically fail-safe. 'Flava' is a golden yellow variety equally attractive to hummingbirds.

Gelsemium sempervirens Carolina jessamine

> Method of climbing: twining stems
>
> Needs: sun to part shade, regular to occasional watering
>
> Character: tubular, fragrant yellow flowers, to 20 feet; evergreen
>
> Season of bloom: late winter to early spring
>
> Hardiness: zone 7
>
> Possible drawbacks: poisonous

Excellent trailing ground cover as well as screen for dull fences and walls.

Wisteria sinensis Chinese wisteria

> Method of climbing: twining stems
>
> Needs: sun to part shade, ordinary soil, regular watering when young, occasional watering thereafter
>
> Character: long clusters of white or lavender-blue flowers hang from stout vines with pale green leaves divided into many leaflets
>
> Season of bloom: early summer
>
> Hardiness: zone 6
>
> Possible drawbacks: needs annual pruning to control size

An adaptable vine that makes such thick woody stems that it can be trained as a shrub or small tree. Give it a good start with adequate water, then leave it dry except during drought.

Trees and Shrubs

This list is rather short, but you can expand it by asking for suggestions at your local nursery. Native flowering trees and shrubs may be little known outside your area, but be perfect for a woodland garden.

Arbutus unedo strawberry tree

> Needs: part shade or sun, well-drained soil, occasional to little watering
>
> Character: hanging clusters of white, urn-shaped flowers followed by red $3/4$-inch fruit, 8–30 feet (tallest in warm climates); evergreen
>
> Season of bloom: fall and winter
>
> Hardiness: zone 8

A large shrub or small tree, this has reddish flaking bark and a neat habit that makes it ornamental even when out of bloom. Flowers and fruit appear together to brighten dull months.

Mahonia aquifolium Oregon grape

> Needs: part shade, little watering
>
> Character: tight clusters of yellow flowers, followed by edible dark-blue fruit, upright stems with glossy, spiny leaves, bronze new growth, to 6 feet
>
> Season of bloom: spring
>
> Hardiness: zone 5

This has a strong vertical dimension, though the leaves spread horizontally, that makes it useful among more rounded shrubs. Can be kept to 4 or 5 feet by cutting out the oldest stems.

Nandina domestica heavenly bamboo

> Needs: part shade, sun in cool climates, best in good soil, regular to occasional watering
>
> Character: airy, white clusters of flowers, light green divided leaves, purplish new growth, upright stems to 8 feet
>
> Season of bloom: late spring, early summer
>
> Hardiness: zone 7

This is also useful for vertical lines, but more airy and delicate than Oregon grape. Planted at entryways for good luck in Japan.

Pittosporum tobira tobira

> Needs: part shade or sun, occasional watering
>
> Character: clusters of white flowers with fragrance of orange blossoms, whorls of shiny dark green leaves sometimes variegated with white, to 10 feet
>
> Season of bloom: spring
>
> Hardiness: zone 8

A compact bush, even when tall, that grows well in seashore conditions.

Ribes sanguineum red flowering currant

> Needs: part shade or full sun, good drainage, occasional watering
>
> Character: drooping clusters of small, pale to deep pink flowers followed by blue-black berries, to 10 feet
>
> Season of bloom: spring
>
> Hardiness: zone 5

One of the most spectacular dry shade shrubs, as showy as azaleas in bloom. Look for selections with deep pink flowers if you want it to stand out, paler ones for blending into the background. Needs perfect drainage in warm, humid areas.

Sophora japonica Japanese pagoda tree

Needs: part shade or sun, well-drained soil, occasional watering

Character: small, warm, white sweet-pealike flowers in long sprays, followed by seedpods, finely divided leaves, to 50 feet; deciduous

Season of bloom: summer

Hardiness: zone 4

This is a tough tree for almost any climate, tolerating heat, drought, and city air, rewarding neglect with lavish bloom.

The Least You Need to Know

➤ You'll find fewer showy flowers in dry shade. Use lots of what works for you.

➤ Add interest with complementary textures, including at least three of these types: large and bold, swordlike, fine and ferny, or medium.

➤ To get more flowers, open out trees that block the light by removing unnecessary branches.

➤ Easy annuals and bulbs for dry shade: sweet alyssum (*Lobularia*), lily of the valley (*Convallaria*), bluebells (*Hyacinthoides*).

➤ Easy perennials for dry shade: lady's mantle (*Alchemilla*), red valerian (*Centranthus*), bishop's hat (*Epimedium*), Hosta.

➤ Easy vines, trees, and shrubs for dry shade: trumpet vine (*Campsis*), wisteria, tobira (*Pittosporum*), Japanese pagoda tree (*Sophora*).

Chapter 20

Wet and Wonderful

In This Chapter

➤ What kind of place is this?

➤ Colorful annuals

➤ Dependable bulbs

➤ Lasting perennials

➤ Vivid vines

➤ Good-looking trees and shrubs

Too often a damp or water-soaked spot is seen as a liability. Yes, most of your favorite plants say that well-drained soil is a must. For others, however, wet is wonderful.

In fact, you may be able to grow some luscious prizes, such as candelabra-type Japanese primroses, that are a bother in drier sites. And you don't have to worry about getting someone to water while you're on vacation.

You might even be tempted to create your own mini-bog, just so you can grow some of these treats, or extend the soggy spot near the drain pipe a few feet. Once you find out how lovely wet soil areas can be, anything is possible.

What Does This Garden Look Like?

Wet soil covers a diversity of conditions, from highly acid sphagnum bogs that are home to a specialized set of plants, to the banks of streams and rivers. These have a constant flow of oxygenated water, very different from a stagnant bog or marsh.

Oxygen is important. The roots of many plants can tolerate moist soil if well aerated. Fewer can thrive in true swamp conditions where there is little drainage and almost no oxygen in the waterlogged soil.

Some areas have standing water in winter and spring, then dry out completely in summer. Others are submerged year-round. True water gardening, involving a pond, oxygenating plants and perhaps a few water lilies, is a specialty. Here we'll just look at possibilities for turning wet soil into an asset.

Take Stock

What are the characteristics of your own area? Most important, does water drain through or stagnate? How large an area are you dealing with? How moist and how dry does it get throughout the year? All these factors need to be considered when choosing plants.

Green Tip

To make wetting peat moss easier, use hot water with a little added soap. Then make sure it never dries out again.

Naturally low, wet areas usually have highly organic soil, a product of years of fallen leaves and other debris plus slow decomposition. Add peat moss (acid, hard to wet, but good for artificial bogs), dried leaves or other fibrous amendment if you are creating or extending a wet area to duplicate these conditions.

Making Your Own

Perhaps you have a place that gets extra water naturally, next to a faucet, at the end of a drainpipe, along a drainage ditch or next to a pond. If you want to extend this zone of moisture, the easiest method is to interrupt the natural drainage with a barrier.

Dig down 1–2 feet, making a bowl-shaped hole, then place a moisture-resistant material on the subsoil. Pond liner is durable, but expensive. Plastic garbage bags are cheap, but temporary. One of the best solutions is to mix bentonite clay (available at feed stores) with an inch or two of the soil at the base of your hole, tamp down well, and soak. The clay will swell, closing the gaps between the grains of soil and preventing water from passing through.

Fill your artificial marsh with soil, peat moss, and other organic matter. This will give it the acid character typical of most bogs. Water when dry, though the moisture barrier will keep the soil moist far longer than surrounding areas.

Now let's look at the plants you can grow. Many of these, by the way, do not require wet soil. If they please you, feel free to add them to any regularly watered bed.

Annuals, Biennials, and Tender Perennials Grown as Annuals

Angelica archangelica angelica

> Needs: part shade, moist to wet soil
>
> Character: huge divided leaves, up to 3 feet long, give an almost tropical effect for several summers before the flowering stalk rises to 6 feet and opens flat heads of white blossoms
>
> Season of bloom: early summer
>
> Hardiness: zone 4
>
> Possible drawbacks: its demise after flowering can leave a gap until next year's seedlings appear

Available from herb growers, this is a beauty in leaf and flower. It can be a giant, however, so make sure you have room. Starts easily from new seed.

Angelica (Angelica archangelica) is a biennial that may live for two years or more, especially if the flowering stems are cut off as they appear.

Take Care!

Be sure to sow angelica seed as soon as it ripens to get new plants for next year. Once it dries out, germination will be uneven. As a biennial, it should get a start as early as possible so it will winter over as a substantial plant.

Mimulus* × *hybridus monkey flower

Needs: partial shade, sun if soil is very moist

Character: tubular flowers with flat faces in yellow, orange, red, or bright pink

Season of bloom: spring or summer, depending on planting dates

Informal, fun annuals that complement wild gardens. Good in containers left in trays of water.

Myosotis sylvatica forget-me-nots

Needs: part shade, regular watering

Character: tiny blue, white-eyed flowers on sprawling stems with hairy leaves, to 1 foot

Season of bloom: spring

Possible drawbacks: may seed too prolifically in cool, moist conditions, becoming an attractive weed

One of the best fillers between spring bulbs and perennials, making airy blue pools beneath trees and around shrubs. Easy to pull if it spreads outside of planned boundaries. *Myosotis scorpioides* also does well under these conditions.

Nemophila menziesii baby-blue-eyes

Needs: sun or part shade, regular to occasional watering

Character: clear blue, cup-shaped flowers on light green fernlike leaves, to 1 foot

Season of bloom: spring

Possible drawbacks: dislikes heat and high humidity

Useful for its generosity with seedlings as well as its fine color, Baby-blue-eyes can be a quick cover for bare spots or a filler between taller plants.

Bulbs

Camassia camas

> Needs: sun, moisture, can take fairly heavy soil
>
> Character: spikes of starlike flowers, usually blue though white are available, rise above narrow leaves. *C. cusickii* and *C. leichtlinii* are 2–3 feet tall, *C. quamash* is 1–2 feet
>
> Season of bloom: late spring, early summer
>
> Hardiness: zone 5

Somewhat unusual bulbs that are becoming more popular, these are well suited to the marshy area. In the wild, these grow in both dry and wet situations, though the extra moisture often disappears in summer. Edible, if in the future you have too many.

Fritillaria meleagris checkered lily

> Needs: sun or light shade, good soil, regular watering
>
> Character: nodding, 2-inch bell-shaped flowers finely checkered with brown and purple, 1–1$^{1}/_{2}$ feet
>
> Season of bloom: spring
>
> Hardiness: zone 3

A conversation piece, this one, best in large groups. It's native to damp meadows in Europe and Asia and will survive occasional immersion.

Narcissus poeticus 'Actaea' Poet's narcissus

> Needs: sun to light shade, regular watering
>
> Character: white blossoms with a small yellow cup edged with red, narrow leaves, 2 feet
>
> Season of bloom: late spring
>
> Hardiness: zone 4
>
> Possible drawbacks: poisonous

One of a group called poet's narcissus. While most daffodils prefer good drainage, this one may be safely planted in damp but not stagnant soil.

Zantedeschia aethiopica calla lily

> Needs: sun or part shade, regular watering
>
> Character: a large, white, tubular flower bract surrounds a spike of tiny true flowers, bold, arrow-shaped evergreen leaves, to 3 feet
>
> Season of bloom: spring, early summer
>
> Hardiness: zone 8

This is a good specimen plant, upright and conspicuous. It contrasts nicely with ferns and forget-me-nots (*Myosotis*). The rhizomes don't store well, but it can be grown in pots in colder areas.

Perennials

Aconitum monkshood

> Needs: sun to partial shade, moist to damp, cool, rich soil
>
> Character: flowers in a shade of blue or purple, depending on the species, borne in spikes 2–5 feet tall
>
> Season of bloom: summer
>
> Hardiness: zone 2
>
> Possible drawbacks: very poisonous! Keep away from children, far from vegetable gardens; not for hot, humid summer areas.

Excellent rich color from plants that are easy to grow, given the right conditions. They can substitute for delphiniums in slightly shady areas.

Asclepias incarnata swamp milkweed

> Needs: sun, moist to wet soil
>
> Character: bright pink flowers top strong stems, 3–5 feet tall
>
> Season of bloom: summer
>
> Hardiness: zone 3
>
> Possible drawbacks: poisonous; resents transplanting so buy in containers

Native to eastern and central United States, this is one of the best wet-soil plants. Varieties with white flowers are available.

Aster novae-angliae New England aster

> Needs: sun, moist to wet soil
>
> Character: large clumps, 3–5 feet, bear masses of pink to lilac or purple daisylike blooms
>
> Season of bloom: late summer, fall
>
> Hardiness: zone 4
>
> Possible drawbacks: leaves may mildew, may need dividing every few years to check spreading roots and rejuvenate clumps

Great for fall color, height at the back of a grouping.

Caltha palustris marsh marigold

> Needs: sun or shade, wet soil
>
> Character: 2-inch gold, single or double flowers in clusters, round, bright green leaves, to 2 feet
>
> Season of bloom: spring
>
> Hardiness: zone 3
>
> Possible drawbacks: irritating sap

These are true bog plants, accepting occasional immersion but tolerant to drying out in summer. One place to look for them is water gardening supply stores.

Chelone lyonii pink turtlehead

> Needs: part shade or sun, wet soil
>
> Character: spikes of 1-inch rosy-purple flowers, oval leaves, to 3 feet
>
> Season of bloom: summer
>
> Hardiness: zone 3

This is also a true bog-lover, good for adding color to the edges of ponds and streams. The white turtlehead, *C. glabra*, can take a little less water.

Coreopsis rosea pink coreopsis

> Needs: sun, constantly moist soil
>
> Character: masses of tiny, pink daisylike flowers, fine leaves to 2 feet tall
>
> Season of bloom: summer to fall
>
> Hardiness: zone 4

This is a good ground cover for moist areas, fine and delicately textured. It's creeping roots soon fill in bare ground between taller plants.

Eupatorium purpureum joe-pye weed

> Needs: sun or shade, moist, wet, or somewhat dry soil
>
> Character: large heads of pale purple-pink or white flowers, large, toothed vanilla-scented leaves, 3–9 feet tall
>
> Season of bloom: late summer, early fall
>
> Hardiness: zone 4

This is both tall and eye-catching. One of the best varieties is 'Gateway', growing only to 5 feet with deeper colored flowers and purplish stems. Butterflies love this one.

Filipendula rubra queen of the prairie

> Needs: sun or part shade, rich, moist to wet soil
>
> Character: tall plumes of tiny pink flowers above divided leaves, 4–8 feet
>
> Season of bloom: summer
>
> Hardiness: zones 2–3

This looks like an oversize astilbe, feathery and graceful. Good for backgrounds and informal borders.

Helenium autumnale sneezeweed

> Needs: sun, wet, moist, or dry soil
>
> Character: yellow to bronze daisies on strong stems, to 6 feet
>
> Season of bloom: late summer, early fall
>
> Hardiness: zone 3
>
> Possible drawbacks: taller varieties may need staking

Though drought-tolerant, sneezeweed does best with moisture. The species itself is weedy and not too ornamental. Most plants sold are more compact, attractive varieties, usually 3–4 feet high. Needs little fertilizer.

Iris pseudacorus yellow flag

> Needs: sun to light shade, moist to wet soil
>
> Character: large, bright yellow flowers, long, sword-shaped leaves
>
> Season of bloom: late spring
>
> Hardiness: zones 3–4

This is extra-easy to grow, even under ordinary garden conditions or shallow water. The leaves remain attractive all season, can be used for texture interest in part shade.

Floral Lore

Yellow flag, native throughout Europe, North Africa, and Siberia, was taken by Louis VII as his heraldic emblem in his crusade against the Saracens, becoming the fleur-de-lis.

Ligularia stenocephala 'The Rocket'

> Needs: partial or full shade, moist to wet soil
>
> Character: spires of yellow daisylike flowers above bold, deeply cut leaves, to 5 feet
>
> Season of bloom: early summer
>
> Hardiness: zone 6

Being large and majestic, these are useful for filling in shady wet areas where other plants fail.

Lobelia cardinalis cardinal flower

> Needs: sun or partial shade, moist or wet soil

> Character: tall spikes of deep red, 1-inch flowers, to 4 feet

> Season of bloom: summer

> Hardiness: zone 2

> Possible drawbacks: contains poisonous alkaloids

No one could miss this in bloom. The color is as bright as red as you could ask for. Protect it with a mulch so late frosts don't cut down too-early shoots. Plant groups.

Lobelia siphilitica big blue lobelia

> Needs: part shade, dry shade, moist or wet soil

> Character: lavender-blue flowers in spikes to 3 feet

> Season of bloom: late summer

> Hardiness: zone 5

> Possible drawbacks: contains poisonous alkaloids

A little shorter the its red cousin, this lobelia is a good background or large filler, being enjoyable without asking for admiration.

Lysimachia clethroides gooseneck loosestrife

> Needs: sun or part shade, moist to wet soil

> Character: tiny white flowers in gracefully curving spikes, to 3 feet

> Season of bloom: summer

> Hardiness: zone 3

> Possible drawbacks: spreads by underground roots, invasive

Here's another filler, an enthusiastically spreading one. The interesting flower spikes blend well with larger flowers.

Maianthemum canadense wild lily of the valley

> Needs: part shade to shade, moist, wet, or somewhat dry soil

> Character: small spikes of white flowers, heart-shaped leaves, to 6 inches

> Season of bloom: late spring

Hardiness: zone 3

Possible drawbacks: may be invasive

If you need a ground cover for your bog, try this. The leaves are glossy and neat, making a dense mat that will prevent weeds from sprouting. In bloom, it's enchanting.

Mertensia virginica Virginia bluebells

Needs: part or full shade, moist to damp, rich soil

Character: curling spikes of lavender buds open to blue bell-like flowers, oval leaves, to 2 feet

Season of bloom: spring

Hardiness: zone 3

Like most wildflowers, these are most effective in masses. Use them in drifts between shrubs or among taller perennials. Dies to the ground by midsummer.

Mimulus guttatus common monkey flower

Needs: sun or part shade, moist to wet soil

Character: bright yellow tubular flowers, spreading plant to $1^1/_2$ feet

Season of bloom: summer

Hardiness: zone 5

This makes a cheery ground cover, brightening damp areas with its flowers like sunny faces. Easy from seed.

Monarda didyma bee balm, Oswego tea

Needs: sun or light shade, moist to wet soil

Character: clusters of long, tubular flowers in pinks and reds, sometimes white or violet

Season of bloom: summer

Hardiness: zone 4

Possible drawbacks: subject to mildew when allowed to dry out and in high humidity

Much loved by hummingbirds, these mint relatives have leaves that make a good herbal tea. If you think mildew may be a problem, search out new, resistant varieties such as 'Violet Queen' and 'Marshall's Delight'.

Physostegia virginiana false dragonhead, obedient plant

> Needs: sun or part shade, moist to damp soil
>
> Character: dense spikes of purplish pink or white flowers that look like tiny snapdragons, 2–3 feet
>
> Season of bloom: late summer to fall
>
> Hardiness: zones 2–3

This can extend your flower gardening into fall, it's bright flowers welcome as summer fades. If you'd rather not have purple-pink, look for 'Bouquet Rose' or other varieties with rose-pink blooms.

Primula japonica Japanese primrose

> Needs: part shade, wet soil
>
> Character: $2^1/_2$-foot stems with whorls of white, pink, or purple flowers, 6-inch leaves
>
> Season of bloom: spring through summer
>
> Hardiness: zone 5

This is one of the plants that bring sighs of envy from other gardeners, especially when planted in quantity. Will grow in the edge of ponds, even in shallow water.

Thalictrum aquilegifolium meadow rue

> Needs: sun or part shade, dry, moist, or wet soil
>
> Character: fluffy heads of purple or white flowers, leaves divided into rounded leaflets similar to columbine (*Aquilegia*), to 5 feet
>
> Season of bloom: late spring or summer
>
> Hardiness: zone 4

Tall but airy, this is an excellent plant for almost any situation. It is more heat-tolerant than other meadow rues.

Trollius europaeus globeflower

> Needs: sun to part shade, rich, moist soil, regular watering
>
> Character: round, single, lemon-yellow, gold, or orange blossoms, deep green cut foliage, 2–3 feet
>
> Season of bloom: spring

Hardiness: zone 4

Possible drawbacks: dislikes heat

Globeflowers love damp soil and are some of the most elegant flowers available for the edge of a pond, having the air of a traditional perennial garden rather than a wild-flower meadow.

Vines

Aristolochia macrophylla Dutchman's pipe

Method of climbing: twining stems

Needs: sun to full shade, any soil, average or extra water

Character: large, heart-shaped leaves with 1¹/₂-inch purplish brown flowers shaped like an old-fashioned pipe

Season of bloom: late spring or early summer

Hardiness: zones 4–10

Green Tip

Want more ideas on vines and are willing to hunt a little? Consult one of the gardening encyclopedias listed in chapter 25. There are a few, but none are commonly available.

A vigorous vine whose leaves are excellent for screening, useful in moist or shady situations where few other vines flourish. Deciduous. This is a favorite of the pipevine swallowtail butterfly.

Trees and Shrubs

Clethra alnifolia summersweet, sweet pepper bush

Needs: part shade, moist to wet soil

Character: spikes of sweet-scented, tiny white or pink flowers, up to 8 feet tall

Season of bloom: summer

Hardiness: zone 3

A rounded, bushy shrub, handsome even when not in bloom. Plant it where you can enjoy the scent as you walk by.

Magnolia grandiflora southern magnolia, bull bay

> Needs: sun, moist to wet soil
>
> Character: huge, white fragrant flowers, glossy green leaves, 50–80 feet
>
> Season of bloom: summer, fall
>
> Hardiness: zone 7

A well-known tree in the south, this magnolia has almost everything: good-looking leaves, sweet lemony fragrance, and showy blossoms.

Paulownia tomentosa empress tree

> Needs: sun, moist to wet soil
>
> Character: upright clusters of tubular, lavender-blue spotted flowers, large leaves, fast-growing to 45 feet or more
>
> Season of bloom: early spring
>
> Hardiness: zone 5
>
> Possible drawbacks: invasive roots

Few trees grow faster than this one, sometimes 6 feet in a year. The flowers are both large and conspicuous, giving a show in spring that makes the greedy roots worth the trouble they cause. Site it away from drains, however.

Viburnum opulus European cranberry bush

> Needs: sun, moist to wet soil
>
> Character: white clusters of flowers, small fertile blooms surrounded by larger sterile ones, followed by red fruit, maplelike leaves, to 12 feet
>
> Season of bloom: spring
>
> Hardiness: zone 3

The lace-cap clusters of flowers are unusual and decorative, but the clear glossy red of the fruit is almost as lovely.

The Least You Need to Know

➤ Wet soil is often poorly oxygenated. The better the drainage, even if wetted by constant drips, the more kind of plants you can grow.

➤ You can make your own bog using pond liner or other moisture barrier. Fill with highly organic, somewhat acid soil and water when dry.

➤ Easy annuals for wet soil: baby-blue-eyes (*Nemophila*), forget-me-nots (*Myosotis*).

➤ Easy bulbs and perennials for wet soil: camas (*Camassia*), calla (*Zantedeschia*), New England aster, joe-pye weed (*Eupatorium*), yellow flag (*Iris pseudacorus*), meadow rue (*Thalictrum*).

➤ Easy vines, trees, and shrubs for wet soil: dutchman's pipe (*Aristolochia*), European cranberry bush (*Viburnum*), empress tree (*Paulownia*).

Chapter 21

Barrels, Tubs, and Pots

In This Chapter

➤ Setting the stage with pots and planters

➤ Soil is the foundation

➤ Potted plant care

➤ Choosing plants

➤ A bouquet of popular plants for pots

Containers are artificial environments. You are responsible for providing proper soil, moisture, and nutrients as well as occasional weeding and tidying up. You have more control over the conditions plants receive, but may spend more hours providing them.

On the other hand, containers can bring flowers into places less plant-friendly than a backyard, areas such as decks, entryways, windowsills, and rooftops. You can even hang them from beams and ceilings.

They also offer exceptional design possibilities. From choosing the right pot or planter to adding trailing lobelia to a window box of petunias and marigolds, you're in charge of shaping a small world, an artistic composition. Here's how to do it successfully.

Your Container Sets the Mood

Start by choosing a frame for your picture, one that will suit with its surroundings and set the tone, formal, informal, or offbeat.

Take Care!

Warm weather and constantly moist soil can cause roots to rot. If a plant droops suddenly even though the soil isn't dry, tip it out of its pot and look at the roots. Chances are they'll be brown and decaying. The plant has few roots left to supply the leaves with moisture so it wilts just like one you forgot to water.

Garden Talk

The term *rootbound* means that the roots have reached the side of the pot, and, having nowhere else to go, are circling around the edge, perhaps even bending back into the soil. Before you plant into a larger pot or into the garden, gently pull them free or take a knife and cut the mat of roots in several places. This will persuade them to reach out into new soil.

What can you use for planting? Almost anything that will hold soil, though there are a few requirements. Before you put a plant in anything, from an old shoe to a three-hundred-dollar Italian terra-cotta urn, make sure the container meets these requirements.

The Basics of Pots

Good drainage is critical. The roots of most plants will rot if they are subjected to waterlogged, poorly aerated soil. Make sure your container has at least one hole in the bottom where water can drain out.

This also means that if there's a saucer underneath, the pot must be raised slightly on small rocks or bricks so any standing water stays beneath. If you're growing bog plants, however, the deeper the saucer of water the better. Keep it filled and your plants will stay pleasantly soggy.

Will you be transplanting a growing shrub or clump of perennials to a larger size pot? Make sure that the sides of the pot are straight so that the root ball can slip out easily. Forego the lovely urn-shaped containers with narrow mouths or plant them with annuals. Or plan on sacrificing the plant when it gets rootbound.

Large containers hold moisture longer than smaller ones. If you want to cut your watering time to a minimum, use the largest ones you can afford. Tiny pots may be cute, but unless you're growing sedums or other drought-tolerant plants, pass them up in favor of more substantial vessels.

On the other hand, weight may be a factor. Hanging planters should be made of a material that can be lifted easily, even when filled with soil. Barrels and tubs on a deck or roof garden shouldn't stress the supports beneath them. Most pots need to be moved occasionally, so consider your back when you buy them.

Materials and Other Considerations

Containers are much like furniture. They both complement the surrounding decor and make a statement themselves. Some are bold attention-grabbers. Some add subtle lines among surrounding foliage. But unless they're totally covered by greenery and flowers, they're on display. Here are some types available.

Clay is one of the most attractive materials available. It blends well with both flowers and greenery and can look informal or dignified depending on the shape.

One of its benefits is that you can find pots in all shapes, rectangular, square, with small legs or flat, deep or shallow, or disguised as frogs, birds, or even kangaroos.

Clay pots, however, dry out more quickly than those made of plastic or other impermeable material. This can be an advantage if you're growing cacti or succulents or a disadvantage if you're forgetful about watering. If your pots need to be able to hold moisture for long periods, find a nonporous material. Planters at a weekend cottage, for instance, need to be able to hold moisture between Saturday waterings. If you want a pot for year-round display, make sure that it's weatherproof. Many clay containers crack when exposed to winter weather.

Garden Talk

Terra-cotta is an Italian term meaning "baked earth" and is often used as a synonym for clay. Pots fired at high temperatures are most durable.

Some pots are glazed or painted, becoming both less permeable and more weather-resistant. These can be artistic, gaudy or elegant. Generally more expensive than unglazed clay, they may be worth the price if you want an accent for a special place.

Wood is well suited to informal areas, and looks great with almost any plant. It is, however, subject to decay. Treat it with a stain or other preservative, or paint it.

If you want a short-term, inexpensive container, try a fiber pot, often available from nurseries who use them for potting trees and shrubs. These last a year or two, though paint can add many months to their life span.

Black plastic nursery pots, also available from nurseries, aren't glamorous but if you plant lots of trailing flowers few people will notice the plastic. You can also pop them inside baskets, brass kettles, or other nondraining containers. Use a saucer to catch drips, but be sure the pot is raised enough to allow water to pool below it rather than keeping the soil soaked.

Other, more handsome, pots made of fiberglass, plastic, or other synthetic material are commonly available. These may not have the elegance of terra-cotta, but they are usually lightweight, nonporous, durable and less expensive.

Floral Lore

Container gardening has a long history. The ancient Egyptians used clay containers and the Romans planted trees and shrubs in large terra-cotta olive oil jars called *dolia*.

Concrete is heavy but weatherproof and often attractive, especially when set with small pebbles or given a rough, woodlike texture. It's a good material for very large containers such as those needed for small trees.

In contrast, wire baskets lined with moss are exceptionally light and can have starts of annuals planted all over their surface. They need close attention to watering, however, and so are best used in cool summer areas.

What about the strange and unusual? Washtubs, sinks, old pots, tin cans, hollowed logs, and pumice rocks, just about anything you can think of has been used for holding plants. Even old shoes have been planted with succulents and annuals.

Containers may be as temporary as a milk carton planted with seeds on a windowsill or as durable as a hollowed stone. As long as water can drain away, they will work.

Designing with Pots

When placing and planting containers, consider first the background it will be seen against. If you want the pot to be on display, put it against a simple, uncluttered wall or fence. If you want a more understated effect, use it among other plants, perhaps as an accent in a garden bed.

The more ornate the container, the less complicated the background needs to be. A pot with floral designs painted on it will be lost in front of an intricate trellis. Instead, choose an expanse of dull concrete or siding that needs to be livened up. If the trellis is what you have, stick with a pot of a solid color, perhaps one whose outline is lushly curved.

A single large planter will be effective on its own. In fact, it may be a striking accent. Smaller pots, however, may need to be bunched together to be noticed at all. They may make a poor show when scattered around an area, but seem lively and purposeful when clustered in one place. They'll also be easier to water.

When choosing plants, balance a flamboyant pot with simple lines and a plain one with an prodigality of colors and textures. The pot with floral designs, for instance, needs a single kind of plant, perhaps a marguerite daisy whose finely cut foliage and white or yellow flowers can liven up a dull background without competing with the pot.

If you want the elegant lines or glaze of a special vessel to stand out, choose a plant with a plain texture, perhaps an agapanthus whose narrow curving foliage might seem a little dull in a black plastic. A plain cube or box-shaped planter, on the other hand, might need intricate, fernlike leaves or a profusion of small flowers to bring it to life.

Plain planters can set off intricate compositions of color and texture. Multicolored flowers such as nemesia are excellent when combined with others that share some of the same hues. Blue, small-flowered lobelia, purple, large-flowered petunias, yellow marigolds (*Tagetes*), and gray-leafed dusty miller is a popular combination.

Green Tip

The subtle grays and blue-greens of succulents are particularly lovely when set off by terra-cotta. They grow happily in small spaces, so are well suited for shallow bowls and animal-shaped pots.

Or you can choose a single color and repeat it in different sizes and shapes. Rose-pink impatiens combined with tiny-flowered pink sweet alyssum (*Lobularia*) or the pink-edged leaves of Hawaiian ti plants (*Cordyline terminalis*) can be very effective.

Variegated leaves, such as those of the ti, make excellent fillers in pots. Coleus has red, orange, and yellow shades to add, polka-dot plant (*Hypoestes phyllostachya*) has pink, hosta comes in cream or yellow varieties, and New Zealand flax (*Phormium*) comes in both yellow and red.

If you're planting a large container, you can use evergreen shrubs for year-round interest, or choose a small tree with a graceful branching pattern. Use trailing plants to soften the edge, provide flowers at a different season or in a different color, and contribute a contrasting foliage texture.

Feel free to duplicate designs you see in magazines or books. This is, in fact, a good way to start. A list of plants is usually provided and you can take advantage of someone else's experience by using them. Make sure, though, that the plants suit your climate, whether cool or warm and muggy.

Soil Considerations

Planters are enclosed spaces, interior environments. Just as the air in a room may become stuffy, the soil in a pot can become stale without a constant renewal of air. It needs to be lighter and more porous than garden soil.

Garden Talk

Vermiculite and perlite are both materials that have been heated and expanded, something like popcorn. They hold both air and water.

Light and porous soils, however, are rarely rich in nutrients. This one of the reasons why container plants need regular fertilizing. The other is that roots are restricted to this small area, prevented from seeking outward for better soil.

Packaged soil mixes are usually adequate. Some have little else but peat moss and perlite or vermiculite, both artificial lightweight substitutes for sand, but work well if fertilized frequently. Add more perlite or vermiculite if you're planting succulents or cacti.

Green Tip

Soil polymers are gellike granules that absorb several hundred times their weight in water. Polyacrylamide is the longest-lasting material. Expand the granules with water, then add to soil according to the manufacturer's directions.

Mixes have the advantage of being sterile, readily available, and not too expensive if you're planting an occasional pot or two. If you're filling large numbers of pots, you can make up your own mixture of peat moss, soil, and vermiculite, or add extras to a packaged mix. Steer manure is a possible addition. So is finely ground bark. Experiment with different proportions until you have a loose, fast-draining, fibrous mix.

If you can't water faithfully, you may want to add special super absorbent soil polymers that swell when wet, releasing their moisture to the surrounding soil as it dries out. These can mean the difference between shriveling and survival to plants at weekend cottages. Just be sure to allow them a good drying out period. You could easily overwater pots treated with these.

Potted Plants Need Extra Care

It's easy to forget them, until you see wilted leaves or yellowed foliage. How do you usually jog your memory? With notes on a bulletin board? With reminders in a weekly calendar? Whatever method works for you, use it as soon as you put out your container garden. A few minutes of regular maintenance a week can keep it growing well.

Water Regularly

Water is, of course, a constant concern. Rain helps, but leaves may shelter the pot from all but a small soaking. A well-filled planter may have more roots per square inch than a garden bed, all of them eager for moisture. You're the supplier.

Water thoroughly, until you see some draining out of the pot. This ensures that all the soil is moistened. If the soil is very dry and the root ball has pulled away from the sides, put the container in a pail of water and soak it an hour or two. Then leave it alone until the top of the soil feels dry. Alternating soaking and drying will give the roots both the water and the oxygen necessary for growth.

Fertilize Lightly and Often

Many fertilizers are available. You can add a dilute solution of nutrients every time you water or spread small pellets of a slow-release fertilizer once a season. Or you can fertilize monthly. Choose the method that seems easiest and most convenient, the one you'd have least trouble remembering.

Which kind? These plants are dependent on you for feeding, since their soil mix contains few if any of the minerals usually found in garden dirt. Give them the most complete fertilizer you can, including micronutrients. Give them a feast, but not, however, one that contains too much nitrogen. This element promotes rapid leafy growth and, if used alone, can suppress flowering. A balanced fertilizer, 10-10-10 or 20-20-20, is usually best. See chapter 8 for details on fertilizers.

Take Care!

Fertilizers may build up in potted soil, especially if small amounts of water are added infrequently. Be sure to flush the soil with water occasionally. To do this, just water the plant with more water than usual, until water flows freely out the bottom.

Choosing Plants

There are so many plants available, aisles and aisles of them at a large nursery. How can you find a few that are willing to grow quickly and bloom exuberantly?

You could ask one of the nursery professionals for advice, preferably during a slow period. You could bring a picture with you and try to match its design. You could examine every tag and collect a small group of possibilities in a corner.

Before you buy, however, you have some factors to consider.

Winter Hardiness

Unless you're planting annuals exclusively, resistance to damage during coldest winters is important. Being surrounded by air rather than soil, roots in pots are more susceptible to injury than those planted in the ground. This may alter their hardiness by a zone or more. Ask for local advice.

Containment Can be an Advantage

Some plants are just too vigorous for most gardens. They'll grow so quickly that they overrun everything else. But isn't this what you want? For toughness and adaptability, few others can equal these plants. Look for those listed in encyclopedias as invasive. Here are some suggestions.

Ground Covers and Perennials

➤ *Aegopodium podagraria* bishop's weed

➤ *Campanula poscharskyana* Siberian bellflower

➤ *Cerastium tomentosum* now-in-summer

➤ *Lamium maculatum* dead nettle

➤ *Lysimachia nummularia* moneywort, creeping Jenny

➤ *Polygonum* knotweed

➤ *Tanacetum* tansy

Vines

➤ *Lonicera japonica* Japanese honeysuckle

➤ *Polygonum aubertii* silver lace vine

Green Tip

Bog plants can be simple to grow. A deep saucer is easily kept filled with water, and will keep a pot full of wet-soil-tolerant plants quite happy. Look in chapter 20 for possibilities.

Annuals, Perennials, and Bulbs

Here are some of the most popular flowering plants for containers. You can, of course, add nonflowering types for texture and foliage color. You can experiment with wild or peaceful color combinations. You're the designer. Enjoy yourself.

Agapanthus africanus lily of the Nile

Needs: sun to part shade, regular to occasional watering

Character: heads of large, blue, tubular flowers on $2^1/_2$ foot stems, straplike leaves

Season of bloom: summer

Hardiness: zone 6

This has a sense of simplicity in its arching leaves and whorls of flowers. Excellent for substantial containers.

Begonia tuberus begonia

Needs: part shade, rich soil, regular watering

Character: large roselike leaves in shades of pink, red, yellow, and orange, upright or trailing stems with large leaves

Season of bloom: summer

Hardiness: zone 9

Possible drawbacks: subject to mildew, dislikes heat and low humidity

These give glorious pure color in quantity, a much-appreciated quality in shade. In colder areas, buy the tubers and start them indoors in spring, or buy small plants in bloom. Good air circulation reduces the possibility of mildew.

Chrysanthenum × ***morifolium*** florist's chrysanthemum

> Needs: sun, rich, well-drained soil, regular watering
>
> Character: many flower forms, from single daisies to many-petaled doubles, petals sometimes narrow, spiderlike, or spooned, in yellow, gold, and bronze, sometimes pink and burgundy, 1–3 feet, depending on variety
>
> Season of bloom: late summer, fall
>
> Hardiness: zone 5
>
> Possible drawbacks: many varieties need pinching to bush out, some need staking

Mums seem the perfect autumn flower, their rich tints echoing the fall leaves. If you choose dwarf varieties and give them plenty of nutrients, you'll find them easy and undemanding.

Cymbalaria muralis Kenilworth ivy

> Needs: shade to part shade, average soil, tolerates alkaline soil, regular to little water
>
> Character: round, scalloped leaves are accompanied by tiny lilac flowers that look like miniature snapdragons
>
> Season of bloom: summer
>
> Hardiness: zone 3

A quick-growing, delicate trailer often sold as an annual for hanging baskets. Often seeds itself into cracks in walls and pavement.

Fuchsia × ***hybrida*** fuchsia

> Needs: part shade, rich soil, regular watering
>
> Character: hanging, bell-like or double flowers, often with contrasting sepals, usually in shades of pink to purple and white, upright or trailing stems
>
> Season of bloom: summer
>
> Hardiness: zone 10
>
> Possible drawbacks: dislikes dry heat

Garden Talk

The term *sepal* refers to the usually leaflike, sometimes petallike, parts of the flower just outside the petals. In fuchsias, for instance, they are brightly colored, flaring backward above the hanging petals. In a rose, they are small, green, and inconspicuous.

281

Often seen in hanging baskets, fuchsias also come in upright forms that may be planted in shady beds. They come in hundreds of varieties, so look around to find some favorites.

Lilium true lilies

> Needs: sun (part shade in hottest areas) though they like shade over the roots, average well-drained to good soil, regular water
>
> Character: a thousand shades in many forms, from spires of small, hanging, bell-like flowers, to huge trumpets and flat, upward-facing stars, all on strong stems from 2–8 feet tall, wind-resistant
>
> Season of bloom: late spring to early fall
>
> Hardiness: zone varies according to group, see chapter 12 for details on other hybrids

The Asiatic hybrids are easiest and do well in pots. They bloom from May to early July and are hardy to zone 3. Usually upward-facing, often with a light fragrance, these have myriad colors to choose from.

Shrubs

Remember, these are less hardy in containers than in the ground because their roots are more exposed and lack an insulating blanket of soil around them. If in doubt, move them into a garage or other sheltered area during coldest weather.

Brugmansia and ***Datura*** angel's trumpet

> Needs: sun or shade, regular watering
>
> Character: upfacing or hanging trumpetlike flowers, white, pink, or yellow, large leaves
>
> Season of bloom: summer, fall
>
> Hardiness: zone 10
>
> Possible drawbacks: all parts are poisonous including contact with the leaves

This will wow your friends! Big enough to take center stage on a large patio, these have an elegance that makes them showy but not gaudy.

Angel's trumpet is a tender shrub that will grow well in pots in colder areas. In fall, bring it into a greenhouse or put it by a sunny window.

Rhododendron azalea, rhododendron

> Needs: part shade, good, loose, acid soil, regular watering
>
> Character: tubular to flat blossoms in many colors and shades, large or small leaves, some with attractive felty undersides, from 1–20 feet depending on variety; evergreen or deciduous
>
> Season of bloom: spring to early summer
>
> Hardiness: zones vary by species and variety
>
> Possible drawbacks: leaves are poisonous

Their dense, fibrous root system makes even the largest species of rhododendrons good candidates for containers. Many shades and leaf textures available, so look around before you buy one.

Camellia japonica camellia

> Needs: part shade, rich, well-drained, slightly acid soil, regular to occasional watering

> Character: tidy, slightly waxy, roselike flowers, usually shades of pink, single or double, glossy leaves, usually 6–12 feet, depending on variety

> Season of bloom: spring

> Hardiness: zone 7

Camellias also have dense root systems that adapt well to life in planters. They make dense bushes that may be covered with blooms if not given too much shade. Look for varieties whose blooms drop off cleanly rather than turning brown on the branch.

Lantana hybrids lantana

> Needs: sun, average to poor soil, occasional watering

> Character: bright clusters of tiny blossoms, yellow, pink, purple, cream, orange, or red on a sprawling plant, 2–4 feet

> Season of bloom: all year in frost-free areas

> Hardiness: zone 8

> Possible drawbacks: fruits are poisonous

Few plants give as much color for as little effort as this. Far from demanding rich soil, it will withhold its blossoms if either fertilizer or water are too plentiful. Many varieties available, multicolored or single-hued. Its long bloom season and quick growth makes it valuable as an annual in cold-winter areas.

Rosa miniature roses

> Needs: sun, rich, well-drained soil, regular watering

> Character: inch-wide blossoms in many colors, small leaves, well-branched bushes, to $1^1/_2$ feet

> Season of bloom: summer

> Hardiness: zone 6, zone 5 with protection

These small-flowered roses are both attractive and disease-resistant. Buy them in bloom if you can, so you can choose between the numerous shades available.

The Least You Need to Know

➤ Make sure your pot has at least one drainage hole. Roots can rot in wet soil.

➤ Use porous pots like clay for plants that don't mind dry soil and nonporous ones for those that need even moisture.

➤ Use simple plantings in many-colored pots and sparsely decorated containers for flamboyant combinations of flowers.

➤ Use a loose, well-aerated soil mix.

➤ Use plants one zone hardier than normal if they are to survive over the winter.

Part 4
Expanding Your Enjoyment

Why make a garden and then hurry from house to car without enjoying it? Why look at it only through a window? Here are some easy ideas for bringing a flower bed into your life.

You've never watched birds? Plant a butterfly bush and you'll have both humming-birds and butterflies to give you pleasure. You've never considered yourself a flower arranger? Take some pruning shears into the garden, pop the blooms you cut into a glass jar and discover the joy of seeing flowers at your breakfast table. The possibilities are endless.

Chapter 22

For the Birds (and Butterflies)

In This Chapter

➤ Hummingbirds love flowers

➤ Butterflies love flowers, too

➤ A bouquet for the birds

➤ A bouquet for the butterflies

➤ A bouquet for the caterpillars

A garden full of flowers is a feast, but a garden with hummingbirds and butterflies darting and dipping among the blossoms is like a smorgasbord of desserts, an irresistible celebration.

Some people may have reservations about snakes, toads, and salamanders in their garden, but few would turn away the brilliant butterflies, no more than they would the flowers themselves, or the hummingbirds with their iridescent coloring and ability to hover or dash from one spot to another.

How can you attract these easy to appreciate wild creatures? Give them what they need, including shelter and food for hungry caterpillars. With a little forethought and consideration for their necessities of life, you can have both hummingbirds and butterflies visiting your flowers in abundance.

How to Invite Hummingbirds

Just as you need food, water, and shelter, so hummingbirds have similar needs. Look at your garden from their point of view. Are there flowers to provide nectar and small insects? Is there a place to nest? Is there water for bathing?

A feeder of sugar water may draw hummingbirds close to your window, but they need a variety of foods including both insects and flower nectar, perhaps even sap running down a tree trunk.

When their favorite flowers are blooming, they'll usually choose the plant over the feeder. You might be tempted to plant masses of such well-known hummingbird favorites as bee balm and cardinal flower. Don't. These are in bloom for only a short period each summer. Choose a diversity of perennials, annuals, and shrubs with blooming periods that overlap, then add a feeder for reliability.

Though hummingbirds are certainly attracted to red, they will take nectar from flowers of many different colors. Make sure you have enough red plants to be noticed, but don't restrict yourself to a scarlet-flowered garden.

If you can, tolerate some of the weeds and wild plants that many birds and butterflies use as food. Perhaps a back corner the yard could be exempted from tidying. Or you could leave a small part of the lawn unmown and full of flowers. Or you could plant a wildflower meadow.

Nectar is a hummingbird staple, but insects provide much-needed extra nutrition. Don't routinely spray your garden for bugs. If you can, tolerate those small spiders and the other crawlies. The birds will be most grateful.

Take Care!

Be aware, that a praying mantis is capable of capturing an adult hummingbird with a quick attack. Beneficial as the mantis is in most gardens, consider it a pest when you're enticing hummingbirds to visit.

Shelter is important for nesting, and parents usually choose dense, twiggy bushes to give protection to baby birds. Surround the garden with suitable shrubs and you may have the pleasure of a nesting pair making their home with you.

An adult male hummingbird can be very territorial, attacking other birds, even his own chicks, when they approach a food source he considers to be his. Try to have feeders and hummingbird flowers scattered around the yard, out of sight of each other. That way a male standing guard on one won't be controlling food for others.

Hummingbirds get much of their liquid from nectar, but they also enjoy bathing in a fine spray of water. You can buy small diameter hoses similar to drip-irrigation lines with an attachment that uses only a small amount of water but emits a constant burst of tiny drops. Look for them at stores that sell bird feeding supplies.

How to Invite Butterflies

Many of the flowers that hummingbirds enjoy are also attractive to butterflies. There are, of course, a few other factors to consider. Butterflies usually sit on flower to sip nectar, so flat, easily available blossoms such as daisies are especially good for them.

Give Them Flowers, Sun, and Shelter

Flowers are an obvious butterfly attractant. Many, but not all species, sip nectar from the blossoms. Try to have bloom times overlap so that you have them available all season. Most butterflies, like hummingbirds, need reliable food sources.

Large numbers of a single plant are most easily found by a wandering butterfly. Instead of one aster, group five or ten of them together. Sow nine square feet of sweet alyssum (*Lobularia*) instead of two. Create a large flower bed instead of a small strip.

Which flowers will butterflies in your area like? That depends on the species that's likely to be hanging around. Milkweed, a favorite of monarchs, is useless in areas without the butterflies that prefer it.

Butterflies like flat clusters of flowers that are easily for them to sit on as they search for nectar.

Take Care!

Using an overhead sprinkler can discourage butterflies. They'll avoid your garden if you water during midday sunny flying times. They rarely get out and about before the air warms, so early morning is a better time to soak your garden. This also reduces the risk of fungus diseases.

Get local advice. First find out what common species you can expect to visit your garden, then get a list of the flowers they enjoy.

Choose a sunny area for your garden. Not being warm-blooded animals, butterflies need patches of warm sunlight to sit in on cool mornings. They fly well only after their body temperatures rises. Rocks that catch the heat are also welcome.

Also provide shelter from the wind. A hedge is useful, especially since a loose hedge allows air to filter through, rather than creating a solid barrier behind which eddies form. Fences and walls are also useful.

Do they need water? Some species like to congregate at mud puddles, but many need only nectar.

Don't Forget to Feed the Caterpillars

One of the challenges of butterfly gardening is the easy-to-forget fact that you must consider both larval and adult forms. No caterpillars, no butterflies.

You may certainly attract splashy, brilliant butterflies that have passed their caterpillar stage in a nearby field, but with housing developments taking over vacant, nearly wild land, don't bet on that pleasant state continuing.

Take Care!

Not only are both larva and adult forms extremely susceptible to pesticides and herbicides, but some of the best caterpillar food plants are those many people consider to be weeds.

While some larval host plants are garden ornamentals, many others are trees and shrubs, or common inhabitants of local meadows. While butterflies are often eclectic in their tastes, caterpillars tend to be more specific. Eggs are laid on plants that will provide proper food, and the caterpillar does little roaming. Eating and growing big enough to metamorphose are its main goals in life.

If you have room, a small wild area where some of the less tidy host plants can make themselves at home will benefit birds as well as butterflies. It can become an insect-rich shelter for all wildlife.

Will they attack your ornamental plants? No. Most destructive caterpillars are the larval stage of moths. Some, certainly, turn into butterflies, but their numbers and appetites are rarely large enough to be noticed.

A number of butterflies overwinter as eggs or in a chrysalis (also called a pupa). If you're serious about gardening for butterflies, put off fall cleanup until the following spring to avoid removing them. This, by the way, is an excellent excuse to do less work.

Turn to the back of this chapter for a list of common larval food plants.

Swear off Pesticide Use

Nothing cuts a butterfly population like chemicals. Even some organic sprays such as *Bacillus thuringinensis*, used against destructive caterpillars, should be banned from your garden. If you feel that you need to spray, perhaps you should consider removing the troublesome plant and replace it with something disease-resistant.

Flowers for Hummingbirds

Here are popular nectar sources. Remember that the insects attracted to these plants are also important, so even if you use a feeder add some of these also.

Annuals and Perennials

Aguilegia	columbine
Alcea	hollyhock
Chaenomeles	flowering quince
Cleome	spider flower
Crocosmia 'Lucifer'	crocosmia hybrid
Fuchsia × *hybrida*	fuchsia
Heuchera sanguinea	coralbells
Impatiens	impatiens
Lantana camara	lantana
Lobelia cardinalis	cardinal flower
Monarda didyma	bee balm
Nepeta × *faassenii*	catmint
Nicotania alata	flowering tobacco
Penstemon	beardtongue
Petunia × *hybrida*	petunia
Phaseolus coccineus	scarlet runner bean
Salvia coccinea	red salvia
Tropaeolum majus	nasturtium

Trees and Shrubs

Aesculus × carnea	red horse chestnut
Alibizia julibrissin	silk tree, mimosa
Buddleia davidii	butterfly bush
Lonicera	honeysuckle
Malus	apple, crab apple
Rhododendron	rhododendron, azalea
Weigela	weigela

Vines

Campsis radicans	trumpet creeper
Ipomea	morning glory
Lonicera	honeysuckle

Flowers for Butterflies

All of the previous lists will be welcomed by butterflies as well as hummingbirds. Simply add the following to the list.

Annuals and Perennials

Achillea	yarrow
Ajuga	bugleweed
Armeria maritima	thrift
Aster	aster
Chrysanthemum	chrysanthemum
Coreopsis	coreopsis
Dianthus	pinks, carnations
Eupatorium maculatum	joe-pye weed
Helianthemum	sun rose
Hemerocallis	daylily
Hyacinthoides	English bluebells

Lobularia maritima	sweet alyssum
Origanum	oregano
Phlox	phlox
Scabiosa	pincushion flower
Sedum	sedum
Solidago	goldenrod
Tanacetum	feverfew
Thymus	thyme

Vines

Aristolochia macrophylla	Dutchman's pipe

Trees and Shrubs

Caryopteris	bluebeard
Escallonia	escallonia
Lavandula angustifolia	lavender
Potentilla	potentilla
Syringa	lilac
Viburnum	viburnum

Plants to Host Caterpillars

Some of these may host only a few species of butterflies. Get local advice on which ones are most useful in your area. In general, native plants are your best bet. The butterfly population has evolved with the native flora and they are well suited to each other.

Grasses and Sedges

Antirrhinum	snapdragons
Aster	aster
Betula	birch
Ceanothus	blue blossom, wild lilac
Celtis	hackberry

Cirsium	thistles
Crataegus	hawthorn
Daucus carota	Queen Anne's lace
Dicentra	bleeding heart
Lupinus	lupines
Malva	mallow
Medicago	alfalfa
Petroselinum	parsley
Plantago	plantain
Populus	aspen, cottonwood
Prunus	wild plum
Quercus	oak
Rumex	sorrel, dock
Salix	willow
Urtica dioica	stinging nettle
Viburnum	viburnum
Vicia	vetch
Viola	violet

The Least You Need to Know

➤ Hummingbirds are attracted to red, but they enjoy nectar from flowers of many other colors also.

➤ Hummingbirds need the nutrition given by small insects found in blossoms. Sugar water solutions are a supplement not a replacement for flowers.

➤ Plan your butterfly garden for a sunny area. Butterflies rarely visit shady gardens.

➤ Find out which butterflies frequent your area and plan your garden to include their favorites.

➤ Feed caterpillars as well as butterflies. Their tastes are quite different. Again, find out what your local species enjoy and provide it.

Chapter 23

Bringing the Garden Indoors

In This Chapter

➤ Flowers for vases

➤ Easy dried flowers

➤ Forcing bulbs and branches

➤ Flowers in salads and soups

➤ Houseplants from the garden

When you create a garden of flowers, why not get all the pleasure you can out of it? With just a few snips taken as you're wandering, you can have flowers for the table or the salad. You can dry many others for long-lasting bouquets with just a few more minutes trouble. And when the temperature outside dips below freezing, a few Impatiens or fibrous Begonias, quickly dug and potted, can continue the show in your living room.

Some plants are better for cut flowers than other, of course. And knowing which flowers are edible and which are poisonous can prevent unpleasant mistakes. A bit of knowledge here, as in most subjects, can make the extra few minutes seem relaxed and enjoyable rather than simply another chore.

Here are ideas for using the fruits of your gardening labors to bring color and life to your house, from cutting branches of forsythia to provide a display a week or two before they open outdoors, to potting a half-dozen bulbs for growing indoors. Here are ideas for getting the most out of your garden.

Blossoms and Branches for Fresh Arrangements

A trip to any florist's will soon increase your appreciation for the flowers in your own garden. Beautiful as they may be, florist's arrangements are expensive. One summer's flowers on a rose bush, for instance, may be worth more than the purchase price of both the bush and any fertilizer you've used.

And flowers bring life to a room. No wonder those without gardens spend extra money for the privilege of enjoying them close up. Few man-made objects can equal the subtle shading in a chrysanthemum, the vivid blue of a spike of delphinium, or the cheerfulness of a bowl of daisies.

And fragrance is the specialty of flowers. Long-lasting lavender, spicy or sweet rose, sweet peas, lilies, jonquils, and many more all add a presence that can't be duplicated artificially.

The Basics of Harvesting Flowers

To get the most from cut flowers, you need to treat them properly. Let's start with the basics of cutting.

For long life indoors, blooms need to stay firm and filled with water. That means a constant supply through the stem. Water needs to enter the stem easily at the base, entering the tubelike vessels that carry sap to the leaves and flowers. Keeping these channels open starts with using a sharp tool when cutting.

Green Tip

Pay attention to which blossoms seem to complement each other. You may find that perennials on opposite sides of the yard seem to light up when placed side by side. Note these discoveries down for next year.

You can use either a knife or pruning shears, but make sure that whatever you use cuts rather than crushes the stem. If you tear some of the tissue as you gather, cut it again with a sharp knife when you get indoors.

When cutting any flower stalk, treat it as a pruning operation. Take the whole stalk off at the base and shorten it later if it's too long. Remove any extra leaves that would be covered by water in a vase.

When taking roses or other flowering branchlets, always cut to a bud that faces outward. A new branch will sprout from below the bud so you need to choose one that will grow in the proper direction. Never leave a stub. This will simply die back to the next bud, possibly further.

Conditioning Your Blooms

It's best to get stems into water as soon as possible. If you can't carry a bucket with you as you roam around the garden, be sure to put them into a large container as soon as you go inside. Again, always treat the tubelike vessel openings at the base of the stem carefully. You want to keep them open and able to transport water.

You should have six inches to a foot of lukewarm water in the container, enough to thoroughly saturate the stems. Let the flowers sit in this water for a few hours or overnight, then put them in vases, bowls, jars, bottles, or other containers.

For longest blossom life, add commercially available cut flower food to this water or a homemade mixture of 1 tablespoon sugar, 2 teaspoons chlorine bleach, and 1 teaspoon vinegar for each half gallon of water. The sugar gives energy, the vinegar keeps the water acid, and the bleach keeps vessel-blocking bacteria from forming.

Be aware that daffodils have a poison that dissolves in water, injuring other blooms. Keep them by themselves.

Arranging the Flowers

Flower arrangement can be a high art or a professional skill. It can also be a casual gathering of whatever is available. How much time you want to spend on it is entirely up to you.

Don't feel, however, as though you can't do an arrangement just because you haven't studied the craft. An informal bouquet of mixed colors and textures can be just as rewarding as a carefully thought out composition.

First choose your vase or other watertight container. This can be an exquisite blown glass creation or an attractive jar that used to contain mustard. Just suit the jar to the setting. Avoid metal containers if you're using a flower preservative; these may adversely react with the chemicals.

You can either plan your harvest from the garden, or take whatever is available and figure out how to use it later. Don't forget leaves and dried seed heads. These can add interest and fill out the composition.

Most important, gather a mixture of textures. Tiny baby's breath around substantial rose blossoms is a classic combination. Meadow rue or spikes of lavender mixed with large iris or daisies can give a similar effect.

When you place blooms in a container, start with the largest, most showy flowers and add smaller ones until it is filled. You'll be able to judge right away whether your additions give the hoped-for effect.

Good Flowers for Cutting

Give your blooms cool moist air, away from radiators, sunny windows, and air conditioning. Keep them well above freezing. Avoid the TV as a display area. Avoid drafty areas. Avoid putting them near ripening fruits, which give off ethylene gas, possibly ripening your flowers into bare seedpods.

Annuals

Antirrhinum	snapdragon
Calendula	pot marigold
Callistephus	China aster
Centaurea cyanus	cornflower
Cleome	spider flower
Consolida	larkspur
Cosmos	cosmos
Gypsophila elegans	annual baby's breath
Helianthus	sunflower
Lathyrus odoratus	sweet pea
Matthiola	stock
Nigella	love-in-a-mist
Tagetes	marigold
Zinnia	zinnia

Perennials and Bulbs

Achillea	yarrow
Agapanthus	lily of the Nile
Alstroemeria	alstroemeria
Anaphalis	pearly everlasting
Anemone × hybrida	Japanese anemone
Anthemis tinctoria	golden marguerite
Aster	aster
Chrysanthemum	florist's mum
Coreopsis	coreopsis
Dahlia	dahlia
Echinacea	purple coneflower
Gerbera	Transvaal daisy

Gladiolus	gladiolus
Gypsophila	baby's breath
Helleborus	Christmas rose, Lenten rose
Hyacinthoides	bluebell
Iris	iris
Lavandula	lavender
Leucanthemum × superbum	Shasta daisy
Liatris	gayfeather
Lilium	lily

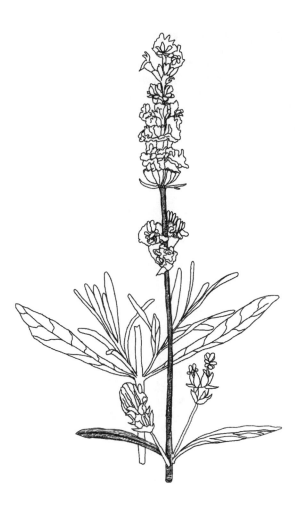

Lavender, with its sweet-spicy scent and spikes of violet to purple flowers, is one of the most popular flowers for both cutting fresh and drying.

Narcissus	daffodil
Platycodon	balloon flower
Ranunculus	Persian ranunculus
Rudbeckia	gloriosa daisy
Solidago	goldenrod
Stokesia	stokesia
Thalictrum	meadow rue
Tulipa	tulip
Zantedeschia	calla

Dried Flowers for Lasting Bouquets

While many flowers may be dried using special techniques, some of the ones you see in commercial dried arrangements practically dry themselves. Often called everlastings, these need to spend only a week or so hanging upside down in a dark, warm, dry room. Some may be tied in small bunches, larger ones need to be hung individually. You can then arrange them just like fresh flowers.

Everlastings

Achillea	yarrow
Allium	flowering onion
Anaphalis	pearly everlasting
Catananche	Cupid's dart
Celosia	cockscomb
Echinops	globe thistle
Gomphrena	globe amaranth
Gypsophila	baby's breath
Helichrysum	strawflower
Limonium	sea lavender
Lunaria annua	honesty

Store dried flowers in darkness, if possible, to prevent fading.

Forcing Spring Bulbs and Branches

In flower arranging, *forcing* means bringing budded flowers indoors where the warm air opens them weeks before they would otherwise. Whole branches and bulbs, full of stored food and nutrients, are chosen rather than individual flowers because it's a lengthy process, from a week to over a month, depending on how close to blooming they were when you started.

Garden Talk

In general, *forcing* means accelerating a plant's development, or pushing it to flower or fruit in a season other than its normal one. Depending on the purpose, forcing can involve warmer than normal temperatures, extra fertilizer, or extra light.

Branches

Shrubs that bloom in April, May, and June may be cut as early as the end of January, or as late as a few weeks before bloom. Put them in vases of water, making sure the water is changed regularly, and wait. A cool room, about 60 degrees, is best. Avoid dry, hot areas that may wither buds before they open.

Some of the best spring flowers shrubs for forcing are:

Cercis	redbud
Chaenomeles	flowering quince
Cornus florida	dogwood
Cornus mas	cornelian cherry
Deutzia	deutzia
Forsythia	forsythia
Halesia	silver bell
Hamamelis	witch hazel
Kalmia latifolia	mountain laurel
Kolkwitzia	beauty bush
Magnolia × soulangiana	saucer magnolia
Magnolia stellata	star magnolia
Pieris	lily of the valley shrub
Prunus	flowering cherries and plums
Rhododendron	rhododendron, azalea
Spiraea	bridal wreath
Viburnum	viburnum

Bulbs for Indoor Bloom

Forcing bulbs is a somewhat different process. Bulbs are potted in rich loose soil, allowed to root well in cool conditions, then brought into cool rooms to open their blossoms. They will need six to eight weeks of 40-degree weather (or the inside of your refrigerator) before you warm them. When brought indoors, they'll last longest at temperatures of 50 to 60 degrees.

Crocus	crocus
Hyacinthus	hyacinth
Narcissus	daffodil
Tulipa	tulip

Edible Flowers

Did you ever realize that the small pansy called Johnny-jump-up tastes purple? Or that nasturtium flowers are spicy but not as spicy as the leaves? Welcome to the study of flowers for salads and soups!

We tend to keep the flower and kitchen gardens separate, but sometimes blurring the lines has advantages. Flowers add color as well as unique flavors and, when used as a garnish, can lift an ordinary potato soup into the realm of gourmet treat.

Yes, there are poisonous plants among the flowers. Don't *ever* eat any blossom whose edibility is in doubt. Stick to the ones on the following lists. Get to know them in leaf and flower and ignore the others.

How do you use them? After your soup or salad in its serving bowl, place the flowers around the edge, or make an artistic cluster in one corner. You could cook them, but they'd lose their color and form. A last minute garnish is best.

You can, of course, use them to garnish other dishes, sweet breads, for instance, or meats. As guests serve themselves, however, they're likely to be pushed to the side.

Now, which flowers can you eat?

Herbs

Any culinary herb is fair game. Many, such as mint, are a bit dull looking but safe. Here are some to consider:

➤ Borage—bright blue, very attractive

➤ Chives—pale lavender-pink clusters

➤ Dill—flat yellow heads

➤ Garlic—white clusters

➤ Lavender—small purple spikes, good in fruit salads

➤ Oregano—pink clusters

➤ Rosemary—lavender-blue

➤ Sage—purple-blue

➤ Thyme—lavender

Vegetables

If you grow any of these vegetables, consider using the flowers occasionally:

➤ Bean—white, purple

➤ Broccoli—yellow

➤ Peas—white

➤ Strawberries—white

➤ Zucchini—large, gold

Annuals

These annuals are easy to grow in quantity, and can be sown outdoors when the soil is still cool:

➤ *Calendula*   pot marigold

➤ *Eschscholzia*   California poppy

➤ *Bellis*   English daisy

➤ *Tropaeolum*   nasturtium

➤ *Phaseolus*   scarlet runner bean

➤ *Viola tricolor*   Johny-jump-up, pansy

Perennials

Others are edible, but taste too medicinal for pleasant eating:

➤ *Hemerocallis*   daylily

➤ *Monarda*   bee balm

Bringing Plants Indoors

It often seems a shame to abandon profusely blooming annuals and tender perennials to frost. What are their chances indoors? With some, quite good.

You can pot up large impatiens, fibrous begonias, ageratum, and sweet alyssum (*Lobularia*) and expect them to succeed indoors for quite a while. Notice that these are all shade-tolerant plants. Indoor light levels are generally very low, and even these need a bright window.

Some shade lovers such as tuberous begonias, primroses (*Primula*), and fuchsias seem to resent the closed atmosphere, rarely blooming for long indoors. An airy cool room or greenhouse is best for holding them over winter. Or you can let them go dormant, give them a cold, moderately dry period, and revive them in spring.

Some sun lover such as geraniums (*Pelargonium*), chrysanthemums, and lantana may give you a good show if you give them as much sun as possible and a fairly cool, moist room.

If in doubt, experiment. After all, when frosts are coming you can hardly lose more than the time it takes to pot them.

The Least You Need to Know

➤ When cutting flowers, make sure the base of the stem is cut as cleanly as possible. Use sharp tools and recut if the stem becomes crushed.

➤ Treat cut flowers as you would delicate plants, shielding them from extremes of heat or cold, dry air, and drafts.

➤ Hang easy to dry flowers in cool dark rooms until brittle, then store them in darkness to prevent fading.

➤ You can bring flowering branches into bloom indoors if you put them in water and place them in a cool room until the buds begin to open.

➤ Bulbs such as tulips and daffodils may be potted and brought into bloom indoors if you give them six weeks at 40 degrees to root.

➤ Many blossoms are edible, but only use those you know are nonpoisonous.

Chapter 24

$2 \times 2 = 4$
$2 \times 3 = 6$
$2 \times 4 = 8$
$2 \times 5 = 10$

Easy Multiplication

In This Chapter

➤ What is propagation?

➤ Starts from seeds

➤ Three plants from one

➤ Getting more of the best varieties

➤ Layering woody plants

Perhaps you're looking at a large clump of Siberian iris and thinking there must be some way to get three plants out of it. Or your favorite penstemon, the sprawling one with pinkish blue flowers, seems to be rooting along the stems and you're wondering if each one would grow on its own.

Congratulations! You've graduated to one of the most enjoyable gardening activities, increasing your own stock of plants. No longer will you be completely dependent on nurseries. You'll be able to get plants for free.

Does this involve a lot of work? That depends. Many plants can be multiplied quite easily. Others demand special conditions that take time and a greenhouse to create. If you start with the easy ones, you can move on to more ambitious projects later.

What Is Propagation?

Welcome to the world of plant propagation! This is the art and science of getting many plants from few. While nature relies on a limited number of techniques, such as seeds, bulblets on stems that grow into new plants when they drop off, and runners that root wherever they touch the ground, humans have developed more. These include such sophisticated procedures as growing an entire plant from a single cell.

Seeds Can Be Easy

The simplest method of getting large quantities of plants, the one most common in nature, is through seeds. You can buy them in packets or you can gather your own. Some generous plants self-sow, or spring up in out of the way places by scattering seeds themselves. You do nothing.

Others need help. Perhaps this is no more than covering the seed with a little soil in spring, letting nature do the watering, and welcoming the small sprouts a few weeks later. Perhaps you need special soil and warmth. Let's review the factors involved.

The First Essential: Proper Soil

Seeds come in all sizes, from dustlike specks to large beans, avocados, and coconuts. Most flower seeds are under a quarter inch in diameter. They need to be surrounded by soil for good growth, but new seedlings can't push up through a hard or deep layer of dirt. They need a light, but moisture-retaining, shelter.

In the garden, break up clods of dirt, forming a layer of even textured soil that will closely surround the seeds. If there are large air pockets, the seeds may sprout but die because they can't anchor themselves properly.

Though some seeds need light to germinate, as a general rule cover them with a layer equal to their diameter. Very fine seeds, such as those of sweet alyssum (*Lobularia*), can be just patted into the soil and watered well. Be sure, however, to keep the surface moist until the seeds sprout.

Garden Talk

The term germination refers to the processes a seed undergoes when exposed to proper warmth and moisture conditions that turn it into a baby plant. The embryo inside the seed begins to grow, putting out a single root then one or two leaves.

You might be surprised at the first few leaves you see. They are often much different in appearance from those of the adult plant, being simple and rounded even on plants with ferny, deeply cut foliage. Be sure you don't pull the new plants up, mistaking them for weeds.

When exposed to the force of raindrops and then dried, most garden soil will form a thin hard layer called a crust. Your seedlings may not be able to crack it. Try covering fine seeds with a layer of sand or potting mix to give small plants an easy job of reaching the sun.

Seeds sown outdoors are rarely bothered by fungus diseases, but if you start your flowers indoors, you'll want to buy a sterile mixture to eliminate the possibility of disease. Though you may be tempted to save money by using soil from the garden, your seedlings will be healthier when grown in a prepared mix.

These are usually fibrous and crumbly. You'll have no trouble with crusting here. They are also light, with lots of air spaces for good drainage. They make excellent seedbeds and, if your garden soil is heavy with clay, you may wish to use them for covering seeds outdoors.

The Second Essential: Warmth

Sow some petunia seeds outdoors in April, when the ground is cold and wet, and you'll get nothing. Sow them in a 80-degree greenhouse and you'll have robust young plants in a few weeks. Forget-me-nots (*Myosotis*), on the other hand, may shoot up quickly when sown in your spring garden. Seeds, obviously have temperature preferences.

Many annuals are sown indoors or in greenhouses because by the time the soil is warm enough outside, it's summer. Gardeners want flowers now, not in two months. Some might not even bloom before frost. These heat-loving annuals are the ones that need a head start indoors.

Inside, you're in charge of providing the proper soil, light and the right amount of water. This may be more trouble than you'd care to take. On the other hand, your seedlings are close at hand and easy to watch out for. Given a sunny window or fluorescent light, most need little more attention than occasional watering.

Green Tip

Proper temperature is like a signal that sends a message saying "The weather's fine. It's all right to grow now." Whenever you plant seeds, first find out what the best temperature is for germination. Then decide whether to start them indoors or outdoors.

The Third Essential: Moisture

To set off germination, seeds wait for moisture as well as the proper temperature. When a seed comes in contact with water, it swells and begins to grow. Once this process has started, any dryness can destroy the delicate new life inside. Constant moisture is important.

Moist but not soggy is the rule here. Oxygen is also important and wet soil has little air to offer. You'll have little trouble keeping hardy, spring-sown seeds watered since nature will often do the job for you. Those sown outside in summer, however, may need frequent misting.

Indoors, you can tie a plastic bag around a small tray of seedlings, or place a piece of glass over a large one to get the needed humidity. As soon as the seeds sprout, however, let them get good air circulation to reduce the risk of disease.

Saving Your Own Seed

You can always buy seed packets in stores or from mail-order catalogs, but saving your own is easy. Simply allow some of the flowers to ripen their seeds, cut the seed heads and place them in a paper bag. The seeds will drop out into the bag and you can then put them in envelopes and mark them with the name of the plant and the date.

How long can you keep them before sowing? That depends on both the type of plant and the conditions under which they are stored. Though seeds have germinated thirty, fifty, even a thousand years after ripening on the plant, most flower seed will last two to three years in a closed dry container on a cool shelf.

Now, for storage, you reverse the conditions needed for germination. Just as moisture and warmth cause seeds to sprout, the warmth and moist air of a kitchen shelf will cause them to deteriorate. Dryness and coolness preserve them.

While some gardeners keep seeds in their refrigerator, a cool basement will do. Just be sure that the inside of the container stays as dry as possible. Commercial desiccants are available but a layer of coarse salt will also absorb excess moisture.

What Is Best Grown from Seed?

Annuals are naturals, of course. For species survival, they depend exclusively on spreading quantities of quick germinating seed. Give them the right conditions of moisture and warmth and you'll be successful.

Many perennials are just as eager to grow from seed. Others, however, may need a period of low temperatures, or warmth then cold, before they sprout. Mix the seeds with moist potting medium, place it in a refrigerator for the proper length of time, then sow the mixture as a unit.

Green Tips

Keeping seeds moist outdoors in sunny weather can be difficult. You can put a cover such as a flattened cardboard box or piece of cloth over them if you're careful to check for sprouted seeds frequently. Most seed packages give an approximate time to germination, but shorter and longer periods are possible.

Garden Talk

The term *stratification* refers to the process used to hasten seed sprouting by overcoming dormancy requirements. In nature, immediate germination may not be desirable and seed wait for a certain pattern of warm and cold to signal the proper time to sprout. Mimicking these patterns with shorter periods in a refrigerator or other 40-degree environment allows you to control germination times. As little as one month or as many as four may be required.

Trees and shrubs may also need this treatment, called stratification. Most packets of seeds give detailed instructions for germination. If not, consult a gardening encyclopedia for needs of specific plants.

Dividing Is Easy Too

As you may guess from the word, division means cutting a single individual into two, three, or five smaller ones. Depending on the type of plant, you may be able to pull it apart with your fingers, or you may need a sharp knife or spade to cut apart a mass of roots and leaves.

Dividing is a technique that works best with perennials, bulbs, or shrubs that form clumps of leaves and stems, clusters of many crowns, or growing points. It won't work with single-stemmed plants, those with a small, tight crown of leaves, or those that have a single long taproot. These have only one growing point that cannot be split.

First dig up the plant and look carefully at the roots and base of the stems. You'll see that there are roots attached to each crown. If you gently pull the growing points apart, you'll find yourself with a number of small separate plants.

Sometimes the crowns and roots are so densely packed that you need to cut them apart. Most clumps can safely be sliced into two or three chunks without losing any blooms next year. But, if you divide them into smaller pieces, each one may require a year or two to grow to flowering size.

Garden Talk

The term *crown* refers to the place where the stem or cluster of leaves emerges.

This technique is best used in early spring or in autumn, seasons when the weather is cool and wet, unlikely to place much strain on damaged root systems. However, consult your gardening encyclopedia for details.

Before or immediately after dividing, cut deciduous plants down within 2–4 inches of the ground. Evergreen plants should have a third of their oldest leaves removed to reduce transplanting stress. Remember, if you remove roots, you need to remove an equal proportion of leaves to keep the top and bottom in balance.

You may be doing the plant a favor by dividing it occasionally. Many perennials continue to create new crowns and roots at the edge of a clump, allowing the inside to die out. Dividing rejuvenates the plant, giving each piece fresh soil to colonize.

Goldenrod has strong creeping stems that can be cut into several divisions each year.

Cuttings: as Many Plants as You Want

Sometimes one plant out of a group of seedlings stands out. It has larger flowers of a deeper yellow, perhaps, or variegated leaves. Seeds from that individual will have as much variation as the original batch and dividing will only increase the stock by a few each year. How can you get ten or twenty?

You take cuttings. These are small pieces of stem or root that, when in contact with moist soil, sprout roots and become independent clones of your original prized specimen. This is a technique plant breeders have developed that takes advantage of a natural survival talent many plants have developed for turning broken pieces into pioneers.

Some trees, shrubs, and perennials need special conditions and techniques to root, while others are easy. Willows, for instance, can grow from a stick thrust into damp ground. Others, such as English ivy (*Hedera*), put out roots when kept in a vase of water. Most plants, however should be rooted in sand or other porous medium.

What Part of the Plant Do You Use?

Cuttings can be taken of soft growing wood, hardened stem wood, or, from some plants, roots or leaves. The easiest and quickest to root are those from new growth. The exact time to take cuttings, however, varies from plant to plant. Again, consult the encyclopedia.

Start with an Easy Plant

As an introductory exercise, let's take an August Impatiens and snip off some of the branches to root for flowering plants indoors in October.

Cut off a piece 3 or 4 inches long. Most important, cut it about a quarter inch below a leaf. The point at which the leaf sprouts from the stem is also the point at which roots will form. A stub left below that point will simply die, perhaps taking the leaf node with it. Make a clean cut with sharp knife or pair of pruners. If the end is crushed, recut it with a sharp knife.

Remove the leaves at that node and the one above it. You want enough leaves to nourish the cutting, but since there are no roots to absorb and transmit water, any extra leaf surface is a water-using liability.

Garden Talk

The term *leaf node* refers to the place where one or more leaves sprouts from the stem or branch. It is usually somewhat thicker than the other areas, often marked with a line. Small buds are usually visible even when leaves aren't present.

Do You Need a Rooting Hormone?

An easy to root plant such as impatiens may not need any help to get roots started. However, dipping the end in a rooting hormone powder will make the process quicker and more reliable. If you're working with cuttings of shrubs or trees, rooting powder is definitely an advantage.

Place Cuttings in a Soil Mix

Garden soil is rarely a good rooting medium. You'll have best luck by placed cuttings in containers of sand or half sand and half peat moss. You can also use perlite or vermiculite alone or mixed with peat moss.

Use your fingertip to make a hole about an inch deep. Place the cutting in it and firm the rooting medium around it. The leaf node should be covered completely.

Humidity Is Important

Now, until roots form, the stem and leaves are dependent on moisture in the air and the rooting medium to keep them from drying out. Keeping a humid atmosphere around the leaves can mean the difference between a cutting that dries out before forming roots and one that stays crisp and green until rootlets can take over the task of gathering water. The best way to do this is to place a small container of cuttings in a plastic bag or cover a larger one with a piece of glass.

Take Care!

Normal household temperature should be adequate to root impatiens, but other plants may be more particular, requiring the rooting medium to be heated to 75 or 80 degrees.

Now, Wait

Predicting how much time is required for rooting is difficult. At least a week, perhaps much longer, depending on the plant. Pulling the cuttings up every few days may damage new roots, so control your curiosity.

After a few weeks, tug very gently on the stem. If you feel resistance, stop. You probably have two or three new roots anchoring the stem. New leaves emerging are also a good indication of successful rooting.

Take the pot out of the plastic or remove the glass. New plants need air circulation at this stage to keep the risk of fungus disease down. If leaves start to wilt, replace it and give them a few more minutes of fresh air tomorrow.

Allow cuttings to stay in the rooting medium until they are well rooted and starting to put out leaves. You can then pot them up or place them outside.

Congratulations! Once you start rooting plants, you've passed from beginner to intermediate gardener. Celebrate your achievement, perhaps by treating yourself to another trip to the nursery. You can't have too many flowers, can you?

Garden Talk

Layering is the process of rooting a shoot or branch while it is still attached to the parent plant.

Layering Woody Plants

You can also take advantage of the root-forming inclination of leaf nodes in a process called layering. Instead of completely cutting off a piece of the plant, you persuade the node to root before removing the top from the parent plant.

Why do this rather than take cuttings? The process is more certain of success because the new plant remains attached to the old one until well rooted. It also allows you to turn branches up to half an inch thick into new plants. You may not make as many of them, but they'll be larger.

Sprawling shrubs and perennials can often be layered by simply weighting a branch with a brick and mounding earth over it, but if you want to try this trick on a taller shrub or tree, you'll have to bring the rooting medium up to the branch.

Slice part way through a stem or branch, about a quarter inch below a node from which you have removed the leaves. Use a matchstick or other small piece of wood to hold the incision open, preventing the wound from healing.

Moisten a handful of peat or sphagnum moss and wrap it around the branch, completely enclosing the leaf node and cut. Cover this with clear plastic wrap and tie the ends tightly.

You'll have no need to guess whether or not your branch is rooted. You'll be able to watch the whole process through the plastic. When the ball of moss is filled with roots, cut the entire rooted branch off, remove the wrap and pot in soil.

Make sure you don't overwork your new root system. If there are too many leaves on the new plant for it to support, pluck off about half of them. New ones will soon sprout to replace them.

The Least You Need to Know

➤ Give seeds moisture, proper temperature, and loose, well-aerated soil for germination. Some need light to germinate, some need darkness. Cover if needed and firm the soil around them.

➤ Make sure seeds never dry out after sowing. Don't keep the soil soggy, however, or they may rot.

➤ You can divide plants that make clumps of stems or leaves into two or more individuals because each growing point, or crown, is served by separate roots. Simply cut or pull the crowns apart.

➤ Cuttings are small pieces of stem with a leaf node at the base. When inserted in soil or potting mix, the node puts out roots, turning the cutting into an independent plant.

➤ Layering persuades a stem still attached to the parent plant to also root at a leaf node. You make a cut halfway through the stem or branch, then pack moistened soil mix around it, removing the rest of the branch when rooted.

Continuing
the Quest

You know what you want. How do you get it? Or you've fallen in love with daylilies and want to know more about them. Or you simply want to know more about the fascinating pastime called gardening. This book is an introduction. Where are the best places to continue your learning?

Before long you'll find that there are millions of pages of information out there. There are hundreds of nurseries you can buy from. There are countless opinions on every facet of gardening, some of them contradictory. How do you navigate your way through the maze of possibilities?

The best way is to let someone else simplify the task. Whether you're exploring the Internet or looking for a some good books on perennials, choose a few resources and let them guide you.

Finding the Plants You Need

The primrose you've decided is exactly right for your damp, shady corner is out of stock, or your nursery doesn't carry it at all. Frustrating, isn't it? Unfortunately, most stores have room for only the most popular of the plants available, and even those may be in this week, gone the next. What do you do?

Changing Your Mind

You may want, or need, to plant something soon. Your nursery probably has a few other plants that would fit your situation. Is substitution your best option?

Take Care!

Never buy a plant whose preferences clash with your garden's soil, water, and sun patterns. If you do, you'll find yourself with a potential problem plant that can cause you extra work and still turn up its leaves and die.

That depends. You can get a lot of pleasure from the presence of a few plants you really love, the rose you saw on the garden tour, the primrose whose soft yellow complements your pink bleeding heart, the bright blue grape hyacinth you prefer to the common darker ones. They're the ones worth waiting for.

On the other hand, a background planting of azaleas may not need the same careful thought. If one's a bit taller than another, or a slightly different shade of pink, you aren't going to care much.

Perhaps you just want a growing border by the end of summer. You like flowers but aren't particular about the individuals that make up the picture. In this case, go for quick color. You'll find it much easier to plant a whole bed all at once than gather pieces here and there.

Fill in with Annuals

Take Care!

When a nursery professional suggests a possible addition to your garden and your first thought is "Yuck" you can always go on to something else. If it would annoy you every time you walked by, don't let yourself get talked into buying it, no matter how perfect a match it is for your spot.

Saving a place for a special plant can be frustrating, but you can always add a placeholder in the form of an annual, long flowering, bright and sometimes as big as shrub you're waiting for. Sunflowers (*Helianthus*), cleome, nicotiana, cosmos, gloriosa daisies (*Rudbeckia*), four-o'clocks (*Mirabilis*), and dahlias (a tuber, but substantial as an annual) are all good choices.

Don't forget vines, either. A few strings laden with morning glories can make a bare spot an asset.

Obtaining Your First Choice

First, check with your nursery professional to make sure this plant is really well adapted to your climate. Next, ask if it can be special ordered, or if will be available later. You'll get your best results working through a local source, if possible.

Next, call other nurseries in your area. Be sure to give them the exactly scientific name, a jawbreaker perhaps, but essential for accuracy.

Mail-order catalogs can bring unusual plants such as saffron crocus into your garden.

You Can Get Almost Anything By Mail

One of your best resources could be *Gardening by Mail: A Source Book* (5th ed.) edited by Barbara J. Barton and Ginny Hunt. You can look up specific plants or types of plants and get a list of who might carry them.

If you feel confident and patient enough to try seeds, B & T World Seeds (b-and-t-world-seeds.com), an online company that carries 37,000 varieties, is your best bet.

If you're just interested in exploring possibilities look for ads in gardening magazines, or search the Internet. You may end up acquiring a library of catalogs from specialty nurseries, from orchid and wildflower growers to bulb merchants. You can also find companies carrying a wide range of perennials, shrubs, and trees. Some send black-and-white lists, some full-color catalogs.

Be warned, though, that you'll find hundreds of fascinating flowers offered for sale. Catalogs can be hazardous to your pocketbook.

Books, Books, Books!

Your library is a good first place to check for more advice. Books have been published on every facet of gardening, every viewpoint, every field of interest. You'll probably find three or four to get you started in any direction you're inclined to go.

Once you explore the library's offerings, you'll know which you want to buy to refer to again. Be sure you buy at least one good general gardening encyclopedia (see Resources, page 321). Detailed information on every plant you're likely to come across will help you plan your garden and keep you from planting unusual finds in the wrong place.

You can also buy the latest books on whatever subject interests you long before your library acquires them. And if you have a passion for out-of-the-way plants such as species tulips and other wild bulbs, you may be able to indulge yourself in books for fans of these specialties, books a library with a general audience would rarely purchase.

Even if you're an Internet addict, books have the advantages of quicker searches, easier browsing, and portability. So why search the Net?

Online Information

Information, lots of it. More than you want to know, probably. Sorting through it could take time.

Yes, it's fun and you can dive into any facet of gardening as deeply as you have time for. You'll gain benefit from others' experience, find local resources quickly, ask for catalogs, get help on plant problems, order garden supplies and check out online magazines. But information is no substitute for hands-on experience.

Gardening is about feeling the sun on your back, listening to robins and wrens sing, getting to know the texture of your soil, and smelling the rosemary that brushes your hands as you weed. Information is usually valuable only as far as it helps you put plants in proper places. Once settled it, most will do an excellent job of growing without any interference from you.

With that perspective, and a gardening encyclopedia in hand, use the Internet as an expansion of your bookshelf. Use it to follow a new interest, learn a new technique, find new plants and new books, or argue with others over the best way to grow dahlias. Just be sure to spend more time in your garden than on your computer.

Some companies have online catalogs that are fun to explore. If you like what you see, you'll probably want to get on their mailing list since you'll find turning pages quicker than downloading them onto the screen.

Going Farther with Roses, Daylilies, Dahlias or . . .

One way to learn more about plants that fascinate you is to talk to others with more experience at growing them. You can get information on the best varieties for your area, tips for creating the best growing conditions and help with any problems you encounter.

How do you find such like-minded people? You can ask the white-haired woman selling daylilies at the local plant sale. You can ask questions at your local nursery. You can call your local Cooperative Extension Service. If you're on the Internet, you can look up organizations that can steer you to local chapters.

Are there any specialty growers near you? You may be able to find small-scale nurseries, often no more than a large backyard, run by people whose enthusiasm for wildflowers or succulents or herbs has turned a hobby into a business. Sometimes open by only by appointment, they can be invaluable sources of plants and advice.

Many areas have plant shows, anything from afternoon exhibitions at a local library to three-day extravaganzas with a thousand exhibitors. A trip to one of these will give you a good idea of what's going on in the local gardening world. You can talk to an orchid grower or a native plant devotee. Gardeners are always eager to talk about their favorites so don't be shy about asking questions.

Green Tip

Your most useful Internet resources could be plant selection databases. These can give you names of specific plants that match your requirements of garden conditions, height and color. One of the best is (www.clr.toronto.edu/cgi-bin/ GROVER/htgrover?fields) from the Center for Landscape Research, University of Toronto.

Resources

Here are some pathways into more knowledge. First start with a good gardening encyclopedia. Some possibilities are:

American Horticultural Society Encyclopedia of Garden Plants, Christopher Brickell, editor

Wyman's Gardening Encyclopedia, Donald Wyman

Sunset National Garden Book, editors of Sunset Books and Sunset magazine

Time-Life Plant Encyclopedia, online: www.vg.com/cgi-bin/VG/vg

Gardening magazines are fun to look through and educational besides. Start off with a selection of these:

The American Gardener (from The American Horticultural Society, 7931 E. Boulevard Dr., Alexandria, VA 22308-1300)

Fine Gardening (63 S. Main St., Box 355, Newtown, CT 06470-9989)

Garden Design (1401 Connecticut Ave. NW, Suite 500, Washington DC 20008-2302)

Horticulture (PO Box 51455, Boulder, CO 80323-1455)

National Gardening (from the National Gardening Association, PO Box 51106, Boulder, CO 80321-1106)

You'll find numerous clubs to join, from local garden clubs to local and national organizations devoted to specific kinds of plants. Here's a selection:

American Hemerocallis (Daylily) Society, Elly Launius, AHS Executive Secretary, 1454 Rebel Dr., Jackson, MS 39211

American Iris Society, Marilyn Harlow, PO Box 8455, San Jose, CA 95155-8455

American Rhododendron Society, PO Box 1380, Gloucester, VA 23061

American Rose Society, PO Box 30000, Shreveport, LA 71130-0300

North American Rock Garden Society, Jacques Mommens, PO Box 67, Millwood, NY 10546

Internet information runs the gamut from carnivorous plant specialists to home gardeners bragging about their tomatoes. Here are some useful places to start:

The Gardening Launch Pad, www.tpoint.net/neighbor/

The Garden Gate: What's Coming Into Bloom, www.prairienet.org/garden-gate/whatsnew.htm

The GardenNet, gardennet.com

The Internet Directory for Botany, www.helsinki.fi/kmus/bothort.html

The Virtual Garden, www.vg.com

The Least You Need to Know

➤ If you just want color, take what a nursery has to offer. If you're looking for a special plant, hold its place with annuals until you find a source.

➤ Start your library with a good gardening encyclopedia and let your interests lead you on from there.

➤ When stepping into the Internet, find a few pages of links to keep you form getting lost.

➤ Look for plant shows and sales. You'll find lots of people who can give you advice on what grows best in your area as well as info on local nurseries, organizations, public gardens and other resources.

Terms and Definitions

Annual   Plants that sprout, bloom, and die in one year.

Cotyledons   One or two leaves put out by a germinating seed, often much different in appearance from the plant's adult leaves, being simple and rounded even on plants with ferny, deeply cut foliage.

Crown   The place where the stem or cluster of leaves emerges.

Deadheading   The removal of faded flowers before they ripen seeds, a process that often sends a signal to the plant to stop blooming. Seed formation may also use energy gardeners would rather channel into growth.

Deciduous   Refers to a plant that will drop its leaves in fall, overwintering as a skeleton of bare branches.

Drought-tolerant, drought resistant   Descriptions of plants that can survive with little or no more water than nature usually provides. Obviously, a plant that is drought-tolerant in Oregon may need extra water in Arizona. And a plant that has had only a year to become rooted will need more water than one that has had ten.

Evergreen   Refers to a plant that keeps its leaves all year. The oldest leaves, however, will be shed occasionally, often in late summer.

Everlastings   Plants whose flowers tend to be drier than most, with petals that keep their shape and sometimes much of their color even after the plant has wilted.

Forcing   Accelerating a plant's development, or pushing it to flower or fruit in a season other than its normal one. Depending on the purpose, forcing can involve warmer than normal temperatures, extra fertilizer, or extra light.

Genus   A classification division usually composed of many species. Tulips are all members of the genus *Tulipa* but there are many different species within that genus, for example, *Tulipa tarda*, *Tulipa greigii* and *Tulipa clusiana*.

Germination   The processes a seed undergoes when exposed to proper warmth and moisture conditions that turn it into a baby plant. The embryo inside the seed begins to grow, putting out a single root then one or two leaves called cotyledons. These are often much different in appearance from the plant's adult leaves, being simple and rounded even on plants with ferny, deeply cut foliage. When those are fully grown, the seedling puts out true leaves.

Harden off   To condition plants to low temperatures or low humidity. Seedlings raised in a greenhouse, for instance, need gradual exposure to drier air and cooler nights before planting them outside. Woody plants go through a natural preparation for winter temperatures. Early frosts, for instance, may injure them more severely than later ones because they haven't had enough time to harden off and prepare for low temperatures.

Hardiness   A measure of a plant's ability to survive your winters. This depends not only on the type of plant, but on whether or not it has time to ripen and become completely dormant before a hard freeze. Extra early frosts can kill branches and roots that aren't prepared for them.

Humus   The end production of decomposition, the dark brown, gummy substance that leaves, wood and animal matter becomes. It's excellent for holding water and nutrients. What most people call humus, however, is the partially decayed product, still fibrous and good for aerating the soil.

Layering   The process of rooting a shoot or branch while it is still attached to the parent plant.

Leaf node   The place where one or more leaves are attached to the stem.

Nutrients   The elements that plants need to carry out a plant's growth processes. The six needed in largest quantities are nitrogen, phosphorous, potassium, calcium, magnesium, and sulfur.

Organic matter   The remains of once-living organisms, usually fibrous material such as rotted wood and dead leaves. In a partially decayed state it can loosen heavy soil and hold moisture. When completely decayed it is humus.

Perennial   Plants that grow a permanent root system but without woody stems.

Perlite   A mineral that has been heated and expanded, something like popcorn. Holds both air and water.

Pinching   Taking off the terminal bud of a stem or branch. This allows the buds at the side to sprout, making the plant more bushy.

Rootbound   A plant whose roots have reached the side of the pot, and, having no where else to go, are circling around the edge, perhaps even bending back into the soil. Before you plant into a larger pot or into the garden, gently pull them free or take a knife and cut the mat of roots in several places. This will persuade them to reach out into new soil.

Self-seed   Plants that are masters at growing without the help of gardeners. Without any help from you, they sprout and grow in all sorts of odd places. If you wish them to stay put, cut off the fading flowers before the seeds ripen.

Species   A subdivision of a genus. Tulips are all members of the genus *Tulipa* but there are many different species. Species tulips refers to those that are close to the wild types, quite different from those that hybridizers have created with their breeding programs.

Stratification   The process used to hasten seed sprouting by overcoming dormancy requirements. In nature, immediate germination may not be desirable and seed wait for a certain pattern of warmth and cold to signal the proper time to sprout. Mimicking these patterns with shorter periods in a refrigerator or other 40-degree environment allows you to control germination times. As little as one month or as many as four may be required.

Terminal bud   The bud at the tip of a stalk or branch that is responsible for continuing the growth of that stem. The buds at the side of the branch often remain dormant until the terminal bud is removed. When you take off the bud without any of its stem, the process is called pinching.

Vermiculite   A mica, a mineral, after it has been heated and expanded, something like popcorn. Holds both air and water.

Colors of Flowers

When you work with flowers, you work with color, with subtle to intense shades and a thousand variations of colors. Here's a selection of flowers grouped into some of the categories you'll be using in your designs.

Bright Blue Flowers

True, sky blue is a treasure in the garden, not rare, but not common either. As a cool color, it seems to recede into the distance, giving a sense of space to small gardens, but its brilliance is noticed immediately.

Some of these plants may have forms of pink or white, but blue is what they're known for:

Anchusa	alkanet
Brunnera	brunnera
Centaurea cyanus	cornflower
Ceratostigma	dwarf plumbago
Consolida	larkspur
Cynoglossum	Chinese forget-me-not
Delphinium	delphinium
Ipomoea tricolor	morning glory
Linum perenne	perennial flax

Lobelia erinus	lobelia
Myosotis	forget-me-not
Nemophila	baby-blue-eyes
Nigella	love-in-a-mist
Salvia azurea	blue sage
Salvia patens	gentian sage
Scilla siberica	Siberian squill
Veronica	speedwell

Lavender-blue to Light Purple Flowers

Many of these are called blue, but it's a cool, shy blue, blending in to the green foliage background. Some are definitely lavender and others a bright purple.

This is one of the largest color groups in nature, close to the cool pinks and mauve that are so common. Use them with both warm and cool colors. They'll set off golds as well as rose-reds:

Agapanthus	lily of the Nile
Ageratum	flossflower
Anemone blanda	anemone
Aster	aster
Camassia	camas
Campanula	bell flower
Caryopteris	bluebeard
Catananche	Cupid's dart
Ceanothus	blue blossom
Centaurea montana	centaurea
Chionodoxa	glory-of-the-snow
Cotinus coggygria	smoke tree
Eryngium	sea holly
Felicia	felicia
Geranium (some)	Cranesbill
Hyacinthoides	bluebells

Hyacinthus	hyacinth
Hydrangea	big-leaf hydrangea
Lavandula	lavander
Linaria purpurea	purple linaria
Limonium	sea lavender
Lobelia siphilitica	lobelia
Mertensia	mertensia
Muscari botryoides	grape hyacinth
Nepeta	catmint
Paulownia	empress tree
Platycodon	balloon flower
Polemonium	Jacob's ladder
Rosmarinus	rosemary
Scabiosa	pincushion flower
Syringa	lilac
Tradescantia	spiderwort
Triteleia 'Queen Fabiola'	triteleia
Verbena bonariensis	Brazilian verbena
Verbena canadensis 'Homestead Purple'	purple verbena
Wisteria	wisteria

Purple Flowers

Rich velvety purple, is unusual. It often needs to be sought out among plants with lavender-purple as their main show. Some varieties of lilac (*Syringa*) and butterfly bush (*Buddleia*), for example, are darker and more intense than others. But the search is worth it. Use it with everything, from blue to orange-red. Here are places to start:

Aconite	monkshood
Aster (some)	aster
Buddleia	butterfly bush
Clematis × *jackmanii*	clematis
Crocus (some)	crocus

Delphinium	delphinium
Heliotropium	heliotrope
Hyacinthus	hyacinth
Iris sibirica	Siberian iris
Iris reticulata	iris
Syringa	lilac
Petunia	petunia
Salpiglossis (some)	painted tongue
Salvia × *superba*	perennial sage
Viola	pansy

Cool Pink to Rose-red Flowers

From pale pink to deep rose, these all mix together beautifully. You could have one bed of just this one group, with pink and perhaps some true blue to accent it. With no lack of pinks to choose from, let your imagination wander freely:

Abelia	abelia
Alibizia	silk tree
Allium schoenoprasum	chives
Anemone japonica	Japanese anemone
Armeria	thrift
Bergenia	bergenia
Cercis	redbud
Cistus	rock rose
Clematis montana	anemone clematis
Colchicum	autumn crocus
Cosmos bipinnatus	tall cosmos
Cyclamen	cyclamen
Dianthus	pinks
Dicentra	bleeding heart

Echinacea	purple coneflower
Erica	heath
Gaura	gaura
Kalmia	mountain laurel
Kolkwitzia	beauty bush
Lamium 'Beacon Silver'	dead nettle
Lathyrus latifolius	perennial sweet pea
Lobularia	sweet alyssum
Lycoris	spider lily
Magnolia × *soulangiana*	saucer magnolia
Malva	mallow
Matthiola	stock
Origanum	oregano
Pelargonium peltatum	ivy geranium
Physostegia	obedient plant
Prunus	ornamental cherries, plums
Ribes sanguineum	red-flowering currant
Rosa rugosa	rugosa rose
Saponaria ocymoides	soapwort
Schizanthus	poor man's orchid
Weigela	weigela

Warm Pink to Coral Flowers

Here's another tone you'll have to search for. It's common in mixtures and among plants with many colors such as Shirley poppies (*Papaver rhoeas*) roses and daylilies. Some of the cool pinks have warm pink varieties and some of the orange-reds have salmon varieties. Use with blue, lavender-blue, purples, and, of course, white:

Chaenomeles	flowering currant
Impatiens New Guinea hybrids	impatiens
Papaver orientale (some)	oriental poppy

Warm Red Flowers

These are perfect partners for the yellow-gold-orange group, though they have their own character. These are so intense, though, that you may want to use them in small quantities liberally mixed with greenery. Or tone them down with large quantities of gold.

Though this list is short, you can find others among roses, dahlias, and other flowers that come in many shades:

Crocosmia 'Lucifer'	crocosmia
Hemerocallis	daylily
Lobelia cardinalis	cardinal flower
Monarda	bee balm
Papaver orientalis	oriental poppy
Pelargonium	geranium
Phaseolus coccineus	scarlet runner bean
Salvia splendens	red sage
Tropaeolum	nasturtium

Gold to Orange Flowers

This must be one of nature's favorite sets of colors. You'll find them wherever you look. Mix them all together, add some reds and purples, and you'll have a stunningly fiery display. Warm colors such as these seem bring their bed closer to the viewer. They can make deep yards seem smaller, distant corners seem nearer. Wherever you put them, they'll be noticed:

Achillea	yarrow
Allium moly	golden garlic
Anthemis tinctoria	anthemis
Asclepias	butterfly weed
Calendula	pot marigold
Campsis radicans	common trumpet vine
Caragana	Siberian pea shrub
Chrysogonum	golden star
Coreopsis	coreopsis

Cornus mas	cornelian cherry
Corydalis lutea	golden corydalis
Cosmos sulphureus	yellow cosmos
Crocosmia	crocosmia
Doronicum	leopard's bane
Erysimum cheiri	wallflower
Eschscholzia	California poppy
Forsythia	forsythia
Gaillardia	blanket flower
Gazania	gazania
Gelsemium	Carolina jessamine
Geum	geum
Helianthus	sunflower
Hemerocallis	daylily
Impatiens New Guinea hybrids	impatiens
Iris pseudacorus	yellow flag
Kerria japonica	kerria
Laburnum	golden chain tree
Ligularia	ligularia
Lonicera sempervirens	scarlet honeysuckle
Lysimachia nummularia	creeping Jenny
Mahonia	Oregon grape
Narcissus (some)	daffodil
Potentilla fruticosa	shrubby cinquefoil
Rudbeckia	black-eyed Susan
Sanvitalia procumbens	creeping zinnia
Solidago	goldenrod
Tagetes	marigold
Thunbergia	thunbergia
Tropaeolum	nasturtium

Light Yellow Flowers

Pale yellow is an exceptionally useful shade, a good companion for cool as well as warm pinks. It's not as common as deeper yellows, so, again, do some searching among varieties of other colors:

Achillea 'Moonshine'	yarrow
Aquilegia (some)	columbine
Chimonanthus	wintersweet
Coreopsis verticillata 'Moonbeam'	threadleaf coreopsis
Helianthemum 'Wisley Primrose'	sun rose
Hemerocallis (some)	daylily
Meconopsis cambrica	Welsh poppy
Narcissus (some)	daffodil
Oenothera missouriensis	Missouri evening primrose
Potentilla fruticosa (some)	shrubby cinquefoil
Primula (some)	primrose
Tagetes (some)	marigold
Trollius europaeus	globeflower

White Flowers

There are few plants that don't have at least one variety available. This is useful if you like the form of a particular flower, but the color clashes with the rest of the best. Here, though, are the standard whites, the ones you don't have to search for:

Allium neapolitanum	allium
Amelanchier	shadblow, serviceberry
Anaphalis	pearly everlasting
Anemone japonica	Japanese anemone
Anemone sylvestris	snowdrop anemone
Arenaria montana	sandwort
Aruncus dioicus	goatsbeard
Cerastium tomentosum	snow-in-summer
Chionanthus	fringe tree

Cimicifuga	black snakeroot
Clematis armandii	evergreen clematis
Clematis paniculata	sweet autumn clematis
Cornus	dogwood
Crataegus	hawthorn
Deutzia	deutzia
Galanthus	snowdrop
Gallium odoratum	sweet woodruff
Gypsophila	baby's breath
Halesia	silver bell
Hydrangea anomala	climbing hydrangea
Iberis sempervirens	evergreen candytuft
Lobularia maritima	sweet alyssum
Lysimachia clethroides	gooseneck loosestrife
Magnolia stellata	star magnolia
Nicotiana alata	flowering tobacco
Philadelphus	mock orange
Polygonum aubertii	silver lace vine
Spiraea	bridal wreath
Stewartia	stewartia
Sutera cordata	bacopa
Viburnum opulus	European cranberry bush
Zantedeschia	calla

Flowers Available in Many Colors

Some plants never stick to one shade. Though a few are found wild with this talent for variation, most have been bred into diversity by hybridizers. As a gardener, you'll find that they simplify color selection. Want purple? Look here. Want red? Look here. All will satisfy the most color-hungry of gardeners:

Antirrhinum	snapdragon
Begonia	tuberous begonia

Bougainvillea	bougainvillea
Celosia	cockscomb
Chrysanthemum × morifolium	florist's chrysanthemum
Crocus	crocus
Gerbera	gerber daisy
Iris (bearded)	bearded iris
Lantana	lantana
Lathyrus odoratus	sweet pea
Lilium	lily
Nerium	oleander
Papaver nudicaule	Iceland poppy
Portulaca	moss rose
Petunia	petunia
Ranunculus asiaticus	Persian ranunculus
Rosa	rose
Rhododendron	rhododendron, azalea
Tulipa	tulip
Zinnia	zinnia

Your Flower Notebook

Your garden notebook is a place to summarize what you have now and what you want to work toward. Take it with you when you shop for plants and use it as an opening for brainstorming sessions. Or, start to create your own using the information contained here.

What do you have to work with?

Sun _____

Shade _____

Soil _____

Rainfall _____

Wind _____

Humidity _____

What hardiness zone do you live in?

Zone _____

Description _____

What types of background do you have?

House Color _____

Hedges _____

Fences _____

Flowers (and colors) _____

Shrubs _____

What gardening styles do you like? _____

_____

What types of combinations are pleasing to you? _____

_____

What colors do you like? _____

_____

What types of ground cover do you like? annuals? bulbs? perennials? vines? shrubs?

trees? _____

_____

_____

_____

What went right? _____

_____

_____

_____

What went wrong? _____

_____

_____

_____

What improvements can you make? _____

_____

_____

_____

USDA Plant Hardiness Zone Map

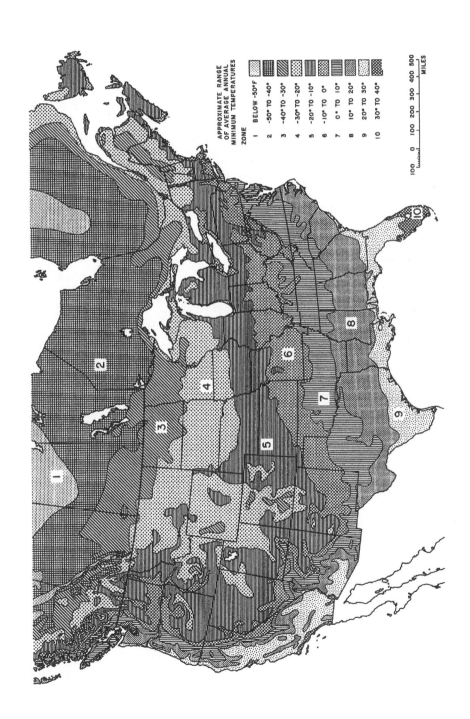

APPROXIMATE RANGE
OF AVERAGE ANNUAL
MINIMUM TEMPERATURES
ZONE

1 BELOW -50°F
2 -50° TO -40°
3 -40° TO -30°
4 -30° TO -20°
5 -20° TO -10°
6 -10° TO 0°
7 0° TO 10°
8 10° TO 20°
9 20° TO 30°
10 30° TO 40°

MILES

Index

Notes

Notes

Notes

Notes

Notes

Notes